A Departed Music

Readings in Old English Poetry

Walter Nash

Anglo-Saxon Books

Published 2006 by
Anglo-Saxon Books
Frithgarth
Thetford Forest Park
Hockwold-cum-Wilton
Norfolk   IP26 4NQ   England

P L

© Walter Nash

All rights reserved. No part of this publication may be reproduced or transmitted in any form or by any means, electronic or mechanical including photo-copying, recording, or any information storage or retrieval system, without prior permission in writing from the publisher, except for the quotation of brief passages in connection with a review written for inclusion in a magazine or newspaper.

This book may not be lent, resold, hired out or otherwise disposed of by way of trade in any form of binding or cover other than that in which it is published, without the prior consent of the publishers.

British Library Cataloguing-in-Publication Data. A catalogue record for this book is available from the British Library.

ISBN 1–898281–37–8

A programme note

Like us, they were conscripted to defeat.
Their luck assigned, they had no room to choose
sickness or blind mishap, ambush or fire.
They gloried in the wars they had to lose.
See, useless at the buried captain´s feet,
the brittle armour and the broken lyre.

Mourning in exile by the wintry sea,
fearing the enemy beyond the wall,
they had no pressing reason to rejoice.
Knowing the fates of men, they shared the fall.
Still beyond sorrow, in an ecstasy
the music-maker lifted up his voice -

And that´s the power that knits the scholar´s frown
over bleared pages: he may only guess
at things long out of mind, far gone from sight,
preposterous things; but in the heart´s distress
hears melodies that ease the tumbledown
through the long overwhelming of the night.

Contents

Foreword 7
1 the poetry business 9
2 of cruel battle and the fall of kin 29
   An affair of honour 29
   Pomp of a battle won 31
   Circumstance of a battle lost 34
   For services rendered; or there's for thy pains 44
   Kith and kin, name and fame 48
3 exiles and lamentations 53
   A maiden in the marsh 53
   A woman in the woods 56
   A lady in luck 57
   A soul at sea 59
   "How doth the city sit solitary" 68
4 rulers of the darkness 73
   News from Niflheim 74
   The nature of the beast 84
   The sleep of reason 89
5 avenger and redeemer 95
   Scenes from a popular script 96
   The style and the message 103
   A different kind of soldier, a different sort of war 104
6 tunes on a broken lyre 113
   The scripting of the song 118
   Alliteration: art and artifice 121
   The state of the art 124
   Compositional styles 128
   Words, words, words 131
   At the close 137
Postscripts 139
    Scop – "scoff" 139
    The happy harpist's "sounding nail" 139
    Rings and things 139
    Snorri Sturluson, c.1179-1241 140
    About Maeringaburg 140
    The dating of Deor 140
    The meaning of wóðbora 140
    Fuþark 141
    On Christ and Ingeld 141
    Re the bearlike Beowulf 142
    Ship design and Frisian seamen 142

Monastic Riddle	142
ealdormon	143
Did they know this was Tryggvason?	143
On armies, ours and theirs.	143
More about "wound gold".	144
"Sister's son".	144
The meaning of ceorl.	144
A ring-giving by firelight.	144
Demands and rewards.	145
A biblical note on dóm.	145
Hávamál, "The Words of the High One"	146
Conjectural readings in Wulf and Eadwacer.	146
"Impersonations".	146
"Those who hope for name and fame".	147
Ubi sunt - "where are...?"	147
"There were giants on the earth".	147
The identity of Cynewulf?	148
The Later Genesis and Paradise Lost	148
Sir Thomas Browne	148
Aspidochelone - "shield turtle"	148
marram grass	149
The land of the Finns	149
"a widow woman, her hair tied back".	149
Judith	150
Hair styles	150
Tempering a sword.	150
Maldon - Beginning the battle.	150
Is The Dream of the Rood a "heroic" poem?	151
Understating.	151
Robert Graves, The Crowning Privilege	151
George Puttenham on "stirre".	151
Sweet on Sievers.	152
Siever's "five type" model of Old English poetic rhythms	152
Matters of metre.	152
Stops and spirants and things.	153
On the question of intention	153
Poetic diction.	154
Brunanburh	154
wunden - "curves are beautiful".	154
"broad and brown-edged".	154

Samples 155
   I   Poetics 156
      1. *Caedmon's Hymn*: A poet's awakening 156
      2. *Widsith,* lines 50-67, 135-143: A poet's travels 158
      3. *Deor*: A poet's troubles. 160
      4. Riddle 28: The Harp 166
      5. A Charm, *Wið færstice* ("For a sudden stitch") 170
      6. *Beowulf,* lines 855b - 874: Poetry in praise 172
  II   Wisdoms 174
      7. *The Wanderer*, 62b-72, 106-15. 174
      8. *The Fortunes of Men,* 178
      9. The Exeter Maxims, 93-106 182
    10. *The Whale*, 49b-70 : 184
    11. *Beowulf,* 1758-68: The mortal pride of war 186
 III   Elegies 188
    12. *Wulf and Eadwacer*: A fenland tragedy 188
    13. *The Wife's Lament*, 21-41 192
    14. *The Wanderer*, 73-97: 194
    15. *The Ruin*, 1-11; 25-37 198
    16. *Beowulf,* 2247-2266. The fall of pride 202
 IV   Heroics 206
    17. *The Battle of Brunanburh,* 57-73 206
    18. *The Battle of Maldon,* 42-61; 309-319 : 210
    19. *The Later Genesis,* 277-296 : 214
    20. *Judith,* 96b - 121   Maidenly vengeance 216
    21. *The Dream of the Rood,* 39-56 220
    22. *Beowulf,* 3156 - 3182 A hero's burial 224

Select Bibliography 227
    1. *Basics* 227
    2. *Beowulf: text, editions, translations, commentaries* 228
    3. *Poetic texts in translation: heroic, elegies, wisdoms, riddles, allegory* .. 228
    4. *Critical editions, commentary, and "background"* 229
    5. *Poetics, literary theory, textual criticism* 231
    6. *Allusions and quotations* 232

Foreword

Here are some poems, written in a language we no longer speak, though it belongs to us, in times that were not so much worse than ours, though they seem far worse, by people as miserable or as happy, as serene or impassioned, as pragmatic or idealistic as we are inclined to be. Soldiers are here, and saints, and sinners, and poets exulting in their craft, and men prostrate before the Cross, and lonely women mourning their plight, and great ladies fighting their people´s cause, and learned monks propounding wisdoms and riddles, and simple folk looking to the medicine man to cure their aches and pains. It may not quite amount to William Langland´s "fair field full of folk" – they were most of them living behind palisades – but it is a lively world, nonetheless

I have presented these poems as "readings", in diverse methods and perspectives: as translation, as paraphrase, as critical commentary, as the exposition of a cultural context, as linguistic and stylistic apparatus. In the plan of the book, the first five chapters consist of **Readings** (translation, paraphrase, commentary) on the chosen poems, the sixth is a brief account of **Anglo-Saxon poetics**, metre, diction; the section called **Postscripts** accommodates notes that were originally considered too discursive and beside the point to have been included in the chapter footnotes. (see 1st para. p.139) The long section entitled **Samples** is a sequence of short selections from original texts cited in translation or commentary earlier in the book. These selections are furnished with yet more notes, on language and grammar, on emendations, on disputed meanings and possible variants. My hope is that such annotations will be helpful, especially to anyone beginning an acquaintance with Anglo-Saxon texts. I know, however, that for scholars, editors and such, the making of notes is often a happy self-indulgence, for which I may have to apologise. The final section is a **Bibliography**, of works which should be accessible in academic libraries, or in some cases available through the larger bookshops (including the on-line Amazon.)

The translations in chapters 1 – 6 are of a kind I would not wish to call "free" (ie renderings "in the spirit of the thing"), neither do I regard them as bound to the letter of the text.. The method (if any) is to cleave to the substance of the text, to follow as far as possible the sequencing of the words, and in difficulties to attempt an equable exchange of sense for sense. In the annotations to the **Samples,** on the other hand, I have given precedence to literal translation. As to metre, I do not attempt anything like an imitation of the Anglo-Saxon metres discussed in chapter 6. The translations have a syllabic pulse, normatively of decasyllables or octosyllables, but on occasion contracting or expanding in response to the type or narrative drive of the text.

There is a story about Louis Armstrong, who was asked to define the appeal of jazz and replied that if you had to ask, you wouldn´t understand the answer. That could never be said about Anglo-Saxon verse. You have to ask, and ask repeatedly, and often laboriously. But by and by the appeal is felt, and understanding comes, and the poets speak clearly, in a language that belongs to us, about times not wholly unlike ours, and people whose dealings and natures we recognise as not impossibly remote from our own. And that is a great happiness.

Walter Nash, Tenerife, February 2004

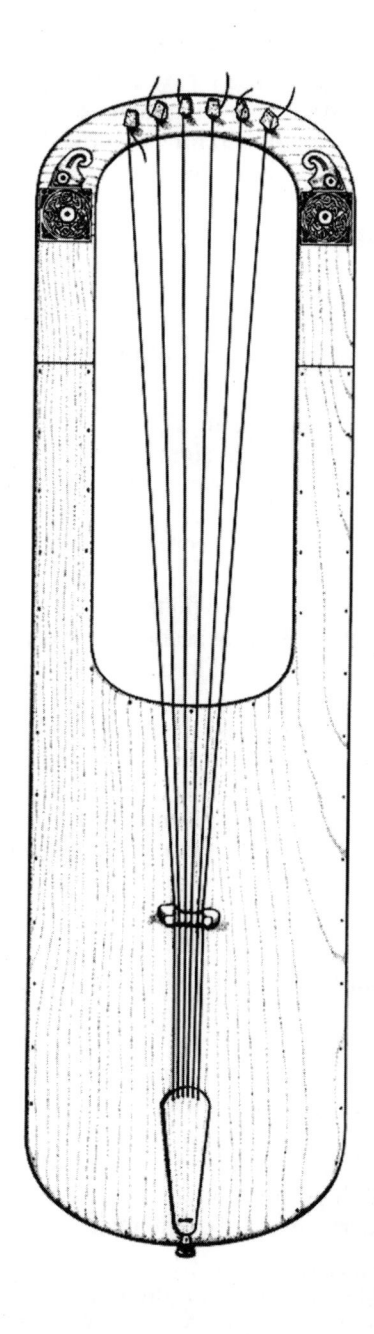

Reconstruction of a lyre from Sutton Hoo
Drawn by Lindsay Kerr

1 the poetry business

The poets' name for a master-poet was *scop*. It is a little term for a large calling, the vocation of one who lives among kings and captains, bearing witness to heroic fame and tragic destiny. Its etymology - as with so many simple, primary words - is obscure. Some dictionaries cite an Indo-European root related to "scoff", perhaps suggesting the boastfulness of satire, or the disdainful taunting of rivals, but the scop's concern was with shaping, with making, rather than mocking.[1] He was essentially a maker in an oral tradition. He could memorise songs and stories, and improvise on them, taking his harp to the feast and telling his tale as he had rehearsed it, or as it came to him. He sang, perhaps for the pleasure of it and certainly for the profit of it; and his professional business was to celebrate his patrons, the tribal chiefs and mighty men who gave him houseroom and paid him to sing, for his supper and his status.

Described in those terms, the scop appears necessarily as a court poet, if the word "court" appropriately designates the simple stronghold of an Anglo-Saxon chieftain's heall, the "hall". In that context the scop may have been no more than a gliwman, a "gleeman", a "minstrel", one of the chief's retainers who had some talent with the harp and could put verses together, for the diversion of his master and his companions in the tribal hall. A poem called *Be monna wyrdum*, "The Fortunes of Men", gives a charming picture of him as the music-man absorbed in deft instrumental skill:

> This one sits at the feet of his lord,
> sits with his harp, and has his pay,
> and ever swiftly plucks the strings
> as the plectrum leaps, the sounding nail.
> Such joy is his.[2]

lines 80-84 The Fortunes of Men

---

[1] Etymologies: *skeubh* related to "scoff", etc. This is the etymology suggested by the OED and Webster's New World (which defines *scop* as "a maker of taunting verses"). It is conceivable that a thread of inner sense runs from "scoff" to "mock", in the sense of "imitate", "mime" (as in 'mocking bird'). Then part of the scop's business could be seen as *mimesis*, imitation; the craft of original invention being *poesis*, "making".

[2] The happy harpist's "sounding nail". The text reads *naegl neomegende*, "sweet-sounding nail" - a transferred epithet, for of course it is the harpstring, not the plectrum, that makes the sweet sound. The "nail" here is a fingernail, or something resembling one. The Old English word for plectrum is *sceacol*, "shackle", suggesting a device in some way fixed (bound, tied) to a finger's end. The MS of the Vespasian Psalter has an illustration of David playing a harp - a lyre of the six- or seven-string type found among the treasures of the Sutton Hoo ship burial. The illustration shows clearly the function of the two hands in playing the Saxon lyre, the right hand to pluck the strings, the left to "stop" or "fret" the sounds. This illustration is copied and enlarged in http://www.cs.vassar.edu/~priestdo/lyre.html. See at that source an informative paper, "The Saxon Lyre: History, Construction and Playing Techniques", by Dofinn Hallr-Morrisson and Thora Sharptooth.

1 The Poetry Business

This is a touchingly intimate, homely picture. Our general notion of the *scop*, however, is more elevated. We have the impression, on the strength of one or two well-known poems or references in poetry, of the *scop* as bard, as artist vagrant, seeking his fortune from court to court, dependent on patronage, but always a free spirit proudly conscious of his calling. Such an itinerant is represented in the fictional character of Widsith, whose name, like the epithet *polytropos*, which Homer applies to Odysseus, means "far-travelled". Here indeed is a singer whose gift of song, if we are to believe him, has taken him far and wide. He claims (impossibly) to have known the great ones of all the world, that is, of all the world after the fall of Rome, during the centuries of migration when Hun and Vandal, Goth and German, moved westward from their original lands, jostling for power and possession. He can claim acquaintance - if only by hearsay - with all the chiefs of all the tribes of those Dark Ages:

> Attila ruled the Huns, Eormanric the Goths,
> Becca the Banings, the Burgundians Gifica.
> Caesar ruled the Greeks, and Caelic the Finns,
> Hagen the Holmrygas and Heoden the Glomman.
> Witta ruled the Swabians, Wade the Helsings,
> Mearca the Myrgings, Marcheall the Hundings.
> Theodoric ruled the Franks, Thyle the Rondings -   *lines 18-24 Widsiò*

and so on, *ad* (almost) *libitum*. We might be forgiven for thinking that this recital of chiefs and tribesmen qualifies as verse by virtue of its rhythms, and as poetry by little else, unless, possibly, in the sonorities of names that must once have evoked a glamorous tale. But metrical catalogues of tribes, or persons, or objects, are standard components in ancient literature - in Homer, for example, or in the Old Testament - where they serve purposes beyond modern notions of the poetic. The Germanic *scop* apparently had functions beside those of a weaver of cunning words; he was also the custodian of folk-memories, one who carried and kept alive the histories of heroes and of peoples in migration and dispersion. In *Widsith*, his place in the halls of the powerful is described:

> And so I can sing, and recite my tale,
> in the mead-hall make known to many
> how great men honoured me with their gifts:
> I was with the Huns and the conquering Goths,
> with the Swedes and the Geats and the southern Danes...   *lines 54-57*

He works this theme methodically, through a tally of Hunnish-Gothic-Germanic tribes, not failing to mention the generosity of chiefs in noble gifts conferred on the singer for his pains in praising them:

> ... and with the Burgundians, a ring I had,
> by Guthere granted, a splendid treasure
> rewarding my song. No miser, that king!   *lines 65-7*

1   The Poetry Business

The king is judged by his munificence; a niggardly prince will have no honour. The recital continues:

> I was with the Franks, with the Frisians and Frumtings,
> the Rugi, the Glomman, the dwellers in Rome... *lines 68-9*

Rome having become, by the end of the 5th century, an outpost of the Germans or the Goths. Then, even less credibly extending his reported circuit:

> I was with the Scots, with the Picts, with the Lapps,
> Lidwicingas, Leonas, Langobards... *lines 79-80*

And with total unlikelihood:

> With Israelites I was, and Assyrians,
> with Hebrews, Indians, Egyptians... *lines 82-3*

Until, after many wanderings:

> And I was with Eormanric all his reign,
> the King of the Goths who paid me well,
> the Lord of that people; paid with a torc
> worth thirty shillings of purest gold *lines 88-92*

For his pains of recital and commemoration in song, the poet is paid with munificent gifts. This is nothing quite so ordinary or regular as a *wage*; it is more in the nature of a bounty - for which the simple Saxon word is *ár* - bestowed at the chieftain's pleasure. The *ár* might be a gift of land or property, a place to live, by grace and favour. Or it might take the form of jewels or artefacts of precious metal. From Guthere the *scop* receives a ring of great price; from Eormanric likewise a sumptuous *béag*.[3] The marks of such lordly favour were commonly *béagas*, "rings", whether bracelets, armbands, or collars of wrought gold. This generosity in return for services rendered is in the tradition of Germanic tribal organisation. The chief's "companions", his inner circle or household guard, serve him with unquestioning loyalty, and he is expected to reward them unstintingly. The poem of *Widsith* concludes with lines that confidently, and no doubt

---

[3] Rings and things. The text says "a ring worth six hundred 'sceatts', reckoned in shillings". A 'sceatt' was a twentieth part of a shilling, six hundred "sceatts" being therefore equivalent to thirty shillings This costly *beag* was probably of the variety known as a *torc*. Torcs, or "torques" were artefacts made of thin strands of precious metal, twisted or "braided" into short pliable lengths, with at each end a solid gold terminal or clasp. For a fine example see, among the treasures of the British Museum, the Snettisham Great Torc. (See online at http:www.thebritishmuseum.ac.uk/compass) Tacitus (*Germania, cap.14*) mentions *torqui* among the customary gifts and barter payments of the Germanic chiefs, adding, with Roman irony, "we have now got them to take cash". On *wunden gold* - "wound gold" - and related matters, see further Chapter 2, page 35, note 21.

1 The Poetry Business

wishfully, assert a symbiotic relationship, an interdependence, of the *scop* and his tribal lord, in which the *scop* is by no means the inferior party. He is portrayed as, in part, the wanderer, ever driven to move on from court to court, to please new masters with gifts of praise, but also as a man sovereign in his own gifts, a "maker and shaker of the world". In return for the generosity of his lords, he makes them famous, through the recital of their deeds:

> So in their wanderings, driven by fate,
> through many lands the poets go,
> make known their needs, and pay their thanks
> northward or southward forever finding
> some patron of song, one gracious in gifts,
> whose wish is, before his bravest men
> to gain repute with glorious deeds,
> till all is ended, light and life
> together. He who strives for praise
> wins, under heaven, a lasting fame.
>
> *lines 135-143 Widsith*

A warrior chief strives for praise, or repute - the word is *lof* - but the poet's words ensure for him "a lasting fame" - then the word is *dóm*, the settled, immutable judgement of posterity and after (the "doom" of "doomsday"). (See also page 49) The *scop's* function, then, is to praise his noble patron, laud his deeds, raise him in the esteem of his followers, stress his place of authority among the surrounding peoples. There is an assumption that he speaks nothing less than the truth when he tells his master's story, for he tells it - so to speak - to his chieftain's face. This is a point made by a great Icelandic writer of the 13th century, Snorri Sturluson, in the Preface to *Heimskringla*, his Histories of Norwegian Kings. He makes the remarkable claim, that his vividly detailed, circumstantial sagas are largely based on the testimonies of court poets:

> We rest the foundations of our story principally upon the songs which were sung in the presence of the chiefs themselves or of their sons and take all to be true that is found in such poems, about their feats and battles; for although it be the fashion of *skalds* [poets] to praise most those in whose presence they are standing, yet no one would dare to relate to a chief what he, and all those who heard it, know to be false and imaginary, not a true account of his deeds, because that would be mockery, not praise.[4]

---

[4] Snorri Sturluson, c.1179-1241. His *Heimskringla* (so called from the opening phrase of its preface, "Kringla heimsins...", "The circle of the world") is quoted here from the text of Samuel Laing's (1844) translation, published in 1907 by the Norroena. Society. Electronic edition at http:sunsite.berkeley.edu/OMACL/Heimskringla The most recent (excellent) translation is that of Lee M. Hollander. See Bibliography, Section 4.

1 The Poetry Business

From that, we may judge that the court poet was obliged to exercise some discretion in praising his chief, and even, it might be, some tact in praising others. A passage in *Beowulf* describes a *scop* singing the praises of a great man who has come to rescue the Danes from a peril against which their own king, the ageing Hrothgar, is powerless. This great man is Beowulf himself, and he has just wrestled to death a marsh-haunting, anthropophagic monster called Grendel, whose nightly incursions have reduced the land to misery. On the day after this encounter, some of the jubilant Danish braves race their horses in the liberated fields, while others listen to the commemorative recital of a *scop*, who has a poem for the occasion:

> A thane of the king's
> supremely gifted, versed in story and song,
> who knew so many of the ancient lays,
> ventured another, matching fact with fact,
> composed a tale held in the bond of truth.
>
> *lines 866-70 Beowulf*

A textual problem here is a phrase in the original, *sóðe gebunden,* literally "bound [up] with truth" or "truthfully joined together". Translators and commentators have suggested, variously, "founded upon fact", "in the bond of truth", and even "correctly linked" (or articulated, implying a comment on the poet's versifying skill). Of these, each of them possible, "founded upon fact" seems most plausible, since it is evident from the context that one good tale deserves another. The art is to make an allusive match - "com-position" in a literal sense. It is Beowulf's heroic feat that the king's *scop* sets out to celebrate, but he does so indirectly, *allusively*, in the context of, or in terms of, another story, the story of Sigemund Waelsing, also a killer of monsters, an ancient hero of the Scyldings (the Danes), whose son appears in Eddaic versions of the Volsung story as Sigurd, the dragon-slayer (and in Middle High German Nibelung tradition as Siegfried). The "fact" upon which the poet's new narrative is based is in part the fact of the Sigemund story, accepted as tribal history - "our glorious past", as it might be; and in part the fact of Beowulf's deed, with which the old history is implicitly compared. Beowulf the Geat becomes by adoption a Dane, a defender of the national honour. So the heroic rescuer is praised, with no loss of face to the grateful rescued.

The example suggests that the professional *scop* had need of a memory stored, not only with recognized historical fact, but also with legend and myth instructively taken for fact. To invoke the past is to illuminate the present position. This is the compositional technique of a poem called *Deor*, a poem possibly maimed and certainly obscured through the hazards of transmission, but a fine poem still, a poem that homes on the perennial truth quaintly expressed by the 20th century American poet, Archibald MacLeish: "a poet's life is hard - a hardy life with a boot as quick as a fiver" [5] It presents the image of a court poet displaced by a rival, deprived of the benefits of grace and favour, and obliged to

---

[5] Archibald Macleish, "Invocation to the Social Muse". Collected Poems, New York, Houghton Mifflin, 1952.

1 The Poetry Business

move on and re-make his life elsewhere. We in our turn, as readers of the poem, are obliged to *move on* in imagination, through a sequence of mythic examples of misfortune, until we reach a painful confession at the close:

> Welund in Värmland knew exile's pain,
> such toil that steadfast earl endured,
> sorrow and longing were comrades then,
> wintercold care; many his woes
> since Nithhad bound him in supple bonds,
> maiming the thews of a nobler man.
>
> That sorrow passed; and so may this
>
> Beadohild less for her brothers grieved
> than for herself when it was plain
> she was with child; nor dared she think
> boldly, what might become of that.
>
> That sorrow passed; and so may this
>
> Many have heard of that rape of Hild.
> Unfathomable the grief of the Geat,
> till the sorrow of love stole all his sleep
>
> That sorrow passed; and so may this
>
> Theodoric for thirty years
> held Mæringaburg; that was well known.
>
> That sorrow passed; and so may this
>
> Wolf-soul of Eormanric we knew,
> Lord of the Goths; a cruel king.
> Many a man sat sorrow-bound,
> nursing his grief, with a deep heart's wish
> that the kingdom might be overthrown.
>
> That sorrow passed; and so may this
>
> Man sits in sorrow, bereft of joy,
> darkened in spirit, telling himself
> that the tale of trouble has no end.
> Let him think, through all the world,
> God, the all-wise, works change on change,
> bestowing gifts on many an earl,
> to this one glory, to that one grief.

1 The Poetry Business

> As for myself, this I will say:
> a poet I was, the Heodenings' *scop*,
> dear to my lord, Deor my name.
> Long winters this fair state I kept,
> with a gracious lord - till Heorrenda came.
> He, skilled in song, won grants of land
> the protector of earls once made to me.
>
> That sorrow passed; and so may this   *Deor*

Apart from the intrusion of some lines that read like Christian homiletic on the problem of evil (the lines beginning "Man sits in sorrow"), this is a poem which turns on pagan legend, and on historical semi-legends, that an Anglo-Saxon audience might be expected to recognize. We cannot respond in the same unprompted way without benefit of commentary, and even that can be little better than tentative. Problems of interpretation persist, and the version offered above raises problems of its own, mostly arising from a disputed reading of the manuscript in the third strophe. (On this, see Samples, p.164). What is at least clear is that the poem cites, in a sequence of strophes with a recurrent refrain, examples of people who have had their bad times - some cruelly bad times - and surmounted them; leading to a final strophe resignedly mourning the worst of all bad times for a poet, to fall from favour and be dismissed by his patron. A poet's life is hard indeed, and a boot, or eviction order, as quick as a fiver. But even that can be lived down.

Deor begins with the story of Welund (Weland, "Wayland") the fabulous smith, abducted by Nithhad, King of Närike, who holds him captive and hamstrings him to prevent him from taking his creative talents elsewhere. On the modern map of Sweden, the province of Närke will be seen to lie between Värmland, to the north-west, and Västergötland, to the south-east; this was in early times "Gothic" - "Geatish" - territory, making Nithhad by kith, or folk-identity, a Geat).The story of Welund's suffering is told at length in an Old Norse version called the *Völundarkviða,* the "Song of Welund". His revenge is terrible. He kills Nithhad's two sons, and in a parody of exquisite craftsmanship, makes their skulls into jewel-studded bowls, which he presents to their father. Next, he rapes Nithhad's daughter, Beadohild, having drugged her. She cannot share her father's anguish over the deaths of her brothers; she can only think - yet scarcely knows what or how to think - of the master-slave who has forced this "love" upon her. There is an irony in her misgivings as to "what might become of that", for what became of it was a heroic son called Widia (or Wudga), one of the mighty Germanic men Widsith names in the account of his travels. "We have heard of this", says the poet, using a verb favoured in Anglo-Saxon *scopcræft,* ("poetics"), the verb *frignan,* "to hear tell", "to hear/know by report". The way of the *scop* is not to claim private, or "privileged" knowledge of the facts he relates; he is only the sounding-board, resonating hearsay, telling everybody what all well-informed people must surely have heard. So, "we know all this", he says, "and very terrible it was; but the suffering passed." More than that: out of the ill event came the goodly consequence.

1   The Poetry Business

From "what we have heard of" in legend, he goes on to "what we know" from history, or rather, history made legendary. Theodoric the Ostrogoth (c.AD 454-526) and "Eormanric" (Ermanaric, d.375) were not historical contemporaries and were never involved with each other as rivals or enemies. Medieval literary tradition, however, has linked them as coevals, contending examples of good and bad lordship - Theodoric as brave, generous, great even in exile and adversity, Ermanaric as a tyrant, cruel, grasping, murderous, feared by his own kith and kin. The poem *Widsith* is unusual in praising at least the noble munificence of Eormanric[6] , who is remembered in Germanic tradition as having exiled his nephew, Theodoric of Verona. The story of Dietrich von Bern ("Bern"= Verona), called in an Old Norse version, the *Þiðrekssaga*, establishes Theodoric as hero and condemns Ermanaric as unspeakable villain though the two men (as noted above) could never have met in real life. The poets heard of them, however. *We geáscodan*, says the *Deor* poet, concerning Eormanric's fame, and he uses a verb *ascian*, meaning "ask" - "we asked", but more fully, "we have learned by asking". Like *frignan*, it has the sense of *being told upon enquiry,* and indicates that the poet is drawing upon well-known sources. Unfortunately for our understanding of Theodoric's tribulations, the laconic reference to *Maeringaburg*, "the city of the Maerings" is obscure.[7]

The recital moves on (after an interpolation which requires further comment) to the conclusion of Deor's lyrical business, which is to tell the world that he, though maybe not so gravely ill-used by fortune as Welund, who was hamstrung by Nithhad, or as the sad girl Beadohild, who was raped by Welund, or as noble Theodoric, who endured a long exile, or as the poor terror-stricken fellows who suffered in silence under the reckless tyranny of Eormanric, is none the less hard done by. He tells us his name, *Deor*, in a line that comes close to suggesting a homophonic pun: *dryhtne dyre, me waes Deor noma* - "dear to my lord, Deer was my name". Is this a real person, or a poetic fiction, a scribe's invention of the myth of a *scop*?[8] He names his tribe, however, the Heodenings, with whom,

---

[6] The word of praise is indeed unusual, as indeed is Widsith's claim, elsewhere in the poem , that his best times were spent among Eormanric's "hearth companions". Even Widsith, however, reproves Eormanric as a *wráþ wáerloga*, "a cruel trothbreaker"

[7] About Maeringaburg: it seems, from learned commentary, that the Maeringas were the Ostrogoths. A runic inscription from 10th century Sweden calls Theodoric *skati marika*, "Lord of the Maeringas". In that same inscription the Adriatic is called "the Gothic sea" Towards the end of the fifth century Italy had been under the control of the Germans under Odoacer; but in 493 Theodoric, at the command of the Byzantine emperor Zeno, led an Ostrogothic invasion and took the city of Ravenna. It is possible that Ravenna is "Maeringaburg". Theodoric "held" it, and all Italy, for 33 years, until his death, still in exile from his homeland, in 526. Perhaps these are the "thirty winters" the poem refers to - but only perhaps. The text is too laconic to allow of more certain conjecture.

[8] The dating of *Deor*. The question, "Is this a real person, or a poetic fiction, or a scribe's invention of the myth of a *scop?*" is asked in passing, but raises a substantial point about the dating of this text, and a few others which might be called "personations", because in them the author adopts a *persona*, conceived in an appropriate style. There are two possible views of *Deor*: one, that it is indeed an old poem, somehow surviving from the 7th century, originally composed by a poet calling himself *Deor*; the other, that it is a fiction, composed in the 9th or 10th century, by a Christian writer impersonating the character and style of a pre-Christian *scop*. Choose either way, or both ways at once; it typifies the difficulty of settling the OE literary calendar.

1 The Poetry Business

under a gracious lord, he has held the position of court poet, "for many winters", until, abruptly, he is displaced by a more famous *scop*, one Heorrenda. We know something of this artist; he turns up in Snorri Sturluson's *Skaldskaparmál* as Hjarrandi, and in the Middle High German poem of *Kudrun*, as Horant, a bard whose sweet verses, it is said, could charm the birds out of the branches. Deor simply calls him *léoðcræftig monn*, "a man skilled in song", but records, as a matter of more immediate importance, that all the rights of land tenure previously granted to Deor by his gracious lord have now at a stroke been rescinded and transferred to Heorrenda. This is his plight; he is not only out of office but out of a home and (consequently) given the key of the great outdoors, after so many years of faithful service. But...everything passes. *O passi graviora*, as Aeneas tells his men when the going gets rough, *haec olim meminisse juvabit*, we have seen worse, and one day even this will be a pleasant memory.

The mood of the poem is obviously one of pagan stoicism, its sadness offset by the lyric charm of the refrain form. *Scopcræft*, or to borrow a phrase from Tennyson, "measured language", has its consolatory uses. Pagan philosophy and crafted form, however, are alike disturbed by a foreign body of text, for the passage beginning "Man sits in sorrow..." and ending "to this one, glory, to that one, grief", a passage of general commentary, not marked by the characterising refrain, is surely an interpolation, a pious *scholion* by some cleric occupied with the ever-recurrent question, "why does God let bad things happen"? The poem in general may possibly be old enough to have been a work known in oral transmission; at some point, however, it came to be written down, in the scriptorium of an abbey or monastery, where its commission to writing - and therefore permanent record - could be justified if it were seen to contain something of explicit doctrinal value or significance, an example, a morality, a "message". The primitive message of *Deor*, which might be paraphrased as "Too bad; but that's life; these things happen, and one way or another they come to an end", is not tolerated by the intrusive lines, which assert a different view of human ills. This reconstructed "message" is that prosperity and suffering alike are *gifts*, allotted by God, who alone can know their purpose. This is the tenor of some lines in the poem *Be monna wyrdum*, quoted earlier; a poem which similarly puts a Christian spin on some pre-Christian themes. The lines read:

> This man is fated in youth, by the power of God,
> to make a wreck of all he labours to do,
> and then, in age, to come to his own again,
> to know his days of delight, enjoy his wealth,
> the jewels, the wine-cups, sitting among his folk,
> more than any man might have and hold.
> So variously does our Almighty God
> through all the earth deal out His gifts to all,
> allots, apportions, shapes the fates of men,
> to some grants wealth, to others misery.   *lines 85-92 Be monna wyrdum*

The point here is that human fortune and misfortune are not a matter of blind happenstance, the unreasoned tumble of life. God is in control; He allots what men are and what they shall be, and knows why. This is the message of the lines just quoted. It is also the tenor of the lines interpolated into the lyric of *Deor*; and whatever the pagan roots of the poem, those lines must surely have been written by a poet with a Christian moral to draw.

A companion poem to *Be monna wyrdum*, called *Be monna cræftum*, "The Gifts of Men", also identifies the character of the poet, but does so in two distinct perspectives. It duly presents him in the expected form, as a musician, a harper:

> This one turns his hand to the harp;
> his joy is deftly to finger the lyre.   *lines 49-50 Be monna cræftum*

He is the "gleeman" who sits at his lord's feet, sweetly singing. But "The Gifts of Men" also speaks of another aspect of the poet. "This one is a *wóðbora*", it says, *giedda gieffæst* - "gifted teller of tales"- or recitalist - or proponent of riddles - or wise words - or sermons - depending on one's understanding of *giedd*, which is glossed as "*song, poem; saying, proverb, riddle; speech, story, tale, narrative; account, reckoning, reason*".The word *wóðbora* signifies "one gifted with eloquence", or "an orator", and the element *woð* somewhat resembles in sense the Welsh *hwyl*, the inspired rhetoric, the passionate persuasion of pulpit or political platform.[9] *Scopcræft*, old style, records, remembers, repeats, reminds, re-shapes; *wóðcræft* has broader pretensions, to a claimed originality, a privileged inventiveness. The *scop*, as we meet him in *Beowulf* and elsewhere, frequently implies the recorder's honest pledge of "So we hear", "I have been told"; the stance of the *wóðbora* often suggests "So it appears to me", "In my view". Thus the author of a poem called "The Whale" prefaces his narrative with this statement of intention:

> I'll make a tale now of the fishy kind.
> I mean to choose my words with poet's art,
> and speak my mind concerning the Great Whale.   *lines 1-3 The Whale*

The expression he uses for "poet's art" is *wóðcræft,* and his indeed eloquent tale, a pulpit oration, comes *þurh módgemynd*, "from (my) thoughts"; an accurate characterisation, as it turns out, for his tale is no saga of the sea, but a view of what he would like people to think about whales, or in essence a discourse on the Great Whale as theological symbol. It may seem that we are dealing with two words that are after all only synonyms, and possibly interchangeable. Between supposed synonyms there is always some difference, however, and if there is a

---

[9] The meaning of *wóðbora*. The glosses here are supplied by Clark-Hall, John R, and Herbert D. Merritt, *A Concise Anglo-Saxon Dictionary*, 4th edn., Cambridge 1960. As to a resemblance to the Welsh *hwyl*, my conjecture is that *wóð-* is from a Germanic root signifying "out of one's mind", "impassioned" (as in Middle English "wod", "wood"). It is related to Latin *vates* ("seer", "poet"). It is also related to the *od-* of Odin, the god of war and eloquence whose Anglo-Saxon name is Woden.

difference between *scop* and *wóðbora* as terms for "poet" it could perhaps be identified as the distinction between *performer* and *author*; including, eventually, the contrast between the vocal and the written, and the kinds of invention and compositional technique appropriate to these modes.

Obviously, all the Anglo-Saxon poetry we know has come to us through the instrumentality of written form; it could hardly be otherwise. Long though the oral tradition may have persisted, it had to reach frontiers of change; and when the spoken was at some point committed to writing, it entered into a practice governed by the *bóceras*, the "bookmen", or scribes - meaning, mostly, the servants of the Church. There is little if anything in the Old English poetic records, even in the spells and folk-remedies of pagan origin, even in the catalogues of ancient proverbs and wiseacreage, that bears no sign of a clerical touch, bringing ageless pagandom into the frame of something like devotional orthodoxy. At the very least, the supervisory power of God is always acknowledged. Before the days of manuscript and clerical control, the Anglo-Saxons were not wholly illiterate; some of them, at least, could write the *fuþark*, ["futhark"] the ancient Germanic letter-code used mainly for carving "runes", private or personal or privileged information, in wood, stone, or other solid material.[10] Runic letters would eventually occur even in manuscript, as a kind of shorthand or signature. It was a laborious way of recording, however, and it is hard to conceive of a runic *text* of any great length, though the hint of one exists, in fragmentary form, in panels on the shaft of an elaborately ornamented stone cross, dating from the late 7th or early 8th century, at Ruthwell, in Dumfriesshire. Those fragments are quotations from the poem now known as *The Dream of the Rood*. The poem as a whole we know from a late 10th century manuscript forming part of the collection called the *Vercelli Book*, after its discovery (in the 19th century) in the chapter library of the cathedral at Vercelli, in northern Italy.

The presumed course of things is, then, that the *scop*, our heroic once-upon-a-time man, by and by gives place to, or merges into, another kind of composer, with different themes, different ambitions, a different context for his recitals. He keeps the old poetic metres, this new composer, and the traditional arts of diction, but because he has recourse to writing, explores a dimension that can make differences to metre and diction alike. The transition from one state to the other can hardly have been abrupt, and there must have been a time, no doubt quite a long time, when gleeman and scribe existed side by side, the gleeman's song eventually fated to oblivion, the scribe's composition granted the durability, such as it was, of text. How and by what degrees the transition took place we cannot know, but we may think it began as early as the 7th century, if we are to accept the account of the poet Caedmon, as presented with characteristic charm by Bede in his *Ecclesiastical History of the English People*. He tells the story of a simple layman, a cowherd,

---

[10] Fuþark - from the first six symbols of a runic alphabet, representing the sounds of f, u, th, a, r, k. The "Common Germanic" or "Elder" futhark dates from the 2nd century AD, and is the form used in inscriptions from Low Germany and Scandinavia. The Anglo-Saxon runic alphabet, adapting to sound changes, is a futhorc and includes symbols not in the older versions. "Alphabet" poems on runic letters - along the lines of "A is an archer who has a big bow" - are extant from Norway, Iceland and Britain. A *futhark* and a *futhorc* are shown on p.141.

1 The Poetry Business

who until he was of mature years "had never learned any song". For that reason, Bede says, he shrank from participation in festive gatherings when, as fellowship warmed, the harp was passed from hand to hand and a song required from each guest in turn. As he saw the harp approaching him, he would be embarrassed and quit the company. Then one night, when it was his turn to watch over the cattle and he had gone to lie down in the shippon, a messenger appeared to him in his sleep, with the command "Caedmon, sing me something". "I can't sing", said Caedmon, "that's why I left the party." "But you can sing for me, " said the stranger. "What shall I sing then?" - "Sing me the Creation". And so, says Bede, he began to sing verses and words he had never heard before, "their purport being as follows":

> Now let us praise the Protector of Heaven,
> the might of the Maker, the thought of His mind,
> the work of the glorious Father - each wonder that he,
> the eternal Lord, established of old.
> At first He gave to the children of earth
> heaven for a roof, the Holy Creator,
> and then the world, the Guard of mankind,
> the Lord eternal, went on to make,
> a home for men, the Master Almighty.
>
> *Cædmon's Hymn*

Since this is reputedly the first piece of religious verse in the English language, it may be worth stressing that Bede does not claim to be reporting Caedmon verbatim, but says that the poem went "something like this", or "along these lines". (*Hic est sensus, non autem ordo verborum*) That is perhaps apparent from a text which, if the truth be told, does no more than hint at the possibility of a poem. In verses that suggest the formulaic repetitions and rhythmic phrase-patterns of the Germanic minstrel, it elaborates the proposition that God created the world for man to live in. God is named, or evoked by periphrasis, in nearly every line. He is named in *essence*, as "Maker", "Father", "Master", "Lord", "Creator", and in *function*, as "Protector of Heaven", "Guard of mankind". The recital is, to say the least, reiterative, and it is hard to believe that these expressions were "words he had never heard before", though perhaps he had never heard them worked into metre. Caedmon's case, however, was brought to the notice of a remarkable woman, the Abbess Hild of Whitby, who on hearing of his dream and his sudden fluency in song, adjudged the gift as being from God, but set him a test by recounting to him a passage from scripture, which he was to put into verse overnight. Next day he returned with this material duly transformed and adorned, and the abbess, rejoicing, ordered him to enter the monastic life and devote his days to the conversion into poetry of whatever he might gather from the biblical scholars in her house. It was an inspired appointment. He listened, he memorised, and then (Bede archly compliments his cowherd), "ruminating, as it were, like some cleanly beast, turned all into the sweetest song." This he did with such success, says Bede, that many were persuaded, as a result, to put aside worldly things and enter the closed life. He adds, that although other would-be poets among the English began to attempt devotional verse, there was no one as successful as Caedmon, because his talent was not purloined from singer or scholar, but came essentially as a gift from God.

Caedmon's story is almost a parable of the transition, in poetics, from *scopcræft* to *wóðcræft* or the shift from "minstrel" to "author". The middle-aged, unlettered cowherd would like to be a gleeman but does not know how. It is not clear whether he could play the harp at all, but that might be taken as read, since he knew no songs; useless to attempt an accompaniment if you have nothing to accompany. He had never learned any songs, or the things that songs were *about*. Now the essence of *scopcræft* is its "we have learned", "we have heard"; it is receipt and transmission. When Caedmon quits the benches and refuses to take the harp, it is because he has learned no songs; he denies the receipt and has nothing to transmit. But then comes his dream. He is visited in sleep by a messenger who persuades him that he has something to sing about, something he knows without benefit of enquiry because it is there in the evidence of his senses and in the feeling of his heart. When he awakes, he is a changed man. He is inspired, he has a theme; and he has no apparent difficulty with technical matters of style and versifying, of working the theme into a form, because that grows out of the enormous subjective power of the theme itself. So the ideas of "inspiration" and "originality" begin to displace the principles of "transmission" and "convention". Then, under the guidance of Hild, Caedmon is encouraged to look for for the material that will henceforth inspire him. There is a period of gestation, or as Bede amusingly puts it "rumination" before the work is finally drafted and published. Thus an author emerges, a man with his own sources - in Caedmon's case, divine sources. "The Word of God as Told to Caedmon", the bookjacket might have read, had such an absurdity existed in his time.

*   *   *   *

It can be said without irreverence that in a long period of three hundred years and more, between the 7th century and the 11th, "The Word of God as Told..."whether in Biblical paraphrase, or Apocryphal narrative, or Saints' Lives, became what one irascible commentator used to call "a devastating industry".[11] The Church - again, be it said without irreverence - corners the production; for obvious reasons, things of useful import, and for the soul's good, get into script, while the myths and legends of the past, the stories of mighty men, the exemplars of the tribe, fare less certainly, not being guaranteed a copyist. *Quid Hinieldus cum Christo?* the great scholar and teacher Alcuin raged at clerks with a taste for heroic tales: "What has Ingeld to do with Christ?; the house is narrow, there is not room for both".[12] Ingeld and his like could find room in the house only if such

---

[11] Bruce Dickins, in the preface to his *Runic and Heroic Poems,* Cambridge, 1915, in specific reference to the "School of Cynewulf" in the 9th and 10th centuries. He complains that the "battle pieces", so vivid in poems like "The Fight at Finnsburg" became "a theme worn threadbare by dull mechanical prentice-work in later Anglo-Saxon poetry, when versifying the scriptures became a devastating industry."

[12] On Christ and Ingeld : *Alcuini Epistula 124.* (in *Monumenta Alcuiniana*, ed. Jaffé, Wattenbach & Dummler, Berlin 1873; published in the *Bibilotheca Rerum Germanicarum*) Alcuin of York, 735-804, in his day among the most eminent of European scholars and teachers, was master of the Cathedral School in York, and later head of Charlemagne's Palace School in Aachen. He wrote, in Latin, devotional verses of a sort more dutiful than inspired. The anger expressed in Letter 124 was apparently excited by reports of young clerics' enthusiasm for heroic narratives.

tales could be made to reflect a godly tendency. The prime example of this revision under God is the continuity of the great poem *Beowulf*, sometimes spoken of as the first English epic, though it has next to nothing to do with the English and their history. Its *dramatis personae* are obscure figures from the Dark Ages of the 4th and 5th centuries, Goths and Germans and Scandinavians, transmigrants from Eastern Europe who had fetched up on the North Sea margins, in Friesland or Denmark or Schleswig or the south of Sweden.

Their tales of monsters and battles came to Britain with the first Anglo-Saxon invaders, in the 6th century, and we assume that their *scops* fashioned this material by and by into a saga of "The Bear's Son" - that is, *Beowulf*.[13] This would have been the poem in its oral phase. By the 8th century - in the time of Bede and Alcuin - some of it, at least, must have existed in written form, in an Anglian (Northumbrian) dialect; but the ravages of the Vikings destroyed the old northern culture, and when the poem makes a definitive appearance it is in the 10th century, laboriously copied into West Saxon, the southern dialect which in fact preserves the majority of Old English literary records. At this point the poem emerging from that laboriously copied text presents every appearance of "authorly" inspiration, of *wóðcræft*. It is not simply a loose transcription of an old tale, or a variety of old tales. It is arguably the unifying work of one man, editing the transmissions of saga and oral legend. He is a learned man, versed in literary rhetoric, with some knowledge of Latin literature. Above all else, he is a Christian, and in his re-shaping of a complex of ancient narratives loses no opportunity of transforming the primitive recital of monsters and ordeals into an exemplary prefiguring of Christian chivalry in the conquest of evil.

This is a major, outstanding example of a general case. By the 10th century, poetic literature is "Christianised", even in its pagan remnants, the fragments and hints of a folk-culture. Conversely, the Christian argument of devotional narrative is conventionally "militarised", with the old heroic language of thaneship and battles transposed into the context of spiritual experience and religious institutions. "Put on the whole armour of God" - Paul's exhortation to the Ephesians - was an instruction the Anglo-Saxon poet/clerics were well prepared to take. This narrative mode is the "high art" of pre-Conquest verse, a canon of comparison for things less weighty and less ambitious, products of an art less "high" than "homely". The minor poetry makes annotations on small lives in particular circumstances. It observes the facts of the world, is folk-wise, reflects on commonplaces and the paradoxes of perception and experience. Some of it is poetry by special licence, some of it poetry by anyone's judgement. There are pieces and passages that make a modern reader thank God or the muses for things that have escaped the canonical prescriptions, things that ordinary observation has quickened into extraordinary life.

---

[13] Re the bearlike Beowulf. In 1910 the German philologist and folklorist Frederick Panzer published a study of more than 200 folk-tales with elements akin to the fantastic or supernatural parts of *Beowulf*, notably in the Grendel episodes. These stories came to be know collectively as "The Tale of the Bear's Son." F.Panzer, *Studien zur germanischen Sagengeschichte: I, Beowulf.* Munich 1910. For a brief discussion of this material, see the Introduction (pp xxii-xxiii) to C.W.Kennedy's *Beowulf: the Oldest English Epic*, OUP 1940; further, *R.W.Chambers, Beowulf: An Introduction to the Study of the Poem,* 2nd edn, Cambridge UP, 1932

1   The Poetry Business

We may take for example, the compiler of the Exeter *Maxims*. (Or *Gnomic Verses* as they used to be known) His object is to record, more or less disconnectedly, a sequence of proverb-like utterances, expressing the proper character of things. "A man must rule with a strong mind", he tells us, and in the next moment, "The sea often brings storms"; likewise "Wise men guard their souls" and "A sick man needs a doctor". Yet, embedded among these pronouncements of the wearily obvious, there are sallies of humour and pointed insight, as in this little discourse, on the old prescriptive theme of "a place for everything and everything in its place":

> A shield for a champion, a shaft for a robber,
> for the bride a ring, for the scholar his books,
> for holy men, housel, for the heathen - their sins.
>
> *lines 129-131 Exeter Maxims*

("Housel" being the eucharist; the heathen can go unhouseled). But certainly the most charming lines from the Exeter *Maxims* are those describing how happy the sailor's wife is to have her man home from sea:

> Happy the Frisian wife when the fleet returns:
> his ship is in, her welcome guest is home,
> her own provider; she brings him into the house,
> washes his soiled clothes and gives him fresh.
> Love's wishes are his to make when he lies ashore
>
> *lines 944-99*

The Frisians had a reputation as seafarers; the *Anglo-Saxon Chronicle* records how King Alfred, when he began to build ships for a navy, evolved an original design, following - significantly - "neither the Frisian nor the Danish models."[14] The Frisians were sailors to be reckoned with. But how touching these lines are in their celebration of the unpoetic commonplace. Nowhere else, in all the passages of Old English verse that mention the ocean and its voyagers, do we find any symbol of journey's end as persuasive as this; home from sea, a man fetches his dirty laundry, and his woman affectionately does it for him. The wry realism of the image is softened by the melodic lyricism of the last line.

The same gift of wry observation appears in a passage from *The Fortunes of Men* describing the sad destiny of one who is doomed to meet his end, not in battle, not in time of famine, not in confrontation with wolves, though all these

---

[14] Ship design and Frisian seamen. The long Chronicle entry for the year 826 describes King Alfred's attempts to create a fleet to fight the Danes. The ships he designed were "very nearly twice as long" as the Vikings' ships, and also "faster, more manoeuvrable and of deeper draught". They were constructed "neither on the Danish model nor the Frisian, but as he himself considered most apt for their purpose" Serving in the squadron that first encountered the Danes off the Dorset coast (conjecturally, round Poole Harbour) were Frisian seamen, some of them mentioned in despatches: Wulfheard Friesa, Æbbe Friesa, and Æþelhere Friesa. These three were all killed in the battle, and never came home to their wives.

"fortunes" are mentioned in the poem, but by unheroically falling out of a tree. The event is as closely remarked as any piece of "war-play" in a battle scene:

> This one, in the forest, from a tall tree
> must fall, without feathers; yet he is in flight,
> swings in the air, until there remain
> no branches to bounce him; then to grassroots
> plunges, poor fellow, and gives up the ghost,
> drops to the ground and departs in death.   *lines 21-27 The Fortunes of Men*

The detail is charming - a strange commendation perhaps, given the sad subject; what charms is the conviction that this is accurate, that this is how it would have been, that only someone who had actually witnessed a fall from a tree could have presented it so exactly. The poor victim is in a kind of flight - he "swings on the air" - bounces from branch to branch, almost playfully, until there are no more branches and he plunges to his death. This fatal fall might remind a reader of the playful descent from a tree described by Robert Frost in his poem *Birches*. The narrator in that poem describes how a boy would climb the birch trees on his father's farm for the pleasure of launching himself from the top and swinging down, using the "give" of the branches:

> Then he flung outward, feet first, with a swish,
> Kicking his way down through the air to the ground

Frost's lines are to be admired for their precision, their objectivity, their cunningly playful rhythm; hardly less objective, playful and precise is the observation of the Anglo-Saxon poet.

The seeing eye can also be subjective, practising a playful deceit with presentations of things as they might seem to be. This is the poetic method of the Anglo-Saxon *Riddles*, ninety-five of which are to be found in the Exeter Book. Their apparent popularity suggests, possibly, a feeling for their value as a compositional exercise; or further, as a form of rhetorical training in the methods of allegory, or exegesis (the explanation of texts or other phenomena with a "hidden" meaning); or again - why not? - as *fun*, an intricate word-game for literate fellows. An example:

> Often I struggle with waves, fight against winds,
> battle with both together, whenever I seek
> Bourne-under-Billows - a country strange to me.
> In the struggle I am strong - if I just hold still;
> if I fail in that, then they are stronger than I,
> they tear at me, and soon put me to flight.
> They want to carry off what I must keep.
> I can resist that, if my tail holds hard,
> and strong against my strength the stones grip fast.
> Now you may ask yourself - what is my name?   *Riddle 16, Exeter Book*

1 The Poetry Business

The name of this strange creature, a zoomorph whose strength is in its tail, is "anchor". It is presumably an anchor of a simple kedge pattern, with a fluke that drags along the sea-bed until it catches under large stones. No ship is mentioned, except in the periphrasis "what I must keep"; and since anchors are properly at home in ships, "bourne under billows", the home beneath the waves, is for the anchor a strange place where its struggle against the elements is enacted. A technique of equivocation, of misleading by leading, is apparent in this as in most other riddles. . .

Riddles, a popular form in all cultures, were esteemed by the Anglo-Saxon scribes, with the encouragement of their ecclesiastical elders.[15] The poets of the scriptorium devised them in play, no doubt (a few deal in naughty double entendre), or sometimes, through imitation and translation, turned them into a learned mode, with classical and biblical antecedents. The riddle could be an ingenious *exercise* in creative writing, or a way of interpreting the world, with a moral in the background - or both. Its position in the scribal culture of West Saxon is rather different from that of another popular mode, freely "adapted" rather than "adopted" by the Christian copyist: the spell, or "charm", called a *galdor*. A *galdor* was useful if cattle strayed, if your horse was stolen, if the crops were poor, if your bees swarmed; and most necessary in cases of common sickness when the spell could be part of a "leechdom" or medical recipe. We have all at one time or another experienced the discomfort called a "stitch", a sharp pain in the side just below the ribs. The Anglo-Saxons took this seriously. Their recipe *wiþ fáerstice*, "for a sudden stitch" begins with the recommendation to "take feverfew, and red nettles that grow in the wall, and dock leaves, and boil in buttermilk". This is the prescription, but before its administration the *galdorgálend*, or "spell-caller", must perform this chant:

> Loud were they, oh, loud, as they rode over the hill,
> dauntless they were, as they rode over the land.
> Shield yourself now, that you may survive this assault.
> Out, little spear, if herein you be!
>
> Light-guarded I stood, under linden shield,
> when the furies attacked, with might and main,
> whistling spears they flung at me,
> I will forestall them, I will send
> a flying arrow, in return.
> Out, little spear, if herein you be!

---

[15] The pioneer of the monastic riddle was Aldhelm of Malmesbury, Bishop of Sherborne, d. 709. He wrote his verses in Latin, and encouraged others to do so; his riddles were based on those of the 5th century poet Symphosius. After Aldhelm, Archbishop Tatwine (d.737) was the author of 40 riddles; then Eusebius (Hwaetberct, Abbot of Wearmouth and Jarrow from 716) increased the total to 100. For further information, see M.R.James' review of "Latin Writings in England to the Time of Alfred", Chapter V of Vol.1 of *The Cambridge History of English Literature*.

A smith sat, making a little blade,
a weapon of iron, wondrous strong.
Out, little spear, if herein you be!
Six smiths sat, making battle-spears -
Out, spear, not *in*, spear!

If herein be any piece of a blade,
a witch's work, then it shall melt.

Were you shot in the fell, were you shot in the flesh,
were you shot to the blood or shot in the bone,
be there never a threat to your life.

Were it sent from the gods or sent from the elves
or by a witch sent, I will help you now.

This is to cure the cast of the gods, this is to cure the cast of the elves,
this the witch's cast. So I help you now.

It flies away to a mountain top.
Hail! The Lord God be your help! [16]   *Charm "For a sudden stitch"*

The text closes on a brief direction to the practitioner: "Take the knife and dip it into the liquid" (ie the milky infusion of feverfew, nettles and dock). Whether this denotes an act of sympathetic magic, an object (the knife) representing the complaint being "treated" with the medicine (representing the "melting" of the witches' blade) or whether it prefigures some kind of surgical procedure - eg an incision - is not clear. Undoubtedly this, like other leechdoms, is a compound of primitive medicine and pagan supersition. The "mighty women" (so called in the original; here translated as "furies") who come galloping over the rise, flinging their spears, immediately suggest the Nordic *valkyrjor*, the Valkyries, who choose those who are to die in battle. The victim here is vulnerable, and so is the medicine man - he is like a warrior protected with the lightest of shields - but the sufferer is not going to die, if the medicine man can help it. The personae of Nordic myth are further present in a line *gif hit wære esa gescot oððe hit wære ylfa gescot,* "were it (ie the 'shot') sent from the gods or sent from the elves". In Norse cosmology, one of the nine provinces, or "homes" that make up the universe is occupied by a race of gods called the *Æsir,* whose overlord is the god Odin; another province is the domain of the *Álfar,* the elves, practitioners of crafts and mischief. Here they are, as Anglo-Saxon *ós* and *ælf,* in the genitive plural forms *ésa* and *ylfa,* invoked by the shaman-physician who also speaks of *hægtessan,* "witches".Only in the last line of the chant is a Christian power invoked, in a Christianised word, *drihten,* "Lord". The wording of the chant suggests that its curative effort concludes in the hey-

---

[16] This layout of the text is mine, with the object of reflecting the dramatic phases of the treatment ritual. The Anglo-Saxon *Hál westu* is a conventional salutation ("Hail"!) which here, however, might be rendered literally as "be well!"

presto of the penultimate line, "It flies away to the mountain top". ("Off it goes! Soon better!"). The last line, however, looks a good deal like a quasi-liturgical addition by a Christian clerk. (*Hál westu,* "Hail"= *Salvete; helpe ðin drihten,* "the Lord be your help"= *Dominus tecum*). The church gets into the chant at the very close, and makes the rigmarole respectable. This appears to have happened with many of the charms; in some, furthermore, the ritual gestures and repetitions of the pagan spell have undoubted resemblances to the actions and trinitarian repetitions of the Mass. It is a work of accommodation. It may well be that the church knew something of the words good folk would like to have said over a gumboil or a failed crop, and would countenance their saying, but with rubrics that made them safe; though with that modification, something of their primitive oddity and and scariness, the poetry of unease, the spell of the spells, may be lost. It is not in the province of the occult to be merely quaint.

But who composed the spells in the first place? This, surely, was not *scopcræft*. Was the local medicine man, the "leech", with his herbs and simples and recommended procedures in any real sense a poet? Or was he one who in his practice instinctively fell into the rhythms and repetitions most efficacious in impressing and sedating the patient? (Which, indeed, is what poets sometimes do to their readers and priests certainly do to their congregations). Or what of those who recorded the proverbs, the maxims, the edifying examples? Did they begin as copyists and become occasional poets by sudden inspiration, or the chance connections of the text? The riddlers were clearly poets, as technical practitioners, and some riddles have the legitimate status of memorable poems, though others may rate no higher than competent versifying. What must appear to anyone reflecting on the wealth and variety of the Anglo-Saxon written records is the existence of a poetic climate, an acceptance of verse-making, for purposes great or small. Not everyone is a renowned *scop* or an eloquent *wóðbora*, a maker of large and lofty things, but the gift of making - or call it, sometimes, the *knack* of making - is known and honoured, and its products, whatever their original function, can in the long view of time bring to a reader peculiar pleasures as keen as those conferred by the study of the major artefacts. We, perhaps, create the poetry from our own supplies of perception and feeling. This is not an argument for promoting the study of "the minor literature" over that of monumental works. It is only a reminder of the difficulty of defining the poetry business, in which we ourselves, with our preferences, tastes, and vested interests, are shareholders.

2 of cruel battle and the fall of kin

An affair of honour

In its entry for the year 755AD, the *Anglo-Saxon Chronicle* tells of a man called Sigebriht, king of the West Saxons; a dangerous man apparently, a violent man, guilty of "wrongful deeds", because of which he was deposed by a rival, one Cynewulf, at the instance of his *witan*, or Council of State. Sigebriht was deprived of his lands, the *Chronicle* says, but allowed to keep the lordship of Hampshire, until he killed a nobleman called Cumbra, his oldest servant. Then he suffered a penalty arguably worse than death: banishment and outlawry, as a man landless, powerless, and unprotected. Exiled to the great forest of Andred, the ancient weald of Sussex and Kent, he did not long survive. At a place the *Chronicle* calls Privet's Flood, he was stabbed by a herdsman, who, the chronicler says, "avenged the earl Cumbra".

Cynewulf prospered in his kingship for full thirty years, but still the business with Sigebriht remained unfinished. There was an *æþeling* - a man of noble rank - called Cyneheard, a man Cynewulf was planning to drive into exile; and this Cyneheard was Sigebriht's brother. Even after thirty years a blood feud makes its demands. So when Cyneheard learned one day that Cynewulf was to be found at a place called "Merantún", *lítle werode* - "with a small guard" - and *on wífcyððe* - "in female company", as the *Chronicle* delicately puts it, he rode there with a guard of his own and no friendly errand in mind. Merantun (now Merton, in Surrey), would seem to have been an estate with a central hall and outbuildings in a compound enclosed by a gated rampart, of stone or, more probably, of timber and turf. Cyneheard and his followers arrived there at night, entered the compound unresisted, and surrounded the lodge where Cynewulf and his lady were abed. The king, immediately alerted, sprang up and took a resolute stance in the doorway, defending himself effectively in this position, where his attackers could come at him no more than one at a time. Yet when he caught sight of the rebel Cyneheard, rage overcame defensive prudence and he rushed out at him, wounding his enemy grievously, but laying himself open to a collective attack. He fought hard, but they were too many. And while they fought, the lady screamed.

Her screaming at length awoke the king's guard, who had been sleeping soundly in the hall. "They came running as quickly as they could", says the *Chronicle*, "each as soon as he was ready".[17] The situation is imaginable: the rummaging in the dark for clothing and kit, for sword and buckler at least, a helmet perhaps, a ringmail shirt maybe, and then the stumbling, by ones and twos, towards the source of that shrill alarm, and getting there only to find their lord the king cut

---

[17] "They came as quickly as they could, each as soon as he was ready". *Beowulf* (1288-92) presents a vivid and apposite account of men hastily arming for a night alarm: "Then, in the hall, sharp swords were snatched from the wall above the benches, and many a broad shield clutched in hand; no thought for helmet and mailcoat when terror loomed." This is the situation of Cynewulf's men.

down in fight, with not another sword to defend him. A brief negotiation ensued. Cyneheard, master of the moment, made to each of them the offer of life and money if they would let the matter end there, but they refused him. It was not possible. They were already doomed men, dishonoured if they turned away from their doom. The fighting began again, and presently all of the king's "small guard" lay dead, with the exception of one, a Welsh hostage, who was very badly wounded. (A "hostage" - more, perhaps, a pledge of allegiance than a hostage in the modern newspaper sense - was engaged, in the warrior-code of the time, to fight in the service of the lord who had taken him)

Next day, when word of these events reached those the king had left behind, the *aldorman* Osric, ("[e]aldorman" = roughly, "earl"), and Wiferth, one of the king's thanes, brought a relief force to Merantun.[18] They found the outer gates bolted and barred against them, and Cyneheard on the rampart, ready to parley. Exchanges followed, of almost painful correctness, each side observing the conventional forms, each knowing what the outcome must inevitably be. Cyneheard made to the newcomers the offer of riches and land, if they would grant him the kingdom; adding that some of their kinsmen were on his side and would not leave him. Osric's people replied that no man had been dearer to them than their lord, and that they would never follow his killer; but offered their kinsmen on Cyneheard's side the chance to go away unharmed. These answered in turn that the same chance had been offered to the members of the king's guard, who had refused it; and that now they themselves could have no part of it, "any more than your comrades could, who were with the king." With that, the obligatory concessions to honour had been made, and there was no more left to be said. After fierce fighting round the gates, Osric's party broke into the compound, killing Cyneheard and all his party with the exception of one, who was the earl Osric's godson. His life was spared, although, like the Welsh hostage in the first act of this narrative, he was badly wounded. Thus either side could show one survivor, a concession to pathos, a victim spared.

---

[18] On the word *ealdormon*, also *aldormon*, *aldor*. This is the ancestor of modern "alderman", but the cousin of ancient "earl". The Old English word *eorl* is cognate with the Norse *jarl*, and in the Anglo-Saxon Chronicles of the 9th and 10th centuries invariably signifies a "Danish" chieftain or field commander. The Old English equivalent is *[e]aldormon*, a deputy of the king, in effect a "lord lieutenant". The distinction between English and Danish terms is strictly kept in historical accounts, until the late 10th century and after, when *ealdormon* and *eorl* are sometimes used indifferently, or "equivalently", eg. The AS Chronicle for the year 992, "the king entrusted the leadership of the *fyrd* (the English army) to the ealdormon Ælfric and the eorl Thorod." In the Peterborough Chronicle for the year 1048, *eorl* is used consistently, in reference to people whose names clearly indicate Saxon origin - *Leofric, Godwine* - as well as to others with Scandinavian names - *Swegen, Siward*. But in poetic usage *eorl* is established early, whether as an indicator of rank, or more generally in the meaning "nobleman, noble warrior" - an expression of *caste*. Beowulf has *eorl* repeatedly, and rather less often, *aldor*. In the poem of *The Battle of Brunanburh,* the Saxon king, Æthelstan, is called *eorla drihten*, "overlord of earls", and his ancestors *eorlas árhwate*, "earls eager for glory." In *The Battle of Maldon,* the English commander, Byrhtnoth, designated *ealdormon* in the Chronicle for the year 992, is throughout called *sé eorl*, "the earl".

2 Of Cruel Battle and the Fall of Kin

There are noticeable symmetries in this account of vengeance avenged, such counterpoisings as perhaps tell us as much about the writer's sense of narrative pattern as about the total course of those scrambled events. With all the concision of the report, we miss the significance of the unreported; we are modern readers, trained to the Daily Blether, we look for the broader scope, the "human interest". What of the *híwan*, the domestic staff and working folk of the Merantún community, the "family" of the house - what were they doing, where were they hiding, or running, all this while? And indeed, what of the lady? What became of her? A king's mistress, who sees her lover - her "lord" - killed at her own chamber door - and we do not even know her name, or what befell her. She disappears into the peculiar exile reserved for women who get caught up in men's quarrels. For this is warrior's business, work for men, and what is more, for men of rank. The chronicler knows this, and is not obliged to spare a thought for a woman's terror, or her fate; nor is it his concern, as a recorder of aristocratic histories, to evoke the panic in the kitchens or the alarm in the shippon, when the broadswords come hurling in at the gate.

For students of Anglo-Saxon, that episode in a *Chronicle* text, usually one of the first encountered in their struggle with the language, is an introduction to a central theme of Old English poetic literature, the theme of warrior heroism and fealty. The narrative touches on essential traits: exile ...feud ...kinship ..allegiance ...revenge ...riches ...land. It is the dark stuff of Germanic history, and hence the material of a powerful strain of Germanic poetry - powerful, though not all-encompassing. Anglo-Saxon poetry does not consist wholly of "old, far-off, unhappy things and battles long ago". There are other things on offer - as illustrated in the foregoing chapter - things that have lived, unpredictably, to be written down by monks in their *scriptoria* and to survive, in aftertimes, the usual manuscript perils of flood, fire, the bookworm, and sometimes even the bookbinder. Yet still the images that move in the mind of a reader exploring the facts and feelings of Anglo-Saxon verse are the residual hints of such a drama as that enacted at Merton in the Chronicle's year 755 (actually the year 757): hints of desperate fighting, the misery of exile, the duty to avenge, the defence of home and hearth, of the call of kinship and the absolute demand of lordship. A way of feeling, a warlike temper, pervades everything. This story of Merton is a given view; a prose preface to poetic tales of heroes and heroism.

Pomp of a battle won

The Anglo-Saxons also won battles. They won a very important one in the year 937, under a warrior-king, whose kingdom of Wessex was then in the ascendant. The event is celebrated, with an entry to itself, in the *Anglo-Saxon Chronicle,* and what is more, is celebrated in verse. The entry begins in striking style:

> Here Æthelstan, King, protector of earls,
> gold-giver to men, and with him his brother
> the noble Edmund, glory undying
> attained in fight, by the thrust of the sword
> at Brunanburh.   *lines 1-5 The Battle of Brunanburh*

2 Of Cruel Battle and the Fall of Kin

The note of official pomp, the swagger of the communiqué, is unmistakable. Æthelstan and his half-brother Edward were sons of the West Saxon king Edward the Elder, and grandsons of Alfred the Great. Their lineage and kin were known to all; they had, as the poet/chronicler himself remarks, prowess in their blood. Their enemies at Brunanburh were a faction of diverse forces allied in their will to crush the increasing power of Wessex: Scots under the King Constantine, the Britons of Strathclyde, the Danish colonists of Northumbria, and the Vikings of the Dublin settlement, led by one Olaf Kvaran and his cousin, also called Olaf. (Olaf Sihtricsson). These participants are not severally identified in the poem, where the principal enemy is Constantine, seconded by "Anlaf" - Olaf Kvaran - and his Norsemen.

The site of the battle is a matter of conjecture; general consensus places it in the north-west of England, somewhere north of the estuary of the river Ribble. Local historians in proud Preston argue for the Ribble; their colleagues in Lancaster put the case for the Lune, further north. Anywhere in this area would make a plausible point of convergence for the allies in the coalition of Northumbrian Danes, Scots, and the Dublin Vikings. The fight that followed was a bloody one, lasting from sun-up to sundown, or as the chronicler phrases it, in an impulse of lyricism:

> after the sun
> in the morningtide, the mighty star
> moved over the earth, God's candle bright,
> the eternal Lord's, until that noble shape
> sank down to rest.
>
> *lines 13-17 The Battle of Brunanburh*

The lyrical moment serves the additional - or perhaps essential - purpose of putting Almighty God into a picture from which He is otherwise absent. The poem suggests that after the breaking of the shield-wall the fight became a cavalry action, the Saxons pursuing their enemy *éoredcystum*, "in troops of horse", cutting the fugitives down from behind, as they ran. It seems to have been, quite simply, a slaughter, with no chivalric gestures to ennoble it. The poet's tone is triumphal, close to scorn, at times not far from gloating - "scoffing" - especially as he describes the humiliation of Constantine, the "white-haired warrior":

> Then, too, the Old One was forced to flee,
> away to his folk in the north - King Constantine,
> old skirmisher. No cause had he to rejoice
> in the meeting of swords; of kinsmen reft,
> parted from friends on that field of battle slain,
> he left his own son there, a boy in the wars,
> mortally wounded on that field of death.
> No cause to exult in the clash of swords
> had Whitehair, the old foe - nor Olaf yet.
> They could not laugh to think, they and their swords
> made winner's work of one day in the field,

> with banners flailing, with spears flying,
> the meeting of men, the fighting hand to hand,
> when at the killing place they played war games
> with Edward's heirs.
>
> *lines 37-52 The Battle of Brunanburh*

After this the Norsemen, or what is left of them - *dréorig daroþa láf*, "wretched spears' leavings" - take ship for Dublin, and the Saxon king and prince ride home in triumph, leaving a field strewn with corpses for the birds and beasts to pick at.

> Behind they left, to come to their bait,
> the raven black, all dusky-plumed
> and horny beaked, and the grey eagle
> with its white tail, and the ravening war-hawk,
> and that dark beast, the wolf in the wood.
>
> *lines 60-65*

This is a carnival of the scavengers, a conventional feature of battle-scenes. Throughout the poem the poet handles convention with the flair of a *scop*, using traditional devices, with frequent reminiscences of heroic word and phrase. The animals in this company are not a realistic menagerie. They are accessories to a tale of human victory that allows no quarter to the human vanquished. But the poem's true note of glory unabashed sounds out in its closing lines:

> Was never yet more slaughter on this isle,
> such tale of numbers slain, put to the sword,
> as records tell, old books that scholars keep,
> since hither westward over the wide sea
> Angles and Saxons came, to seek out Britain
> and quell the British; proud in the craft of war
> they came, earls eager for glory, and got them a land
>
> *lines 65-73*

The tenor of these closing lines is unblushingly imperialistic. The earls came "eager for glory" - the word is *árhwæt*, plural *árhwate*, a compound of *hwæt*, "keen" and *ár*, which indeed may mean "glory", but also means "honour", "reward" "favour", "benefice", "livelihood", even "land". And land, called *eard* - "home", "dwelling place", "estate", "country" - they got for themselves, by ruthlessly displacing the native population, in the migratory manner of the dark age peoples.

The author of *Brunanburh* is clearly a lettered man, with a sense of history. He is also deeply versed in the Germanic conventions of poetic recital. Truly, he plays the part of a *scop*, boasting the valorous achievement of tribal chiefs, ironically taunting the defeated enemy, affirming the lasting fame of the ruler. There is *scopcræft*, too, in its language and phraseology, a good deal of which is borrowed from a common poetic stock, but can claim originality in its application. Its eloquence has been rightly praised. Worth noting is its popularity with the Victorians. Lord Tennyson wrote a verse translation, and a very good one, rejoicing in the poem's triumphalist tone. But that was in the high and palmy days of Empire; modern readers tend to find crushing victory less interesting than magnificently qualified defeat.

Circumstance of a battle lost

"Qualified defeat" is a phrase that might be used to characterise a great poem written half a century later than *Brunanburh*, commemorating a lost battle. In the year 991, during the reign of Æthelred the Unready, a battle was fought in Essex, near the fortified town of Maldon, on the banks of the river Blackwater. It was witnessed, or perhaps reported from testimony, very shortly after the event, by someone who would almost certainly have been a monk or cleric. His poem, which we know as *The Battle of Maldon*, commemorates the Christian men who there died in fight against "the heathen", the latter being Viking adventurers harassing the coasts of southern England with menaces of war and havoc only to be bought off with large payments of "tribute". The traditional word for such extortion is "Danegeld". On this occasion the leader of the pack, the man identified in the *Chronicle* as "Anlaf" or "Olave" was not, strictly speaking, a Dane; he was a Norwegian, one Olaf Tryggvason, converted to Christianity during a winter sojourn in the Scilly Isles, and destined, a few years later, to be King of Norway, in which office he embarked, with the same brutally ungainsayable energy he had brought to piracy, on the christianising of his country and its dependency, Iceland. But the poet of Maldon knew nothing, it seems, of Olaf Tryggvason. It has been suggested that he did not even know his name, so narrow was the gap between the event and the poetic composition.[19] (Whereas the *Chronicle,* in its annal for the year 994, has a long entry concerning "Anlaf", who was graciously received by King Æthelred at a meeting in Andover, and went away well paid and well satisfied). He knew only that the Heathen had arrived in brute force and that the Christians had gone against them, in godly fight.

Against the Viking *here* - the "pillaging army" - stood a Saxon *fyrd*, a levy raised for such emergencies,[20] the task being entrusted to the king's *ealdormon,* who had the immediate support of his thanes and household troops, and could conscript others from the surrounding districts. In Essex, the *ealdormon* was one Byrhtnoth Byrhthelmson. We see him at the beginning of the Maldon poem, energetically

---

[19] Did they know this was Tryggvason? But it was hardly the poet's wish, or business, to know the Viking commander's name. There is evidence that even the Viking's own men were not wholly aware of his identity at the time of his raids on Britain; he had his reasons for keeping it secret. According to a distinguished source, Snorri Sturluson's *Heimskringla* (see Chapter 1, p.12) his crews at first knew him only as Ole (familiar = "Olly"), and thought he was Russian. For details, see *Heimskringla*, Life of Olaf Tryggvason, caps. 32, 33.

[20] On armies, ours and theirs. The two armies, "home" and "away", Saxon and Viking, are consistently distinguished by the words *fyrd* and *here* (the latter eytmologically related to *hergian*, "harry, ravage, plunder") A campaign by the native army, called a *fyrding*, could on occasion be as oppressive to the home population as the operations of the *here*. Thus the Chronicle for the year 1005: "Then the king ordered the call-up of all the forces of Wessex and Mercia; and during all the harvest time they were out campaigning against the Vikings. But it was of no more use then that it ever had been, for during all that time the Vikings came and went as they pleased. And the campaign did all kinds of harm to the country folk, so that for them there was no choosing between one army and the other." The words the writer uses here are *innhere* ("in-" for the home army) and *úthere* ("out-" for the invaders).

drawing up his troops, showing them where to stand, and how to stand, and urging them to take a firm hold of their shields and fear for nothing.This description suggests the formation of a typical defence round the *scyldburh*, the wall of overlapping shields, so essential to Saxon battle, but liable to be broken by the superior force of attackers, or by indiscipline among the defenders. Byrhtnoth is clearly anxious that his inexperienced or variously-experienced troops (some of them little more than boys) should understand the importance of keeping up their spirits and holding the shield wall. This done, he takes up his position among his most seasoned and trusted men, his *heorðwerod*, or household guard.While he is thus occupied, a messenger arrives from the *here*, whose ships are moored, or beached, on an island in mid-river. The tide is at the flood, separating the invaders from the defenders, who are taking up their position on the west bank of the river. From the island shore, the Viking spokesman shouts a message which is quite simply a demand for protection money. If the Saxons will send, at the Vikings' reckoning, a sufficient quantity of treasure, in the form of *béagas*, rings, bracelets, "torcs" of precious metal, the seamen will board their ships and sail peacefully away. The "if not..." is left to the understanding of the hearer.

Béagas were a mark of personal distinction and status, or a token of esteem, as much as a sign of wealth; one of the ways in which a noble master might reward a thane for valiant service could be to confer upon him the gift of a *béag*.[21] The impudent demand for *béagas* in return for the favour of going away and doing nothing unpleasant until next time kindles the scorn in Byrhtnoth's reply:

"D'you hear, pirate, what these people say?
They'll send you tribute - spears they'll give you,
point envenomed, ancient sword -
war-gear that will not serve you in this fight.
You seamen's runner, run back with this errand,
go tell your folk a story they will hate -
that here, undaunted, stands an earl with his *werod*,
to shield this homeland, Æthelred's land, my lord's,
the nation and the soil. The heathen shall fall in the fray"

lines 45-55 The Battle of Maldon

---

[21] More about "wound gold". The *béagas* were only one form of tribute, salary or reward (others being weapons, jewels, horses, grants of land) but they are most frequently mentioned in poetry.They were apparently made of "wound gold". The exile in *The Wanderer* (see Chapter 3) complains that his lot is "the way of the outcast", *nalaes wunden gold*, "not the wound (braided, or twisted) gold". In *Beowulf* (lines 1380-83) as the hero is about to combat a monster, King Hrothgar promises to reward him *wundini golde / gyf þu in weg cymest* - "with the wound gold, should you come out alive". So again in the Old High German *Hildebrand*, the central character, facing single combat with his own son, who does not recognise him, offers him *bouga*, "ring", in earnest of his good faith: *Want do ar arme wuntane bouga / cheisurungu gitan so imo se der chuning gap / Huneo truhtin*, "Then he slipped from his arm the twisted ring of imperial gold which the king, the lord of the Huns himself, had given to him." The importance of the *béag* as an emblem of service, honour, and fealty is evident from these instances.

In saying this, Byrhtnoth accompanies his words with a formal, almost heraldic gesture of defiance, repeated throughout the poem by other speakers as they make their heroic intentions plain: he "lifts up his shield and shakes his slender spear". What is apparently a ritual act affirms a speech that skilfully compounds rhetoric in a high style (*point envenomed, ancient sword...to shield this homeland, Æthelred's land, our lord's*) with calculated irony and understatement (*"They'll send you tribute...war-gear that will not serve you in this fight"*) and with flashes of the plain blast-your-impudence colloquial (*"D'you hear, pirate?...go tell your folk a story they will hate"*). This speech, like others that follow in a narrative constructed round alternations of speech and action, purports to be spontaneous utterance, as though reported by our-man-on-the-spot; but that is arguably one of poetry's truthful fictions. What becomes evident by and by is that this is not the method of the poet who says "we have heard" or "as books tell" The poetic account of the events at Maldon is carefully designed, or as modern reviewers say, *crafted*. Its relationship to factual happening is less fact than faction, or docu-fiction. The poet plays the part of a scrupulous, *scop*-like reporter of actions, a "teller" who, however, enjoys an authorial liberty to attribute to his characters credible sentiments and speeches, faithfully conveying the *what* of an utterance, but freely managing the rhetoric of *how*. So with the poem's first great speech, Byrhtnoth's angry rejection of the Vikings' demand for tribute. No one can reasonably doubt that Byrhtnoth replied to the enemy in the strongest possible terms; but the poet's attribution of the terms is an act of invented eloquence.

"An earl and his *werod*" - again comes that word *werod*, central to any account of Anglo-Saxon warfare. In this context it might well signify something as general as "army", "force", all the men of the *fyrd* that Byrhtnoth has raised; except that the lines describing how the earl rides back and forth inspecting his battle-line tell how eventually he "*alighted where he was loved the best, where he knew his companion-guard most true to him*" The "earl and his *werod*" means just that- the noble commander and his *heorðwerod*, his most trusted band of kinsmen, counsellors, friends, tried in fight and bound to him in mutual bonds of service given and favour received. That one line in Byrhtnoth's speech of defiance - "here, undaunted, stands an earl and his *werod*" - announces the theme of *Maldon*, which is the story of how the *werod*, after the fall of its commander, remembered its pledges, kept its vows, fought as one body, and died by ones and twos.

This is the setting of the poem, presented with the detail of a war-report. The battle cannot begin until the tide ebbs, but as it does a "bridge", or roughly paved ford, is revealed, and the Vikings begin to file across this narrow access. The bridgehead is resolutely guarded by three bold men (they are named as Wulfstan, Ælfhere and Maccus) who are so effective that the pirates plead - "cunningly sue", says the poet - for room to cross the ford and draw up their battle. It is a plea that Byrhtnoth, *for his ofermóde*, "out of pride", disastrously concedes. This is the one and only place in the narrative at which the narrator is critical of his hero. *Ofermód* has theological overtones of *superbia*, or *hubris*; and it is a pride for which the brave *eorl* pays with his life. The initial business of positioning his troops to the best effect thus comes to nothing; there is a shift to re-group before Byrhtnoth again speaks his defiance, while his men listen:

2 Of Cruel Battle and the Fall of Kin

> "Now there is room for you. Come quickly to us,
> you men, to this fight. God alone knows
> who shall be masters of the field."   *lines 93-5 The Battle of Maldon*

So God enters the action; it is to be a fight for godliness. The phrase "God alone knows", in the original *God ána wát* - should not be read with the modern nuance of an agnostic shrug - "Who can tell?" It is an affirmation of faith in a controlling power beyond human will, or skill, or chance, or the disposition of troops. Man proposes, Fate exposes, God disposes.

The lines describing the onset of the fight are busy with a phraseology drawn from a conventional thesaurus of battlefield descriptions:

> Then the fight was at hand,
> glory in the fray; the hour was come
> when doomed men were to fall.
> A shout went up. Ravens circled above,
> and the eagle keen for carrion. Below was a clamour.
> They let fly from their hands file-tempered spears,
> the fine-ground javelins. Bows were busy,
> point struck shield. Bitter the onset.
> Warriors fell, soldiers lay dead
> on either side.   *lines 103-112*

This is a poet's view of the landscape of battle. Those doomed men, those ravens and voracious eagles, like the circling vultures in a Western film, those hard-ground spears, can be found elsewhere, in other phrases from descriptions of other fights. (See, for example the setting of *Brunanburh*, previously described) Yet the description is realistic in presenting the opening sequence of a battle. First comes the shout of challenge or defiance; then the spears flung at the enemy host; then the arrow-storm and, on the other side, the shields raised to take or deflect the points. It is the first stage of the engagement. A struggle at close quarters quickly follows. As the Vikings, pushing forward, begin hand-to-hand fighting, one of the first casualties on the English side is a young man called Wulfmær:

> Wulfmær was wounded - took rest from battle -
> Byrhtnoth's kinsman, his sister's son,
> cut to pieces by hacking blades.   *lines 113-15*

The phrase "took rest from battle", *wælraest gecéas,* literally "sought the bed of slaughter", ie "was killed", is a dignified epic formula, almost a euphemism, in odd contrast with the raw realism of *swíðe forhéawen* "cut to pieces" (resembling *swíðe gewundad,* "grievously wounded", the condition of the Welsh hostage in the Cynewulf/Cyneheard episode) Wulfmær is Byrhtnoth's kin, and more than kin: he is *swustersunu,* "sister's son", a relationship of particular importance in Germanic social lore, very much as *godsunu*, "godson", is a relationship of special importance in religious doctrine.[22] The relationship is essentially protective, and carries obligations and responsibilities, but his uncle cannot help Wulfmær now, in these critical moments. The *eorl* himself is hard beset, and it is left to another fighter, a thane of Byrtnoth's household, to avenge the boy.

This brings in a long episode in which the poet describes, in studied detail, at times almost with gloomy relish, Byrhnoth's valorous combat with a sequence of assailants, ending with his fall and death in battle:

> Then one, battle-hardened, hefted his spear,
> and under the cover of his shield
> pressed in to meet his man.
> As resolute came earl to churl,
> either meaning the other harm.
> Then the seaman flung his Frankish lance,
> wounding the warrior prince,
> who bore down with his shield, splintered the shaft,
> and the spearhead sprang from the gash; enraged,
> the warrior with his own spear stabbed
> the insolent Viking who had wounded him.
> So glad was the earl; he let his javelin drive
> through the other's throat; his guiding hand
> made sure of the enemy's life.
> Then as quickly he thrust at another,
> so hard, the man's armour broke; stabbed in the breast,
> through the ring-mail coat, he took to heart
> a deadly point. And the earl was the merrier.
> He laughed, the valiant man. Thanked the Creator
> for this day's labour the Lord had granted him.
> But then, one of the Danes let fly a spear
> that flew too far, and pierced Æthelred's thane.
> There stood at his side a stripling, a mere boy,
> who boldly wrenched from his lord the bloody spear.
> Son of Wulfstan he was, Wulfmær the young.
> He sent the sharp spear flying back again.
> The point went home. And that man fell and died

---

[22] "Sister's son". In his *Germania*, dating from AD 98, the Roman historian Tacitus notes the importance of the "sister's son" relationship among the continental tribes. "The sons of sisters are as highly honoured by their uncles as by their own fathers. Some even go so far as to regard this tie of blood as peculiarly close and sacred, and, in taking hostages, insist on having them of this class; they think that this gives them a firmer grip on men's hearts and a wider hold on the family" (*Germania*, transl. H.Mattingly, cap.20; see Bibliography, section 4)

who had so gravely hurt his lord.
A man in armour then came at the earl,
meaning to spoil his corpse, stripping away
mail-coat, precious rings, damascened sword.
Then Byrhtnoth drew the sword out from its sheath,
broad-bladed, gleaming; struck at the armoured man,
yet all too swift a shipman came between
and caught the earl's arm with a crippling blow.
Then the gold-hilted sword fell to the ground.
Able no more to hold that tempered blade
or wield any weapon, still the veteran spoke,
urging his fighters on, good comrades all.
And then he could no longer stand upright
lines 130-168 The Battle of Maldon

At some 41 lines in the original, that passage must qualify as one of the longest and most circumstantial accounts of single combat in Old English poetry; and one might add, an account distinguished by its unflinching realism. It is central to the poem - centrally placed and central in theme. It focuses on the hero and his stance among his *werod*, those "good comrades all", from the *cniht*, the "mere boy", to the *búrþegn*, "chamberlain", one of the companions round the chief. It reminds us of the ignoble motives of the savage Vikings, bent on plunder. And it also reminds us that the "warriors' lord" is a Christian prince, glad to fight, suffer, and lay down his life in defence of his earthly overlord, and in the higher service of the Lord of Hosts. So Byrhtnoth's dying words are those of one who has done his duty and looks to God for deliverance:

"Thanks be to thee, Ruler of every nation,
for all the joys I have known in this world.
Now, merciful Creator, I have need
that Thou wilt grant my spirit a good ending
and that my soul at last may come to Thee,
into Thy kingdom, Master of the angels,
peacefully entering, and I beseech Thee,
let never hell's marauding devils harm it."
lines 173-80

Then earth's marauding devils finish their work. *The heathen lackeys butchered him*, says the text.

The interpolation of that prayer marks a kind of conversion: *Maldon*, essentially a poem of tribal, "warrior" sentiment, is here committed, by its poet, to Christian feeling. We are left in no doubt that this is a bearing of witness, a martyrdom. The words of the prayer fall easily enough into the rhythms of translation, because the phrasing of the original echoes the measured orisons of the church. But what is "original" about this original? Are we to think that these are the very utterances of the dying warrior, carefully held in someone's memory to be precisely reported in this memorial text? The question almost answers itself. The words are the shaping of the poet-cleric, in a warmth of pious feeling attributing to his mortally-wounded hero appropriate sentiments, in such a turn of phrase as the noble and pure-souled Byrhtnoth deserved to have at his disposal. Accepting the veracity of the event, we accept the artifice of the telling.

That sense of artifice transforming fact dominates the remaining 150 lines of the poem, which commemorate the fall, one by one, of the companions of the *werod*. They have not all been loyal to soldierly vows, taken in their lord's presence, in the hall or at council. By the *béot*, "boast", an act of public commitment, the warrior vows to repay his lord and protector's generosity with service in battle that precludes not only surrender but also the very notion of leaving the battlefield alive when the lord lies dead and unavenged. To do that, says Tacitus, observing the customs of Germanic tribes in the 1st century AD, means lifelong infamy and shame. [23] It is no different in the 10th century. Yet some of Byrhtnoth's *werod* flee when he is killed. They are named - as almost everyone in the poem is named, for Anglo-Saxon heroism demands names, for praising or shaming. The renegades are the sons of one Odda; they are Godric and his brothers, Godwine and Godwig. Godric, evidently the senior, invites particular opprobrium. It is he who first takes to horse,

> deserting that good man
> who often enough had given him steeds enough;
> mounting the steed that belonged to his lord alone,
> with the costly trappings to which he had no right -
> he and his brothers, both of them, ran,
> Godwine, Godwig, cared naught for the battle
> but turned from the fighting and ran for the woods,
> fled to the fort, saved their own skins.
> Others ran, too, beyond all sense of honour,
> had they remembered the many kindnesses
> done to repay their warriorship.
>
> *lines 187-97 The Battle of Maldon*

One of the dwindling company left on the field bewails the consequence of Godric's desertion:

> "Odda's coward son has betrayed us all.
> Too many thought, when he rode away on that horse,
> that noble steed, it was our lord who ran,
> and so here on this field is a folk divided,
> the shield-wall broken"
>
> *lines 237-42*

---

[23] Tacitus, *Germania*, Chapter 14 : *iam vero infame in omnem vitam ac probrosum superstitem princeipe suo ex acie recessisse* – "for indeed, to have quit the battlefield, leaving your chief dead, brings infamy and shame for all your life to come."

2 Of Cruel Battle and the Fall of Kin

And the breaking of the shield-wall, as always, is the beginning of the end. Now the surviving members of the *werod* are left to fight to the last, each for his honour paying the debt to his fallen lord.

The description of their last stand has the quality of a tableau, a scene dramatically staged. The doomed fighters speak in turn, some making the ritual gesture of raising a shield or brandishing a spear. They make known, or are made known by, their names and their kin. They make their last *béot* ("boast"), the vow to avenge their lord or die on the field. They fight on, until strength fails. Thus Ælfwine, son of Ælfric speaks - speaks *on ellen*, "valiantly":

> "Remember the times when we talked over our mead,
> there on the benches, making our brave boasts,
> heroes in hall, talking of fight and hard knocks -
> well, now we are going to see who the hard men are.
> I will make known to all my lineage,
> mine was a noble family, in Mercia,
> Ealhelm my father's name; wise ealdorman,
> rich with the blessings of this world.
> Thanes in that country will have no cause to jeer
> that I was ready to break ranks and run,
> make tracks for home, leaving my master dead,
> cut down in the fight. No insult could be worse.
> He was alike my kinsman and my lord."
>
> *lines 212-24 The Battle of Maldon*

The valiant speech, like others in the poem (see Byrhtnoth's retort to the Vikings' demand for ransom) is a complex of styles, or an alternation of tones. Ælfwine the bold lad, speaking to bold lads: *nu mæg cunnian hwa cene sy*, "now we shall see who the hard men are". Ælfwine indignant: *me is þæt hearma mæst*, "to me that is the worst of insults." Ælfwine in ritual mode: *Ic wille mín æþelo eallum gecyþan*, "I will proclaim my lineage to all" Ælfwine in pathetic cadence: *he wæs ægþer mín mæg ond mín hlaford*, "he was alike my kinsman and my lord". The noble speech is an artifice, the poet's own rhetorical blend, but no less noble for that, and no less moving.

Others similarly take their stance and make their vows, in the face of certain death:

> Leofsunu spoke, lifting his targe,
> his guardian shield, as he called to the men:
> "This I swear, that from hence I will never
> retreat one foot, but I will press on,
> to avenge in fight my master, my friend.
> Brave fellows round Sturmer shall never have cause
> to scoff, that after my friend was dead
> I came home masterless, flinched from the fray,
> but weapons must take me, point and blade."
>
> *lines 265-72*

2 Of Cruel Battle and the Fall of Kin

Sturmer is in Norfolk; Ælfwine comes from yet farther afield, from somewhere up-country, from Mercia. It seems as though, as this poet presents the drama, the men of Essex are becoming the men of England, representative guardians of "Æthelred's land ...the nation, the soil". And unexpectedly, another representative of the nation appears in the aristocratic, lineage-conscious, kin-connected ranks of the *werod*. He is the private soldier, Nobody, son of No-kin:

> Dunnere spoke then - shook his spear -
> a simple peasant - called out to them all,
> urged every fighter to strike for Byrhtnoth,
> "Let no one hold back, or fear for his life,
> who looks to avenge our people's lord"   *lines 255-59 The Battle of Maldon*

Dunnere is not a thane, not a *gesíð*, a companion of the inner circle. By class he is a *ceorl*, "churl", a mere peasant, most probably a freedman.[24] He has no pedigree to boast of, no well-born kin, no broad familiar acres to call his own. He has no well-crafted speech to make; a single sentence speaks his mind, eloquent enough for the occasion, but in sense no more elaborate than a corporal's encouraging cry to the beleaguered platoon. ("Get stuck in, lads") Yet he has a place in the story.

Another outsider with a place on the inside is the *gísl*, the "hostage". Like the Welsh hostage in the Merton episode, he plays a loyal part in the fight. A Northumbrian, of a hardy race, he joins Mercian Ælfwine and East Anglian Leofsunu as a representative of Æthelred's England at bay:

> The hostage gave them ready support.
> He was of tough Northumbrian stock,
> the son of Ecglaf, Æscferth his name.
> He did not falter in the play of battle,
> but loosed his arrows unceasingly,
> now hitting a shield, now finding his man,
> time and again inflicting some wound
> for as long as he could draw his bow.   *lines 265-72*

His role in the battle play is that of an archer, in support of the spearmen and swordsmen. Thence the last line of the passage as translated above. The reading of that line in the original text, however, is *þa hwile ðe he wæpna wealdan moste*, "for as long as he might wield weapons", an elegiac formula signifying "until he died". The assumption of inevitable death is now never absent from the poem.

---

[24] The meaning of *ceorl*. Dunnere is described as *unorne ceorl*, "a simple peasant". "Churl" here has none of the pejorative overtones it has in modern English; it is an indication of social status - the poet's intention being to show that men from all ranks and regions fought on the English side. A note of aristocratic disdain, however, is sounded in the line describing Byrhtnoth's onset with one of the Vikings: *eode swa anræd eorl to þam ceorle*, "as resolute came earl against churl."

2 Of Cruel Battle and the Fall of Kin

One by one, selling their lives dear, the companions go down. They are named, as they struggle and die. Ætheric fights on, and is killed. Offa fights on, remembering a promise made to his lord that they would ride home victorious together, or together lie on the field of battle. He fights, and is killed. *He læg þegenlice þeodne gehende*, says the text, in a beautiful line, "like a thane he lay by his master's side". Wistan, Thurstan's son fights on, kills three men, and is killed. Still they shout encouragement to each other, the brothers Oswold and Ealwold now taking the lead. And at length there comes from the dwindling ranks a cry of ultimate defiance from yet another who "lifts up his shield and brandishes his spear":

> "Firmer the thought, keener the heart,
> courage the more, as our strength grows less"
>
> *lines 312-13 The Battle of Maldon*

The speaker is an old man, Byrhtwold, *eald genéat*, a veteran among the companions. If there is a taste for heroism, that wild shout must touch it. Who cannot respond, even at a thousand years' distance? The nerves respond, the hair bristles at the nape of the neck. Such an utterance becomes emblematic, a sign to cherish in one's own times of trial and crisis. It is at once a cry of despair and a cry of triumph. And yet - is "wild shout", implying spontaneous utterance, a quite appropriate characterisation of Byrhtwold's speech? We come again to that feature that recurs teasingly throughout the poem, the interplay of realistic report and artistic contrivance. This battle cry is a rhetorical figure. It needs a little thought to shape such a construction, a graduation of balanced phrases. We can hardly suppose that it came to the *eald genéat* while he was at the point of exhaustion, fending off spears and parrying sword-thrusts. He may well have said something rather different, to the same effect, equally honourable, though not quite so polished. Yet the words given to him are the words fit for a veteran to use. They touch and convince. Thanks to the art and sympathetic insight of the poet, we accept them as Byrhtwold's own, heard as the heroes fight on and the action fades, with no ending except the sad certainty of a foregone conclusion.

The Battle of Maldon is deservedly prized as one of the finest poems in the Anglo-Saxon canon. Its appeal is general. The newcomer to the study of Old English, a freshman on campus, warms to the vigour of its narrative and its tally of personalities; fifty years on, the *eald genéat*, veteran in the bookstacks, can find in it subtleties unsuspected and be charmed anew by its complexities. For *Maldon* is indeed a complex poem. The complexity lies not so much in the language, the currency of words and shifting poetic meanings, the problems of synonymy, the elusive intonations of Old English speech. (This last is a matter of which we can know very little; we can only guess at possibilities of pitch and accent). What is complex, or complicating, is a depth of theme and structure, a "layering" of many things cunningly composed or implied by the poet's art. At its simplest, *Maldon* is a poem about kinship, lordship, and loyalty, things in themselves not entirely simple. It is a deeply patriotic poem, its shining hero one who unquestioningly chose to defend King Æthelred's land in a time when nearly everyone else, including King Æthelred, chose solutions of ignoble compromise. So it is also a poem about cowardice and compromise and betrayal. It is a poem about morality, about keeping faith with principles, even at the ultimate cost. So it becomes (with a little prompting from the poet) a poem celebrating Christian faith. Most of all - and again, by the devising of the poet - it is a poem that celebrates the individual nature and the individual act. The *werod* is destroyed as an entity, but individuals matter. Each one is named and commemorated, and in the commemoration is justified. In the worst defeat, the poem tells the modern reader, in the collapse of states and citadels and armies, the individual responds, bears witness, keeps faith with God and his neighbour, and, after all, triumphs. This is the complexity of *Maldon*. It is steeped in the language and sentiment of an ancient heroic tradition, but its rhetoric adduces feelings that still move the reader in the twenty-first century. Its grandeur is the truthful fiction of persons finding within themselves the resources to enact their beliefs. We know their names and their deeds on the day they died. We know why they chose to stand, when they must have known that it was a lost battle, and that an hour or two of courage in the bleak fields by the river, to keep faith with a dead master pledged to a distant king, must come to nothing. They are not demoralised. We know their value as persons. *Maldon* tells a personal tale; *Brunanburh* trumpets the impersonal, merciless rage of conquest.

For services rendered; or there's for thy pains

There is a personal footnote from an external source, one man's story in connection with the affair at Brunanburh. It is supplied by a passage in the Icelandic saga of Egil Skallagrimsson, which relates how Egil and his brother Thorolf, travelling abroad ("for their health", it might be said) had taken service under King Æthelstan, and thus took part in the action in which Thorolf was killed. After the battle, Egil had a place of honour in hall, at the hearth, opposite the king's high seat. He was a man of moods, many of them ugly, and on this occasion the face he turned to the king was contorted in a ferocious scowl of displeasure, expressing, possibly, grief for Thorolf's death, resentment at the king's action in assigning the brothers to separate battlefield commands, or possibly a protest at the inadequate recognition of his own services. The authors of the Icelandic sagas never presume to tell us what their subjects are feeling or thinking. No stream of consciousness, no inner monologue for them; they tell us how people look, what they do, and what they say, and leave us to make our own inferences. There sat the ferociously scowling Egil, one eyebrow up at his hairline, the other down on his cheek, with his sword on his lap, fidgeting with the hilt. Then the king, willing to placate his servant, drew from his arm a gold ring and hung it on the point of his sword, which he held out over the hearth. Egil, seeing the intention, took his own sword and, reaching across, engaged the point of the king's. The *béag* was thus transferred to the blade of Egil's sword, and slid down it into his grasp. Then, says the saga, "his eyebrows righted themselves". Honour satisfied, he promptly composed a poem to fit the event, an elaborately figured utterance in a complex metre, for Egil, in the depth of his dark and violent nature, was a *skald*, a poet, an accomplished practitioner of an incredibly intricate style of oral composition. What the king and others made of this poetic compliment; or how well they understood it, is not certain; but a fine sight the action must have been, with the firelight glistening on the ring and the sword-blades, and the courtiers gaping at Egil's audacity.[25]

That testimony from a foreign source is an idiosyncratic account, possibly unique in Northern literature, of a ritual process known in Anglo-Saxon by various names denoting the receipt or conferring of rewards, in anticipation or acknowledgement of faithful service: thus *hringþegu, béahþegu, máððumþegu, sincþegu*, the receiving of rings, armlets, precious objects (*máððum* = "jewel", *sinc* = "treasure"), and correspondingly, *hringgifu, béahgifu, máððumgifu, sincgifu*, the giving of such things, the giver being the *hringgifa, béahgifa, máððumgifa* or *sincgifa*, which terms become poetic synonms for "lord and master". The ceremony of giving and receiving is the outward and visible sign of an assumed economic compact between master and servant. "The chief fights for victory", says Tacitus, "the warriors fight for their chief"[26] - fight for him because a victorious captain is a guarantee of security, a source of wealth and livelihood. The economic link is raised to a bond of honour in another ritual of the Anglo-Saxon mead-hall, the *béot*, commonly translated as "boast", more properly signifying "pledge", or "vow". The vow is made to the *béahgifa*. It pledges, in repayment of his generosity, to win his battles for him or die with him. Its scope is precisely defined in the lines in *Maldon* describing Offa's death:

> Soon in the battle was Offa slain,
> yet he had done what he promised his lord
> when he made his vow to the gift-giver,
> that they would together ride into town,
> come home unharmed, or in battle die.   *lines 288-92 The Battle of Maldon*

---

[25] A ring-giving by firelight. Egil's Saga, attributed to Snorri Sturluson, date c:a 1230; chapter LV. For a serviceable online translation, see http://www.blackmask.com , *Egil's Saga, translated from the Icelandic*, by the Revd.W.C.Green. Other texts are *Egil's Saga*, transl with an introduction by Hermann Pálsson and Paul Edwards, Penguin Books, 1976; also *Egil's Saga*, Everman Library edn, ed. Christine Fell, transl.John Lucas; in Everman Paperback Classics . This may be fairly called an "idiosyncratic account", in that it was written nearly three hundred years later than the events it describes, and is written by a man with a flair for arresting narrative. We are not to take it as wholesale fiction, however. Medieval Iceland preserved its family sagas in oral tradition for many years before they were written down; and to judge by his *Heimskringla*, Snorri was scrupulously respectful of ascertainable fact.

[26] Chiefs and followers. Tacitus: *principes pro victoria pugnant, comites pro principe. Germania*. Cap.14. See *Beowulf*, 2490-93 and 2497-9, as the dying hero talks of his relationship with his chief, Hygelac:

> In battle, with my bright sword, I repaid him,
> as I was able, for such favours given;
> land he gave, a home, a dear dwelling
> ....
> Always, in the host, I went before him,
> as vanguard, all alone - and always thus
> shall I do battle, while this sword shall last.

2 Of Cruel Battle and the Fall of Kin

Then follows the line *he læg þegenlice his þeodne gehende* - "he lay like a thane by his master's side." A thane keeps his vows; and if in such a context as this they begin to read like marriage vows, that is not wholly amiss. We have no reason to doubt the warrior's emotional commitment to his master; when Osric's troop in the fight at Merton repudiated Cyneheard's offer of "wealth and land" with the reply that "no man was dearer to them than their lord, and they would never follow his killer", they were speaking of an unconditional devotion of thane and lord, such a devotion as religious poetry would eventually adapt as an analogue of the feeling of a disciple for the lord Christ. The feeling was genuine enough, whatever its promissory base.

To break a vow was the worst evil, incurring a shame and retribution that might befall not only the renegade, but all his kin. When Godric, the horse-thief, quits the field at Maldon, the judgement on him, pronounced by Offa in the heat and haste of battle, is *Ábréoðe his anginn* which soberly translated means "May he never thrive", but rendered with proper emotional force, "Be damned to him!" The sentiment is elaborated, powerfully, in a celebrated passage towards the end of *Beowulf*, when the old hero is at last overcome in fight with a monster, a fire-breathing dragon, the guardian of an immense hoard of treasure. Beowulf, characteristically, has wished that the danger might be his alone, and has instructed his personal guard, his *gesíðas*, to hold back. But when the fight goes badly against his master, the young warrior called Wiglaf is troubled, and in words like those of Offa at Maldon, he urges his fellows to remember their *béot*, the vows made in hall:

> I remember the time when we drank our mead
> and there in the beer-hall promised our lord,
> who gave us these gold rings for our own,
> we would repay the trappings of war
> if such a need as this should come upon him -
> the hard-tempered swords, the helmets he gave
> when he picked *us* out for this enterprise,
> his own choice from among all his men.
> He thought us fit for fame - and to me he gave
> these precious jewels - he counted us
> good spearmen, hardy fighters, even though
> it was our lord's intent to undertake
> this glorious deed alone.
>
> *lines 2633-44 Beowulf*

Ignoring Wiglaf's insistence that despite their orders they must go and help their chieftain in his hour of mortal need, the men of the *werod* still hold back. Wiglaf then goes to help Beowulf. Together, they slay the dragon, but Beowulf dies. Wiglaf, grieving, addresses the cowardly *gesíðas* in a long speech, a tumbled outpouring of bitter scorn:

> Wiglaf spoke, Weohstan's son,
>   a man sick at heart - stared at them, the unloved:
> "Now, well may he say who would speak the truth,

> that the lord who gave these treasures to you,
> - such glittering gear as you stand there wearing -
> when among the benches so often he gave
> to comrades in hall, the helm, the mail-coat,
> - a lord to his thanes - such gifts beyond price,
> scarce to be be found anywhere in the world -
> that princely gifts of gear were cruelly wasted
> when war laid claim to him.
> No cause had the prince of our people to boast
> of the strength of his soldiers - yet God granted him,
> the Lord of Victories, strength to avenge himself,
> alone, with his sword, when he had need of glory.
> Little enough protection could I afford him
> there in the fight, but nevertheless found strength
> beyond my strength to bring help to my kinsman.
> As I struck with my sword time and again, it was lesser,
> weaker, the monstrous gout of flame, the heat
> flaring out of the fiend. Protectors too few
> thronged round our chief when the evil hour befell.
> But now, the treasure-taking and the sword-giving,
> all the settled joy of you and your kin,
> all hopes, must die; all landed rights
> for the families of every one of you
> will come to naught, when princes far and wide
> shall hear the tale of your flight,
> your infamous act. Better death by far
> for any nobleman than a life of shame."

lines 2862-91 Beowulf

Here indeed is Tacitus' "infamy and shame for all your life after". The word will get out, Wiglaf promises. Gossip's long ears will pick it up. It will jump over dykes and cross oceans. The renegades will henceforth look in vain for employment and favour; no princely master will take such people into his service. They will be landless, masterless exiles; and as they suffer, so their kin will suffer too.

The *béahgifa's* bounty extends beyond gold rings and jewels. It includes weapons and armour ("give me that bloodstained fighting spear!" Tacitus describes his Germans petitioning their chiefs).[27] It includes warhorses and their trappings.

---

[27] Demands and rewards. Tacitus: *exiguunt enim principis sui liberalitate bellatorum equum, illam cruentem frameam,* "from the liberality of their chiefs they demand that warhorse, that bloodstained spear" *Germania,* cap. 14. This picture of a clansman making peremptory demands on the "liberality" of his chief suggests a negotiation rather more aggressive than the courtly *máððumgifu* of the Anglo-Saxon poems. On the subject of spears, Tacitus notes that the *framea,* "fighting spear", is the Germans' principal weapon, ritually presented to their youths on their coming of age, together with a shield.

Godric's particular sin at Maldon was in stealing the horse of a man who had given him many horses; worse, in stealing with the horse the caparison, the steed's costly, elaborately ornamented "tack", to which he had no right. The poet's indignation is almost humorous; it is the retainer's *privilege* to receive gifts of gold and precious stones, not his *right* to seize them unasked. It is a particularly odious theft. The patron's gifts can extend even to grants of land and property, held, as the modern phrase has it, "by grace and favour". The Anglo-Saxon term for such favour is that important word, *ár*; important especially because its secular significance is adapted in the theological vocabulary, with the meaning of "God's grace". The king or ruler makes the grant to the favoured subject and his heirs, and it is passed down from generation to generation but as fortunes change and as words and rules are broken, it can be rescinded. Under exceptional circumstances, even a king can be deprived of his land, as shown by the fate of King Sigebriht, who was exiled *for unrihtum dædum*, "for wrongful deeds". Such an exile has no land, no lord, no kin, hardly a name to call his own. He becomes a non-person, his deeds forever *dómléas* - "unfamed" - "infamous". He lives in conditions of outlawry concisely defined by the Icelandic legal formula: "not to be fed, not to be forwarded, not to be helped or harboured in any need". For a nobleman, as Wiglaf observes, death is preferable.

Kith and kin, name and fame

A traitor or a renegade is a disgrace to his kin, disowned by his kith. In Anglo-Saxon, as still in modern English, *cyðð* and *cynn* denote overlapping meanings, though with the clearer implication that one contains, rather than equates with, the other: "kith" embraces "kin", much as in a biological taxonomy "genus" involves "species". The organisation of Anglo-Saxon society, in its warrior aspect, implies the inclusive, as it were "concentric", strength of kith and kin. In brief, *cynn* implies "family" and *cýðð* involves "folk". The warriors at Maldon are aware of both, and anxious that others should be aware of them: "mine was a noble family, in Mercia, Ealhelm my father's name", "He was of tough Northumbrian stock, the son of Ecglaf, Æscferth his name" Mercia is Ælfwine's *cyðð*, his father Ealhelm the immediate and most important representative of his *cynn*. So also with "Northumbrian stock"and "son of Ecglaf", in the hostage Æscferth's defiant speech. In the Germanic roll of honour, personal names, as a voucher of identity, require additions. They demand the index of the tribe and the registration of kinship; these things *validate*, as we now say, claims to warrior-status.

The usual word for "kinsman" is *mæg*, pl. *mágas*. It can occur in context with another term, *wine*, meaning "friend", and in the composite *winemáeg* signifying "friend and kinsman". The society of the Anglo-Saxon *heall*, the "hall", that robust and rumbustious and seemingly bibulous court, with its "ale benches" where the warriors compete in their vows and receive their lord's bounty, is a close-knit society of *wineas*, *mágas*, *winemágas*; of *þegnas*, "thanes", and *gesíðas*, "companions", a network of ties, bonds and obligations, centring on the most powerful tie, the supreme obligation to the feudal lord, called *hláford*, or *drihten*, or *fréa*. To some of the companions he might be *winedrihten*, "friend and master". To some he might be not only the tribal lord but also a blood relation, therefore with a double claim on the dependent subject. *He wæs ægþer*

2 Of Cruel Battle and the Fall of Kin

mìn mæg ond mín hlaford, says Ælfwine in *Maldon*: "He was alike my kinsman and my lord" - two reasons for fighting to the death. In the moral system, kinsman was committed to kinsman, but that claim lapsed if it conflicted with the duty of the thane to his lord. Witness again the annal for the year 755: "And he (Cyneheard) offered them goods and land, at their own estimate, if they would grant him the kingdom; and told them that their kinsmen were with him, who would not leave him. And then they told him that no kinsman was dearer to them than their lord, and that they would never follow his killer; and they offered their kinsmen [on Cyneheard's side] the chance to get away unharmed. And they [in turn] replied that the same offer had been made to the [other party's] comrades who had been with Cynewulf, and said that they could no more accept this offer "'than could your fellows who were killed with the king'." The old tale makes explicit, with agonised repetitions, the insuperable commitment of thaneship to lordship, a commitment always transcending the claim of kin; for the *hláford*, the *drihten*, is *béahgifa*, the giver of good things, is *sigora wealdend*, the lord of victories, is *folces helm*, the protector of his people, their surety in a world of precarious fortune.

The tribal lord's hope and objective is to make a name for himself - or have his name made through other agencies: the common talk of the region, the records of the scribal chronicler, or at best, traditionally, the art of the court poet, the *scop*. The poem called *Widsith*, described in the preceding chapter, purports to be a recital by an itinerant *scop* whose wanderings have taken him through many lands and most of the tribal courts of Europe in the Dark Ages. He has seen them all, and found favour with their generous lords. His poem concludes with lines commending equally the virtues of lordship and the value of the professional poet:

> So in their wanderings, driven by fate,
> Through many lands the poets go,
> make known their need, and pay their thanks
> northward or southward forever finding
> some patron of song, one gracious in gifts
> whose wish is, before his bravest men
> to gain repute with glorious deeds,
> till all is ended, light and life
> together. He who strives for praise
> wins, under heaven, a lasting fame.
>
> *lines 135-143 Widsið*

The eager chieftain wins lasting fame - and wins it, the implication may be, through the work of the poet himself, who also "strives for praise". The word for "praise" in this context is *lof*; and for "fame", the last word of the poem, *dóm*. (See also p.12) The words often occur in poetic association when the talk is of heroes and their glory, but they are not wholly synonymous. *Lof*, "praise", generally signifies the fame a man wins while he is living; *dóm*, also means "praise", "fame", "glory", but frequently with the particular nuance of "judgement" - the considered judgement pronounced on a man after his death, and hence a condition of his "lasting fame", for good or ill. In the closing lines of *Beowulf* one of these terms, *lof*, occurs explicitly (in the compound *lofgeornost*, "most eager for praise") while the other, *dóm*, is implied in the detail of the context. The passage describes how twelve warriors of noble rank ride around Beowulf's *hláew*, his burial mound on a headland overlooking the sea. "Wishing to speak of their grief", the text says, "to mourn the king, to make his eulogy, *to speak of the man*" (My italics) They praise his valour, his glorious deeds, extol his soldierly qualities, "as it is fitting a man should find words to praise his *winedrihten,* celebrate his spirit, when he must go forth, out of the body":

> And so they bewailed, the Geatish folk,
> his hearth-companions, the fall of their lord,
> saying that among the kings of the world
> he was the mildest of men, and the gentlest,
> most dear to his folk, most eager for praise.   *lines 3178-82 Beowulf*

"Mildest" and "gentlest" as considered assessments might surprise readers acquainted with the youthful Beowulf's enraged demeanour - dislocating and decapitating - in hand-to-hand combat with monsters; but these last words, *speaking about the man*, after paying tribute to the king and the warrior, may suggest something of the pervasive "christianising" influence on this poem, a recital of pagan themes revised in scribal times by clerical hands. The last two lines are a collocation of superlatives, *mildost, monðwærust, lofgeornost,* and the latter, the last word on Beowulf, is indeed the last word of the poem. Here is a man of whom it may be finally said that his life has been governed by the desire for *lof* - "praise", "repute". The riders come to sing his praises; but here, if we understand the closing passage correctly, the whole account of what the twelve men in their ritual circuit do and say in tribute to Beowulf - in final tribute, in farewell tribute - is the *dóm,* the judgement on a whole life. "Let us now praise famous men", says a well-known passage in *Ecclesiasticus,* and proceeds to do so in some detail, until the verse "and some there be who have no memorial", a sentence often misinterpreted and invested with a false pathos.[28] Those who "have no memorial" have, in Anglo-Saxon terms, no *dóm*, no confirming judgement, no candidature for lasting fame, having done nothing to deserve it. Their name does not live for evermore. They are *dómléas* - the adjective Wiglaf throws at the cowardly companions: *éowerne dómleasan dáed,* "your infamous act". The false thane's condition is one of infamy - bad fame; or ignominy - bad name, or worse, no name at all. For them there is no *dóm*, no fame - because they have not deserved it, whether *dóm* means "glory", or "judgement" or, more austerely, "justice".

---

[28] A biblical note on *dóm*. Ecclesiasticus, 44.1, "Let us now praise famous men...such as have borne rule in their dominions, men of great power and endued with their wisdom" --- 44.9, "And there are some of whom there is no memorial: who are perished as if they had never been".--- 44.10, "But these were men of mercy whose godly deeds have not failed" - 44.14, "Their bodies are buried in peace, and their name liveth unto generation and generation." An Anglo-Saxon poet would have taken this as a text precisely on the theme of *dóm*. The "famous men", the powerful, the wise rulers, the merciful whose godly deeds have not failed, who rest in peace, whose names live for evermore, have *dóm*. Others, who have no memorial, and who have perished as though they had never been, are *dómleas*. The word *these* in 44.10 refers to the "famous men", not to those who have no memorial. 44.9 is a stern judgement; no pathos is intended.

2 Of Cruel Battle and the Fall of Kin

Dóm is a word Anglo-Saxon shares with Old Norse, where, as *dómr*, it has comparable implications. The *Hávamál*, the "Words of the High One", a collection of proverbial wisdoms ascribed to "the high one" - the god Odin, no less -, contains these strophes – nrs 76 and 77 – on the subject of name and fame. Number 76 reads:

> *Deyr fé*
> *deya frœndr*
> *deyr sjálfr it sama*
> *en orðstírr*
> *deya aldregi*
> *hveim er sér gódan getr.*

Which is to say:
> Cattle die, kinsmen die,
> and so we die, we too;
> but a good name never dies
> for the good man who earns it

Then follows number 77, with a variation on the theme

> *Deyr fé,*
> *deya frœndr,*
> *deyr sjálfr it sama*
> *ek veit einn*
> *at aldregi deyr*
> *dómr um dauðan hvern*

And that is slightly but significantly different:

> Cattle die, kinsmen die,
> and so we die, we too;
> one thing I know that never dies:
> judgement on all the dead [29]

---

[29] Hávamál, "The Words of the High One", strophe 77. It is a moot point whether *fé* (in old English *feoh*) should be translated as "cattle" (livestock, the principal evidence of bucolic wealth) or more generally rendered as "riches" (goods and chattels, property in general). For the text, most conveniently, see the Runeberg Project, http://lysator.liu.se/runeberg/eddais . (Or go to Google and ask for Hávamál – there are many websites to choose from). This is a much-edited, much-translated poem. Translations include a version in Esperanto, and also , in parody, a "Havamál for New Yawkas". One of the most attractive translations, as a poem in its own right, is that of W.H.Auden and P.B.Taylor. See http://members.iquest.net/~chaviland/Havamal. Their rendering of the last line of strophe 77, *dómr of dauþan hvern,* as "the glory of the great dead", is debatable, however. What is implied is "every one of the dead"; and though *dómr* in Old Norse can certainly mean "glory" (like *dóm* in Old English), the sense here is closer to that of "judgement"

2 Of Cruel Battle and the Fall of Kin

These verse speak of different kinds of fame. *orðstírr*, "reputation", and *dóm*, the final judgement. When the "High One" speaks of *dómr*, he is not speaking of what accustomed cliché calls "undying fame". What then? Is it judgement itself that never dies, the inevitable act and process of judgement, whether by men or possibly by a higher power? Whatever we do, however we prosper, we are judged; that is something that never lapses. In the latter instance, the interpretation of *dómr* seems set to embrace a religious, even a Christian concept of fame. It implies a possibility of fame, true fame, after a truly heroic life, as expressed in Old English in the elegiac poem called *The Seafarer*:

> Praise that the living speak, after a man is gone -
> the best of final words -
> is that he has confronted, here in this world,
> ere he depart, the malice of the fiend,
> with valiant deeds fighting against the devil
> so that the children of men may later praise him
> and his praise among angels last for ever and ever.[30]

The text expounds "the best epitaph" - *lástworda betst*, "the best of last words". It concerns *lof*, "praise", in three aspects: *lof lífgendra*, "the praise of living men", [*lof*] *æftercweþendra*, "[the praise] of those speaking after the man's death", and *lof mid englum*, "praise among the angels". Of these, the last is the only undying fame, the one secure judgement, though the others must necessarily precede it. Thus the Christian poet recovers the word *lof* from its pagan context, and rehabilitates it in an altered version of warrior-heroism. "For we wrestle not against flesh and blood, but against principalities, against powers, against the rulers of the darkness of this world, against spiritual wickedness in high places", says Paul, adding "Wherefore take unto you the whole armour of God, that ye may be able to withstand in the evil day." [31] That would certainly describe the spirit of Old English religious poetry, with its adapted imagery of arms and combat, drawing on a tradition that tells of kinsmen gathered in hall, in the presence of a beloved lord, and the taking of vows, and the firelight glittering on gold ring and precious sword, and the desperate trust that in the evil day the heart will hold out, though the shield-wall breaks and the vaunted weapons fail.

---

[30] *Seafarer,* lines 72-80

[31] St Paul, *Epistle to the Ephesians,* Chapter 6, vv.12-13

3 exiles and lamentations

One of the laws of Ine - in the late 7th century a King of the West Saxons - concerns "men come from afar" who are encountered off the beaten track travellers or strangers leave the common way to go through the woods, and do not shout or blow a horn, they are to be taken for thieves, either to be slain or held to ransom." Another law defines "thieves" as meaning "up to seven men"; from seven to thirty-five is a "troop"; any more than that is "a raiding army". From these provisions it may be gathered that anyone coming through the forest is probably up to no good, because the forest is a place in itself up to no good. The Anglo-Saxons' feeling for nature was, rather like our own, ambiguous. They could love fair weather in pasture and parkland and garden; they could admire flowers in bloom and swans in flight, and could be amused by cuckoos and midges and other small creatures; they revered, as tokens of God's supervisory presence, the sun and moon and stars; the sky had its beneficent place in the order of things; but for anything as forbidding as a forest, or as limitless as an ocean, or dark as a moorland tarn, or grim as a mountain, for all habitations of the unknown and the potential Unthing, they felt the appalled respect, fed by Germanic legend and folk-memory, that many of us still have for the outdoors beyond the outdoors. Nature the Wild was a dark, cold, wet, monstrous, and beset with anxieties and terrors. It was cruelly remote from the protective arrangements of living expressed in Old English words like *tún*, *burh*, *hám*, *heall* (literally "town," "borough", "home", "hall"), words collectively expressing a notion of house and home and security and companionship and the rule of some kind of law.[32] When a crime was committed or a quarrel festered and someone had to pay for unfinished business, they might, like King Sigebriht of Wessex, be driven out of this relatively safe, approximately principled world and into the barbarous wilderness where they would live hard, sleep rough, and be anyone's for the taking.

A maiden in the marsh

The word is *fáehð*, "feud", "vendetta". Anglo-Saxon law tried to circumscribe acts of violence, accidental or intentional, and compose quarrels and grievances with a system of atonements, usually payments in money. If a man was killed in quarrel his kin had the right to exact *wergild*, a payment of compensation measured by his rank and status. This was the best provision the law could offer for satisfaction and conciliation. There were some differences that could not be reconciled, however: the differences that culminated in the *fáehð*, the blood feud, the consequence of which might be inevitably a man's departure for the woods and marshes or places overseas, an outcast with a price on his head and maybe a woman left at home, friendless and at the mercy of her man's enemies.

---

[32] The modern English forms, however, have meanings not wholly corresponding to those of the Anglo-Saxon originals, *tún*, for example, signified an enclosure of some kind, eg a cattle pen, a paddock for crops, a hamlet or small village, a manorial estate, but rarely a "town" in the present-day sense. For that, the usual word was *burh*.

3 Exile and Lamentations

There is a poem with such a feud in the background, called somewhat prosaically *Wulf and Eadwacer,* these being the names of two of the people mentioned in it; a third, the most important, is not mentioned, because she has no name. She is the narrator, and the story she asks us to read lurks enigmatically between the lines of a brief text:

> To my people, it is as though they were offered a prize;[33]
> they will take him for sure, if he comes on a troop of them
>
> It is different with us
>
> Wulf is on one of the islands, I on another,
> an island of firm ground circled about by fen.
> They are fierce and cruel, the men here on the island;
> they will take him for sure, if he comes on a troop of them.
>
> It is different with us.
>
> I had such hopes of the journey my Wulf would make,
> and then it was rainy weather and I sat crying,
> and then the bold Captain took me in is arms,
> and that was heavenly - yet I hated it.
>
> Wulf, my Wulf, it was my pining for you
> made me sick, your coming here so seldom
> broke my heart; never the want of food.
>
> Do you hear, Eadwacer?
> There's a wolf will carry our wretched whelp to the wood;
> *What is easily parted was never truly joined -*
>
> Our song together   *Wulf and Eadwacer*

---

[33] In our reading, "prize" translates *lác*. A possible rendering of *lác* is "offering", or specifically "sacrificial offering". "They will take him for sure". "Take" renders the original's *ápecgan,* a rare word meaning "to take food, to consume". What is suggested here is something like the biblical sense of "devour"; eg Psalm 27 v.2, "When the wicked, even mine enemies and my foes, came upon me to eat up my flesh, they stumbled and fell."

Then - "It is different with us". In the original, *Ús is ungelíc,* (literally, "to us is unalike"),a laconic statement, meaning either "In our situation we are different [from other lovers]", or "Our positions, as individuals, are different" - "Our fates are separate". The same construction occurs in a line (612) of *Genesis B,* when the Tempter, flattering Eve, tells her: *þe is ungelic / wlite and wæstmas, siððan þu minum wordum getruwodest -* "Your figure and form are altogether changed since you trusted my words" Perhaps the tenor of *us is ungelíc* is not so much "it is different with us" as "for us, everything has changed".

3 Exile and Lamentations

This wonderful, haunting poem, with its passionate, reckless cry of a woman scolding the images of her plight, one of the most imaginative and formally original lyrics in Old English, has sometimes been assumed to be a fragment, but nevertheless convinces with a sense of wholeness; for the psychology of interpretation is such that a reader will always feel the compulsion to make complete sense out of an ostensibly incomplete text.[34]

Then let us attempt a reading, reducible to summary and paraphrase, if that is ever possible with poetry of such latent power. The setting is a region of fenland, with "islands" of dry ground above the level of the surrounding marsh. One of these, perhaps the main island, is occupied and fortified by a warrior clan under the lordship [supposedly] of someone the narrator first calls *se beaducafa*, "the bold in battle", and then names as "Eadwacer". The woman's existence is precarious. She is evidently destitute, she is often hungry, and is full of desperate longing for an absent lover, her Wulf, who lives on another island, and can visit her no more than occasionally, alone, and at the risk of his own life, one plausible conjecture being that he is in exile, an outcast to be taken as a prize, killed or captured for bounty. The occasion for his exile - if that is his condition - we do not know. We do know, however, that Wulf has a rival in *se beaducafa*, Eadwacer, "the bold Captain" When the heavy rains come and [presumably] the marshland waters swell and make passage difficult, the woman is reduced to a despair that makes her succumb to the "protection" of Eadwacer; not because of her hunger, but in her physical need, her love-longing. It brings her great comfort, and yet she reviles herself - and Eadwacer - for it. To her distant lover she cries that his long absences, not her hunger, have made her succumb. To Eadwacer she threatens, with a grim pun, that "a wolf [Wulf] will bear our wretched whelp to the woods" - meaning either that Wulf will come and abduct, even kill, the child of their liaison, or, less Gothically, that a vengeful Wulf will arrive and put an end to this union - "our song together" - that was never much of. a union anyway. *What is easily parted was never truly joined*; a ghostly echo of Matthew, 19:6 - "What therefore God has joined together, let no man put asunder".

The language of paraphrase always reflects the gaps in the narration, our awareness that what the text says depends on what it refrains from saying. A summary like the one above fills in the gaps with "supposedly", "presumably", "plausible", "perhaps", "either...or", the evidence of one reader's attempt to place a tale in context and make connected sense of it. Other readings might invite other suppositions. We might choose to suppose, for example, that Wulf the other-islander is not an exile, but a member of a separate clan, the neighbouring enemy, who chances his impudent arm when he comes courting on Eadwacer's island. An unusual courtship

---

[34] "Impersonations". Not the least puzzling thing about *Wulf and Eadwacer* is its unique lyric form. It shares that distinctive quality as a lyric with *Deor*, and the two poems appear together in the Exeter Book, between devotional texts and the Riddles, as if the compilers of this codex themselves hardly knew how to classify these poems. Both poems are "personations": *Deor* the work of someone impersonating a *scop*, *Wulf and Eadwacer* the impersonation of a woman, so convincing in its intensity and open emotion as to persuade the reader that if this was not written by a woman, it was at least the work of a man with a poignant sense of womanliness.

and an unusual affair, but then, as our heroine says, "It is different with us" The abiding fact, however, accommodating different interpretations, is that this sorry affair, and the woman's heart-piercing plight, is the cause and consequence of *fáehð*, the feud, with the attendant masculine notions of tribal honour that govern alike commanders of great armies and the little masters of the marsh. The woman, in the meantime, belongs nowhere, and to nobody; she, truly, is the one in exile.

A woman in the woods

Also caught in the plight of separated lovers, the mistress of an exile, herself an outcast, is the narrator of a poem with the attributed title *The Wife's Complaint*, or *The Wife's Lament*, which suggests the grievance of a woman whose spouse drinks and keeps irregular hours, rather than the grief and terror of someone living in dangerous isolation, in hardship, and in peril of her very life. Hers is indeed a desperate state. "The tale I have to tell", she announces, "is of troubles endured since I grew up, early and late, but never more than now". She tells of her *hláford*, the *léodfruma* - "liege lord" - who is also her lover, and how he has gone "away from this, his folk, away over the sea"; then how she has set out to find him, "I, friendless outcast, in my sorry need"; but her lover's kinsmen have plotted secretly to come between them, forcing them to live "far, far apart, dwelling in wretchedness - and I, in yearning". The exiled man, his mind unsettled, is full of hatred for his enemies, a bitterness extending perhaps even to her:

> My lord sent word that I should take to the woods -
> a dwelling-place where I found very few
> devoted friends. And I am full of grief
> because the man I thought my own now seems
> soul-darkened, melancholy, a dissembler
> purposing murder. We two were once so glad
> in love shown to each other, in our vows
> that nothing would ever part us, only death.
> All overthrown. As if it had never been.
>
> *lines 15-24 The Wife's Lament*

Wherever she turns now, she must endure the feuds that drive her dearly beloved, and must live wretchedly:

> Now I am forced to live in a forest grove,
> under an oak tree, in a house of earth.
> The house is old, and I am full of care.
> Dark the valleys, the hilltops towering,
> the sullen townships overgrown with briars,
> places bereft of joy. So often here
> I rage against the absence of my lord.
> In all the earth fond lovers lie abed
> at dawn, while I am watching here alone
> under an oak tree by my wretched cave.

> Here in the summer-long day I have to sit,
> here I must weep for all I have undergone,
> so many sufferings. And never peace
> for my sad soul, for all my longings, peace,
> for tribulations borne here in this life.   *lines 27-41 The Wife's Lament*

Now follows what looks like a hiatus or jump in narrative continuity, when it seems that she abruptly leaves the contemplation of her sad soul in order to reflect briskly on the principles of manly conduct:

> He must be always grave, a young lord, and
> stern the thoughts of his heart, yes, but then
> he must seem outwardly glad, and the care in his breast,
> the endless tumult of grief, he must keep to himself.   *lines 42-45*

These are sentiments of the "gnomic" sort, the proverbial pointing ("thus should a man be...", "a warrior must...", "it is an earl's way...") that occasionally marks the episodic path of other poems. But the "jump" is not for the sake of moralising; it is arguably a direct psychological progression. She turns from her misery to think of her lover. He is wretched too, she is sure. She can find reasons for his strange behaviour, his cold treatment of her. He is obeying an aristocratic code of dissimulation - endure, hide your thoughts, bide your time. And she imagines his suffering, as an exile in a barbarous landscape, living in a house even gloomier than hers and - of course - thinking of her:

> All his joy in the world may be outlawed
> to a distant land - and so my dear friend sits
> under some rocky cliff, frostbound by storm,
> by water circled, in a dreary hall.
> Much care of mind my love endures, remembering
> too often, a more joyful place. Such grief
> is theirs who have to dwell in love-longing.   *lines 46-53*

So at the end of this sad story there is a kind of reconciliation. The lovers are still exiles, each from the other, but by an act of generous imagining, by realising that her lover endures privations and longings as great as her own, the woman can achieve something like a reunion, a reconciliation in spirit.

A lady in luck

In the poem called *The Husband's Message* (haphazardly associated with *The Wife's Complaint*) the "husband", a further variant of the lover-in-exile, is not the narrative voice. The message is carried by a stick, a stick carved with runic letters for a lady to decode:

3 Exile and Lamentations

> Here I am come to you on the deck of a ship
> to whisper recognition in your mind
> of the heart's love of my lord; and I dare swear
> that you will find in this a glorious faith.
>
> *lines 7-11 The Husband's Message*

In dead-literal translation, the opening sentence reads, "I am now come here from on shipboard, and now you shall get to know how in your thoughts you may think of the heart's love of my lord" - an awkward, angular way of putting it, but then the stick only speaks runic. What follows is only a little less gnarled:

> Bejewelled Lady! He who carved this staff
> bids me - to bid you - to remind yourself
> of pledges often made in former days
> while yet you two were dwellers in one land,
> wardens of one earth, there among festive towns
> forming your friendship.Feud drove him away
> from a warlike people.
>
> *lines 12-19*

She is *sinchroden* - "treasure-laden", "bejewelled", and therefore of a noble caste; she and the sender of the message have known each other in a united, peaceful land, and in cultivated urban society - *on meodoburgum*, "among festive towns"; but faction among his people disturbed the idyll, and *hine fæhþo adraf*, "feud drove him away". So again it is the feuding of the warlike that divides lover from lover, still exiling the woman as much as the man.

But the carved stick brings the lady good news, and instructions for positive action when the harbinger cuckoo gives the signal - that is, when Spring comes:

> Now he wishes you
> to learn, with joy, how you must put to sea
> when you have heard, from the grove at the edge of the scarp,
> the cuckoo's mournful call. Let nothing then
> hinder your going, nor anyone alive
> deter you from your voyage; seek the sea,
> the gull's domain; take ship, and sailing south
> along the seaways, you shall find this man,
> your lord, waiting for you to come.
>
> *lines 19-28*

Here occurs a hiatus, the manuscript being damaged beyond legibility for several lines. But little of substance is lost; the re-emerging text announces a happy ending for the hapless pair. The "husband", it appears, has surmounted his difficulties and triumphed in adversity. He is not a destitute, wandering wretch. He is wealthy, respected; he has, in the modern phrase, "made it", and needs only the beloved beside him to complete his happiness:

> Now he has done with grief,
> no lack he knows of anything desired -
> treasure, steeds, the revels of the hall,
> or any of the riches of the proud,
> prince's daughter! - if only he has you.
> As for those promises between you two,
> he took a solemn oath: by ᚻ (S) and ᚱ (R),
> ᛠ (EA), ᚹ (W), ᚻ (D), I heard him swear
> that he would keep the vows and loving faith
> you two so often pledged in former days.
>
> *lines 29-52 The Husband's Message*

In this translation the roman letters S, R, EA, W, D are transliterations of the runic characters in the original. Runes are secrets held by those who understand them; in this case they are a code devised by the lovers, signifying, perhaps, their conjoined names, perhaps some shared saying or experience from those "former days" - no matter, for the ending bodes well, and the inquisitive reader can afford to mind his own business.[35] The man is so rich, he has either found a *heall* and become an honoured companion under the patronage of a *sincgifa*, a *winedrihten*, or he has himself become a lord and protector in that land somewhere away to the lucky south. That his state is in any case princely is indicated by one word in the Anglo-Saxon text: when he tells her to take ship and come to where her lord awaits her, his word for "lord" is *þeoden*, and that, exclusively taken, means "king" or "prince" Her status is also known - she is *þeodnes dohtor*, "prince's daughter". And so the royal couple are dismissed to happiness at the end of what is probably the most cheerful tale of adversity in all of Anglo-Saxon's fairly considerable catalogue of misfortunes.

A soul at sea

The Wanderer makes no concession to pleasant hopes, for this is an account, couched in heroic terms, of bitter spiritual exile, its narrator a soul at the frontier of salvation. It begins thus:

> Often the outcast yearns for God's grace,
> the Maker's mercy, though sick at heart
> his lot is to wander the ocean way
> and thresh with his hands the ice-cold sea
> in the journey of exile. Fate is resolved.
> Thus spoke a wanderer, mindful of hardships,
> of cruel battle and the fall of kin.
>
> *lines 1-7 The Wanderer*

---

[35] In the Anglo-Saxon runic alphabet, or *fuþorc*, (see Postscript p.141) the names of the letters expressing S,R,EA, W, D, are: for S, *sigel*, "sun", for R, *rad,* "riding", for EA, *ear*, "earth": for W, *wyn*, "bliss"; and for D, *dæg, "day"*. No doubt there is a coded message here, but who shall decrypt it?

These introductory lines turn on words that play with the parallel, running throughout the poem, between heroic images and spiritual themes. They picture the *ánhaga*, "the solitary", physically as an outcast from society, condemned to wander the oceans of the world because it is his inevitable destiny to do so, because *wyrd biþ ful aræd*, "Fate is resolved". Though the manuscript does not supply them, *Wyrd* ("Fate") invites a capital letter, as does *Metud* ("Maker") in the second line; for here immediately is the poem's primary tension, between unrelenting pagan Fate and the Christian possibility of redemption. *Wyrd* in Anglo-Saxon is either more or less than "fate" or "destiny". *Wyrd* is monstrous, like a sphinx. *Wyrd* is unaccountable and unaccounted for. *Wyrd* is how things happen without reference to why they happen. *Wyrd* is inexorable, foreordained and unpredictable. *Wyrd* has much in common with Thomas Hardy's "Immanent Will". *Wyrd* has no mind of its own. Destiny may be enjoyed, Fate lamented; but *Wyrd* has to be endured. (A verb commonly associated with it is *dreogan*, "to endure"; the words are conjoined in the old Scots expression *dree your weird*, "suffer what's destined", or "accept your lot".)

Against the inflexible, impersonal power of *Wyrd* stands the personal intervention of *Metud*, "God the Creator", who is merciful and is the source of *ár*, that recurrent word which in the heroic vocabulary of lordly bounty means "honour", in the particular form of a gift or a grant of land, and in theological transference has the spiritual sense of "grace". The Wanderer *hopes* for the grace of God, though *Wyrd*, unrelenting, *drives* him into the exilic miseries of a laborious voyaging through ice-bound seas. It is in part a voyage of memory, as he recalls "cruel battle and the fall of kin". His great sorrow, he complains, is that he is utterly alone, with no companion to whom he may unburden his soul, although he knows that manly reticence is the approved quality of an *eorl*:

> I know full well it is a noble's way
> to keep the secrets of the heart close-locked,
> think how he may, to keep thoughts to himself.
> Sad spirit cannot alter Fate's decree,
> nor will an angry one afford relief,
> so, those whose hope is set on name and fame
> seal up the dark thought in their souls.[36]   *lines 11-18 The Wanderer*

This is strikingly similar, in sentiment and wording, to the speech of that disconsolate lady in *The Wife's Complaint*, who bewails the fate of her lover, brooding in exile "under some rocky cliff, frostbound by storms, by water encircled":

---

[36] "Those who hope for name and fame". In the text this is expressed by a single word, *dómgeorne*. The meaning of *dóm* in that compound is "repute" (in the world), rather than "judgement" (out of it). A man of noble caste who does not "seal up the dark thought in his soul" is vulnerable to his enemies and detractors, and will be seen as (in the modern phrase) "a loser". This rule of reticence - "shut up and be famous" – is expressed in folk-wisdoms, like the 14th-century *Proverbs of Hending*: "If thou hast a sorrow, tell it to thy saddle-bow, and ride forth singing". That would be the way of the *dómgeorn*.

3 Exile and Lamentations

> He must be always grave, a young lord, and
> stern the thoughts of his heart, yes, but then
> he must seem outwardly glad, and the care in his breast,
> the endless tumult of grief, he must keep to himself.
> *lines 42-45 The Wife's Lament*

The position is so similar, indeed, as to suggest that this theme of self-restraint and dissimulation is a *locus communis*, a "commonplace" in Anglo-Saxon teachings on conduct appropriate to a man of rank and ambition on the downside of his luck.

Then, desperate to unburden his soul, the Wanderer embarks on his confession:

> So I, often wretched, exiled from my home,
> far from my kin, have had to fetter my heart
> since that day long ago, when the darkness of earth
> enfolded my dear lord, and I, sad wretch,
> wintry-heart, wandered over the frozen waves,
> poor outcast, seeking the hall of a giver of gifts,
> searching the world, far and wide, and hoping to find
> one who would know me in my deepest thought,
> or would befriend me in my friendlessness,
> receive me kindly
> *lines 19-29 The Wanderer*

Here they are in tandem, the ostensible fact and poetic figure of the Wanderer's "exile". It happened long ago, his old tale of tribal disaster. His lord is dead - whether killed in battle or feud - and the companion or thane, once held in honour, is now abject, despised, a drifter in desperate search of a kind patron. The literal emblem of his drift is the sea, the sea in winter. It is notable that, in this poetry of exile, seas and encircling waters are images of *sundering*. In *Wulf and Eadwacer*, the fenland flood separates the lovers; in *The Wife's Complaint*, the exiled lord is pictured as sitting "under some rocky cliff...by water circled"; in *The Husband's Message*, the lady is bidden, at the call of the cuckoo, to "seek the sea, the gull's domain, take ship", and come to where her exiled lord awaits her. For her, at least, the sea is kindly, with the prospect of a voyage in Spring, ending in lovers' meeting. For the Wanderer it is savage; he sails in winter, dark winter, and his journey is endless, unless it may end in the grace of God. His plight is that expressed by another anxious poet, writing centuries later:

> In what torne ship soever I embarke,
> That ship shall be my embleme of Thy Arke [37]

---

[37] John Donne, "A Hymn to Christ, at the Author's Last Going into Germany."

3 Exile and Lamentations

John Donne and the Wanderer share this perception of man gone abroad, at sea, endangered beyond hope, unless God chooses to bring him safe home.

"How cruel a companion is sorrow" the Wanderer's plaint continues, "to one who has no dear protector, whose lot is the way of exile, never the braided gold, a barren heart, never the fruits of the earth." He remembers "retainers in hall, the receiving of gifts - how in his youth his lord feasted him" Such human memories are at once sweet and bitter - as Dante defines them: *nessun maggior dolore che ricordarse del tiempo felice* - "no greater sorrow than to recall a time of joy". So it is with the Wanderer. Memory's only refuge is in sleep, but waking brings grief intensified. It is one of the finest passages in a fine, passionate poem:

> But then, the friendless man, waking again,
> sees before him only the sombre waves,
> the seabirds bathing, spreading wide their wings;
> frost and snow falling, mingled with hail.
> All the heavier then are the wounds of the heart,
> the grief for the loved one; sorrow is renewed
> as memories of kinsfolk crowd his mind.
> With glad cries then he greets them, gazes fondly,
> until that band of comrades fades from sight,
> and the mind echoes no more familiar voices
> of airy phantoms. Then care is renewed
> for him, who again and yet again must drive
> his weary spirit across frozen seas.
>
> *lines 45-57 The Wanderer*

The translation struggles here to ape an effect of the original where the phrase-rhythms move and sway fitfully, as though caught in the gust of a feeling too passionate to be contained in measured accents. It marks the culmination of the most "personal" phase of the poem, the Wanderer's cry of grief. With that culmination comes something like a change of narrative stance, or even a change of narrator. The phrase defining the speaker at the outset of the poem is *swa cwæð eardstapa*, "thus spoke a wanderer"; but by the end this definition has changed to *swa cwæð snottor on móde*, "thus spoke one wise at heart"; one of whom it is further said that "he sat apart, in self-communing" - a posture of solitude, certainly, but hardly the desperate, ice-bound loneliness of the exile.

From the moment when the "Wise man" takes over from the "Wanderer", the poem deals less and less in the style of impassioned personal confession, and more and more in the reflections, mournful but resigned, of a philosophical observer. It becomes a kind of commentary, or perhaps a homily, the progression of which is easily traced. The first stage is a sequence of "gnomic" wisdoms (maxims, proverb-like "oughts" and "musts") defining the character appropriate to the noble warrior:

3 Exile and Lamentations

> A wise man must be patient,
> not too zealous, not too quick to speak,
> too soft in action, or too rash,
> too timid, or too servile, too greedy for gain,
> and never too eager to boast of his intent
> before he is sure of his aim.
> A man should hesitate, before a vow,
> until the eager spirit knows for sure
> where the heart's impulse will lead.
>
> *lines 65-72 The Wanderer*

The phrase "before he is sure of his aim" - in the original *ær he geare cunne*, "before he fully knows", "before he knows for sure" - implies the sense "before he is sufficiently experienced", "before he knows what he is boasting about", and so "before he knows where a boast or a vow will lead".[38] The ideal warrior is proof against rash vows, the ready boasts of the mead-hall; he knows he may be called on to fulfil them when the time of trial comes. In saying this, the Wise Man asserts the conventional wisdoms of warrior society. In its confident precepts, the passage recalls the voice of the Wanderer at the beginning of the poem: *I know full well, it is a noble's way to keep the secrets of his heart locked up – think how he may, to keep thoughts to himself.* These are the rules of conduct for warriors, and also for God's servants. They too, by implication, must keep their counsel, must be modest and temperate, must beware of taking vows without understanding fully what the vows imply.

Such discipline may pass for virtue; but of itself it may not be quite enough to fend off the relentless operations of *Wyrd*. When the Wise Man looks about him he sees a world in which the culture of cities is laid waste. The evidence of the past is the testimony of baleful ruin:

> The wise man sees how terrible it will be
> when all the wide world's riches are laid waste,
> so now in divers places on this earth,
> windswept, covered with hoar-frost, stand the walls,
> the ruined mansions. Palaces decay,
> their masters lost in death, robbed of delight;
> here by the wall the chivalry fell slain
>
> *lines 73-80*

Whether the "divers places on this earth" are located in the poet's imagination, or whether his vision is trained by things seen not too far from home - the ruins, say, of Roman or Romano-British occupation - the description still runs on familiar images of Saxon state, the mead-hall, the king, the proud companions. He

---

[38] Like the soldier's *béot* is the monk's vow, also to be circumspectly made: *Ecclesiastes, 5, vv 4-5*: "When thou vowest a vow to God, defer not to pay it. Better is that thou shouldst not vow than that thou shouldst vow and not pay". In Old English, *béot* expresses "promise" and "vow" as well as "boast".

pictures the fallen past in the likeness of his own falling world, but his description of the fates of the fallen thanes invokes surreal, mythic destinies, the eerie dominion of *Wyrd*:

> War seized on some, and led them out of life:
> this one, a bird bore over the open sea:
> this one was marked for death by the grey wolf,
> that one, a sad-faced thane interred in a cave.
> So the Creator ravaged our earthly home,
> until, their keepers given up to silence,
> the work of giants of old stood desolate.
>
> *lines 80-87 The Wanderer*

There is a contradiction lurking in these dramatic lines; they describe (by implication) the remorseless effects of *Wyrd*, the arbitrary, the irrational, the indifferent, but the destruction, the "ravaging of our earthly home" is finally attributed to *ælda Scyppend*, the "Creator of men". It is a moment of doubt in the compassionate Maker whose grace and mercy the Wanderer seeks. God is wrathful. God destroys the presumptions of His creatures. God is - it seems - a dimension of *Wyrd*. Seen in that light, it is a moment of despair, comparable to that human moment in *The Wife's Complaint* when the distressed woman begins to suspect that the man in whose love she has trusted has purposes malign beyond her understanding:

> And I am full of grief
> because the man I thought my own now seems
> soul-darkened, melancholy, a dissembler
> purposing murder.
>
> *lines 17-20 The Wife's Lament*

Such passages express with peculiar intensity an emotion central to the poetry of exile and separation - the pain of doubt: doubt in another's good will, doubt that faith may be kept, doubt that suffering is for a purpose, doubt that all may yet be well. The girl in the marsh struggles with doubt - why does Wulf not come?; the lady in the woods is oppressed by doubt - does her man hate her? The forsaken princess is rescued from doubt - on the assurance of a few marks on a stick. But the gravest victim of doubt, almost beyond assurance, is the Wanderer, for his doubt is not in the good faith of a lover, but in the mercy of Almighty God.

These dark musings lead him towards the assertion that life has no purpose, that the past has no future, that men did their time, once upon a time, and are done with. His cry is a theme that echoes through all the literature of the Middle Ages - *ubi sunt qui ante nos fuerunt* - "where are they who lived before us?": [39]

---

[39] *Ubi sunt* - "where are...?" (as in "Where are the heroes of old?", "Where are the snows of yesteryear?", "Where are Chaplin and Keaton?" - questions which require no answers, though the questioner may go on to supply them). This rhetorical device has had a long life in western

3 Exile and Lamentations

> Where is the steed? Where the rider?
> Where the giver of treasure? The benches at the feast?
> Where the joys of the hall? O burnished cup!
> O warrior armed! O fame of the prince!
> How time has gone, grown dark under night's helm -
> as though it had never been.
>
> lines 92-96 The Wanderer

The phrase "as though it had never been" - in the Anglo-Saxon *swa heo no wære* - is the phrase used by the lady in the woods as she grieves for departed joys. She remembers the lovers' happiness, how gladly they vowed that nothing but death could part them, but -

>   eft is þæt onhworfen,
> is nu swa hit no wære -
>
> lines 23-24 The Wife's Lament

"now all is overthrown, as though it had never been". Past glories give place to present miseries. In the lady's case, the misery is a hovel in the badlands; the prophet of *The Wanderer* has visions of a huger devastation:

> Where once were friends and comrades, now remain
> these strange, high walls, adorned with serpent-forms
> Violence of spears vanquished the earls, ravening weapons,
> *Wyrd* the mighty; and now the blizzard binds
> this earth, these rock-strewn slopes, beaten by storms.
> Winter brings terror when darkness comes
> and the night-shadow blackens, and from the north

---

literature. Its first occurrence is thought to be c:a 525 AD in Boethius' *De Consolatione Philosophiae, eg* Book II, *metrum* 7:"Where now lie the bones of the loyal Fabricius? What of Brutus or Cato the stern?". The passage in *The Wanderer* beginning "Where is the steed? Where is the rider?" is an early occurrence of the *ubi sunt?* trope in English poetry, and arguably the finest. It (the trope) has since been used by poets of all schools and periods. For a fine modern example, see Edgar Lee Masters' poem "The Hill", a section of his *Spoon River Anthology* (New York: Macmillan, 1915):

Where are Elmer, Herman, Bert, Tom and Charley,
The weak of will, the strong of arm, the clown, the boozer, the fighter?
All, all are sleeping on the hill.

One passed in a fever,
One was burned in a mine,
One was killed in a brawl,
One died in a jail,
One fell from a bridge, toiling for children and wife -
All, all are sleeping, sleeping on the hill.

(Compare the lines in *The Wanderer* beginning "War seized on some, and led them out of life, this one a bird bore over the open sea, this one was marked for death by the grey wolf...&c")

> the savage hailstorm hurls its malice on heroes.[40]
> All this earthly state is full of hardship,
> and *Wyrd's* decree subverts the world under heaven.
> Here wealth is fleeting, friends are fleeting,
> man and kinsman both are fleeting.
> All this earthly frame is vanity!
>
> lines 97-110 The Wanderer

The distich beginning "Here wealth is fleeting" (*Her bið feoh læne, her bið freond læne*) has the resonance of folk-saying, and indeed is close in sense and style to the proverbial utterance of the Norse *Hávamál* (previously quoted, chapter 2 pp.51-2):

> Deyr fé,
> deyja fraendr,
> deyr sjalfr it sama
>
> Cattle die, kinsmen die,
> and so we die, we too...

"All this earthly frame is vanity!" the poet declares, apparently echoing the words of the Preacher, "vanity of vanities, all is vanity". The word in the Anglo-Saxon text, however, is *ídel* (= "idle") which may certainly mean "vain" in the preacherly sense ("of no avail", "meaningless") but which can also mean "empty, deserted, desolate". The hermit surveys a world from which, by degrees, all things - objects, possessions, people - are subtracted, leaving at last a mere *void*.

The poem is not allowed to end there, in these nihilistic reflections. A coda is added, introduced by the words *swá cwæð snotor on móde*, "so said one wise at heart". Here a little word becomes directionally important, for where does *swá* = "so", "thus", point? Is "so = as above" intended, or is it "so = as follows"? In a parallel instance at the beginning of the poem, *swa cwæð eardstapa earfeþa gemyndig*, "so said a wanderer, mindful of harships", the sense of *swá* is clearly *prospective*, forward-pointing - "this is what he said". Then at the end of the poem *swá* may be intended *restrospectively*, in the sense of "that was what he said". Yet there is an argument for the cataphoric ("as follows") sense, even here. The seer, for all his pessimism, still has something left to say, an exhortation, a message positive and hopeful in the face of all this gloomy experience. This is what he says:

> Blessed is he who holds fast to his faith.
> Never in haste shall the warrior speak of his grief
> until he finds the way to assuage it,
> a noble man, nobly acting his part.
> Well for him, then, who looks for grace and solace
> to our Father in Heaven, where all our security stands.
>
> lines 112-15

---

[40] "The storm hurls its malice on heroes", *hæleþum on andan,* says the text, but in this case *hæleþ* is a courtesy title for "man". The *hæleþas* are goodfellas, gentlefolk. For a comparable "social" usage of heroic terms, eg *eorl, duguð*, see *The Whale*, discussed in Chapter 4.

3 Exile and Lamentations

It is a summing-up, and in part a recapitulation. It says, "keep the faith"; then it says, "suffer in silence", last as first, knowing *it is a noble's way to keep the secrets of the heart locked up*; but then it says, "it is well" - *well for him who looks for mercy and solace from the Father in Heaven*. Your prayers, in short, will be answered; out of the depths the Lord will hear you. The clear parallel between the opening and the closing lines of the poem is smudged in translation. The Anglo-Saxon text begins, *Oft him anhaga are gebideð, / metudes miltse -* "Often the outcast yearns for God's *grace*, the Maker's *mercy*" (my italics); then closes with the lines *Wel bið þam þe him are seceð, / frofre to Fæder on heofenum -*"well for him who looks for *grace* and *solace* from the Father in Heaven". The important words are *ár* (grace), *milts* (mercy), and *frófor* (solace, also "refuge"). In the context of the poem these are essentially religious terms. At the conclusion of the text we must be wholly aware that this is not the literal narrative of a thane down on his luck and seeking a prince's protection, but rather an allegory of the spiritual exile of a "wanderer" appalled by the world, seeking for grace, longing for refuge in God, our refuge and our strength, a very present help in time of trouble. The penultimate word of the poem, *fæstnung*, is a word of complex meaning. The dictionary records "security", "safety", "protection", "shelter"; but also, in a legal/transactional sense, "bond", "pledge" [41] In the usage of *The Wanderer*, it may take colouring from any or all of these. The exile seeks protection, shelter, safety; at the end of his musings he has assurance that he has a bond or pledge from Almighty God, and that it stands, though the storm howls and the solid, sullied world becomes a phantom.

These poems of exile have in common that they are all texts for living voices crying out of their predicaments. Even if we know little or nothing about Anglo-Saxon stress, accent, intonation, the phrases on the page make the voices speak to us, urgently, appealing to our sympathy. They that have ears to hear, let them hear. It is this intimacy that makes the poems immediately accessible to the modern reader, apart from any difficulties of interpretation that they may offer. In such terms we might speak of our own hopes and fears, our own sense of loss, or have heard others speak of theirs Only in *The Husband's Message* is there no voice of a human appellant - it is "spoken" by a stick, but even so, the stick speaks for a sender, as intimate letters "speak" to those who receive them. The voices speak of separation, of privation, of absence that wearies the heart, of killing doubt, of benumbing fear. The stories of *Wulf and Eadwacer, The Wife's Complaint,* and *The Husband's Message* are all-too-human tales of the faith that is shaken and the bonds that come near to breaking when lovers are too long apart. It is of an exile in the flesh that they tell. It is different with *The Wanderer*. That story is of spiritual exile, of the fear of separation from the love of God, of the privations of the religious life, of faith under trial, of the wistful hope of reconciliation in Heaven. Perhaps "intimate" is not, after all, the right word for the appeal of *The Wanderer*. It has the strict privacy of the confessional, and a sounding of the poem's austere cadences must leave a reader reflecting that, in the words of W.B.Yeats, "only the dead can be forgiven"; and as he adds - "when I think of that, my tongue's a stone".[42]

---

[41] The dictionary being that of J.R.Clark-Hall, see Bibliography, Section 1

[42] Yeats, "A Dialogue of Self and Soul". Collected Poems, London, Macmillan, 1952

3 Exile and Lamentations

"How doth the city sit solitary..."

The ultimate image of exile is that of the ruined city. It is not that man is exiled from civilisation: rather, that the proposition is inverted - civilisations are exiled from man, not to be regained or recalled. The Anglo-Saxons were acquainted with ruins; they lived with the rubble of the past, much as we live with the shells of medieval abbeys or broken manor houses, though theirs was perhaps a greater sense of wonder and misgiving, and their imaginations fed on the awe inspired in them by the work of departed generations. The Cotton *Gnomics* (or *Maxims*, Cotton Tiberius B) sound the theme:

> Cities are seen from afar
> the skilful work of giants on this earth,
> wondrously wrought in stone   *lines 1-3 Cotton Maxims*

The phrase *enta geweorc*, "work of giants" is recurrent in the Old English poetic vocabulary. "The ancient work of giants (*eald enta geweorc*) stood idle", says the Wanderer, contemplating the urban waste. "He sat gazing at the work of giants" (*enta geweorc*), says the Beowulf poet, describing the young thane Wiglaf as he surveys the tomb of the dragon's treasures, an "ancient chamber" with its "stone arches firm on their pillars". The sword-hilt Beowulf brings from the mere-wife's cave to present to King Hrothgar is a miracle of the goldsmith's craft, described as *enta ær-geweorc*, "ancient work of giants".It is inscribed with runes recording ancient strife before a great flood overwhelmed the race of giants, at God's command. The myth of these *entas*, skilled in war and crafts, may well have its origin in *Genesis*, 6:iv: "there were giants in the earth in those days" [ie before the Flood]; "and also after that, when the sons of God came in unto the daughters of men, and they bore children to them, the same became mighty men which were of old, men of renown." [43]

The fall, through pride, of the "mighty men which were of old, men of renown" is an exemplary theme in Old English poems like *The Wanderer, The Seafarer*, and *Beowulf*. The correlate of the broken people is the ruined and deserted city. Thus the poem called *The Ruin* tells of the majestic wreck of a mysterious settlement, *enta geweorc*, conceivably the Roman city of Bath. (There are references in the poem to bath houses and hot springs "gushing in a wide stream"). This city has fallen into lamentable disrepair:

> Ceilings are all caved in, watchtowers in ruins,
> barred gateway breached, mortar fretted by frost,
> the roofs of houses shattered, lapsed, collapsed,

---

[43] "There were giants on the earth". The *entas* were not malevolent giants, like the inhuman *eotenas, þyrsas,* and *gigantas* , but rather "mighty men", in the biblical phrase, the revered ancestors of a dwindled race. In his translation of Orosius' *History of the World*, King Alfred names *Mimbraðsé ent* (Nimrod the giant) as the one "who began the building of Babylon", and *Ercol þone ent* (the giant Hercules) as a demigod summoned to help Europe and Asia in their fight against the Amazons.

> eaten from under by age. Outworn, forlorn,
> to earth's embrace, the fierce gripe of the ground,
> the master-builders sank; till of mankind
> a hundred generations passed away.
> Kingdom on kingdom then this wall outlived,
> lichened, ruddy-stained, storm after storm,
> until the high arch fell
>
> *lines 3-11 The Ruin*

But the lament is not simply a pity for old buildings gone to rubble. It is for what the wreckage represents, the tale of human ambitions and pride going before a fall. It is for the generations, "outworn, forlorn", gone into "earth's embrace", after all their confidence, their success, their wealth, the splendour of their achievements, exiled for ever from the world they once ruled:

> Slaughter claimed many, and the plague-days came,
> death took them all away, the warrior breed;
> their palaces were turned into waste land,
> their citadels crumbled. Those who would build anew,
> those who would fight again, were laid in earth.
> and so these courts sink into ruin, and
> the broad roof-span over the arching beams
> sheds its red tiles. The ground's a town of tombs
> where many a warrior once, high-heart, gold-bright,
> in trappings of splendour stood, in shining armour,
> proud, wine-flushed, gazing on gold and silver,
> on jewels, gemstones, precious possessions, riches,
> on this bright city of a spacious realm.
>
> *lines 25-37*

Wealth is suspect, and transient. The heroic tradition extols the culture of noble wealth and the *máððumgifu*, the munificence of the treasure-givers in their halls.The poets of Christian times repeatedly question this. "I cannot think that riches will last for ever", says the Seafarer (in the poem of that name) and adds:

> To each man always, before his hour arrives,
> one of three things will come to decree his fate -
> sickness, or age, or violence of the sword
> lay claim upon the life of the doomed man.
>
> *lines 68-71 The Seafarer*

Ádl oþþe yldo oþþe ecghete - "Sickness or age or violence of the sword"; these things are the realities of human existence. All men are *fáege*,"fey",death-doomed, and neither wealth nor the pride of conquest can escape that doom. It is the essence of the little sermon King Hrothgar preaches to Beowulf after his youthful successes as a monster-slayer:

3 Exile and Lamentations

> "Let pride alone, great soldier!
> Now for a while your strength is at its peak,
> but time will come when sickness or the sword
> will take away your power, or swirl of fire
> or sudden surge of flood, or thrust of blade
> or arrow's flight, or age, the hideous;
> else the bright eye will fail, its light grow dark,
> and soon, proud champion, death overwhelm thee."
>
> lines 1760-68 Beowulf

Such a reflection on the vanity of human wishes underlies the Wanderer's lament for "the walls, the ruined houses":

> So now, in divers places on this earth,
> windswept, hoar-frosted, stand the walls,
> the ruined mansions. Palaces decay,
> their masters lost in death, robbed of delight,
> here by the wall the chivalry fell slain
>
> lines 75-80 The Wanderer

Nowhere in the whole of Old English literature, however, is the passion of the past, the grief for time irrecoverable, expressed more powerfully than in words from *Beowulf,* spoken by an incidental character, the chieftain who comes to bury, in the grave-mound which will later be possessed by a fire-dragon, all the treasure amassed by comrades and kinsmen now dead:

> "Hold now, o Earth, what man can no longer hold,
> the wealth of earls. Lo, there were good men once
> who won it from thee. Death in battle claimed them,
> fearful carnage; every one of my kin
> departed from this life. They had their feasts
> and have seen the end of them
> No one now tries the sword or brightens the flagon,
> the precious cup; the heroes are departed.
> Now from the sturdy helm's encrusted gold
> the trappings fall. The burnishers are asleep
> whose task it was to gild the battle-masks;
> and see, that armour which in battle bore,
> over the crashing shields, the bite of iron,
> crumbles, the fighter dead. Nor may ring-mail
> rove with the warrior, march among mighty men.
> No joy of harp, sweet music of the lyre,
> no good hawk swings through the hall, no eager steed
> stamps in the yard. Whole generations have gone,
> sent down to violent death.
>
> lines 2247-66 Beowulf

3 Exile and Lamentations

Here is a noble minstrelsy, mournful and exultant, singing "of human unsuccess, in a rapture of distress".[44] Here is the prophet's cry, from *Lamentations*: "How is the gold become dim! How is the most fine gold changed! The stones of the sanctuary are poured out in the top of every street". And always, behind the elegiac grandeur, the voice of the Psalmist: "Except the Lord build the house, their labour is vain that build it: except the Lord keep the city, the watchman waketh but in vain".[45]

---

[44] Quoted from W.H.Auden, "In Memory of W.B.Yeats, III". Collected Shorter Poems, London, Faber & Faber, 1952.

[45] See *Lamentations, 4.1,* and *Psalms, 127.*

4 rulers of the darkness

Remarkably, for an age in which the turning of a verse was an honoured and widely-practised activity, the Anglo-Saxon era has bequeathed us no more than two names of major vernacular poets: Caedmon, whose miraculous story we know from Bede, and Cynewulf, a person of disputed identity. Between them these two appear to have monopolised the genre of religious/scriptural narrative, at least for want of other attribution. Some large assumptions are required. It is hardly likely that Caedmon, in his indefatigable "ruminating" and dictating (see Chapter 1, p.20), could have produced all the works solely ascribed to him, and Cynewulf, who took care to sign with a runic cipher the works he wanted to be known as his, is rather conveniently assigned the responsibility for others. Of Caedmon as a person we know no more than what Bede tells us, and Cynewulf is a figure hardly less fugitive, the object of speculations rather more or rather less plausible .[46] We take these names, consequently, as the convenient designations of "schools" of writing, rather than as poetic personae. There is certainly a Cynewulfian personality, the shade of a melancholy man, a brooding, penitent, even romantic presence, most evident in the first-person passages of the signed poems. His poems differ, in this respect at least, from the Caedmonian writings, along with his learning and the occasional impression of a distinctive polish and fluency in his style. What unites the two "schools", however, is their persistence in the imagery and moral terms of epic narrative, the Germanic inheritance, as defined by one of the contributors to the Cambridge History of English Literature: "It is safe to say that, in both groups, there is hardly a single poem of any length and importance in which whole passages are not permeated with the spirit of the untouched Beowulf, in which turns of speech, ideas, points of view, do not recall an earlier, a fiercer, a more self-reliant and fatalistic age. God the All-Ruler is fate metamorphosed; the powers of evil are identified with those once called giants and evils; the Paradise and Hell of the Christian are as realistic as the Walhalla and the Niflheim of the heathen ancestor". [47]

---

[46] The identity of Cynewulf? We know, from his runic signatures claiming the poems *Crist, Elene, Juliana,* and *The Fates of the Apostles*, how he spelled his name. Otherwise, all is conjecture. It has been suggested, not very convincingly, that he was a Bishop of Lindisfarne; the signature *Cynwulf* attached to the Decrees of the Council of Clovesho in 803 leads to the conjecture that he may have been a priest in the diocese of Dunwich. (On the coast of Suffolk; those who opt for Lindisfarne or Dunwich find circumstantial support in the vivid sea-imagery in parts of his poems). "Abbot of Peterborough" has been suggested. Some scholars have argued for a Mercian origin, some for a Northumbrian. A melancholy or penitential strain in his writing prompts the assumption that he had known the high life as a minstrel at court, and then, as a convert, turned to the monastic life of repentance. Is it likely? The options are discussed - and dismissed - in *The Cambridge History of English and American Literature* (see below, and Bibliography), and in the *Catholic Encyclopaedia* (website at http://www.newadvent.org/)

[47] *The Cambridge History of English Literature* (see Bibliography): quoted from Vol.1, Chapter 4, "Old English Christian Poetry", by M.Bentinck Smith, section 13, p.48.

News from Niflheim

Whatever concept of Paradise soothed pious Anglo-Saxon souls in pre-Conquest times - whatever relish of "everlasting bliss" or "joy with the angels" or "banqueting among the blest" - their imaginings may well have paled beside livelier fancies of Hell. Not much acquainted with any paradise on earth, they had at least some experience of hellishness. They knew its executives, those brawny rapacious men who came to practise extortion, burn villages, rack the godly, ravage the townships and lay waste the land. Hell was an aspect of war. War they understood, and could the more readily entertain the theme of War in Heaven.

The Caedmonian poem called *Genesis*, a work of some 2935 lines contains what is clearly an interpolated passage of 616 lines, now called *Genesis B* or *The Later Genesis*. This interpolation is an extraordinarily powerful episode, describing the aftermath of the War in Heaven, when Satan, enchained, plans to strike back, and sends his emissary to corrupt Adam and Eve The reader who comes upon it in the context of its "parent" poem must feel that here the song has modulated into a new key, or graduated from competence into genius. It is not "Caedmonian" in style; nor is it "Cynewulfian". Suddenly the feel of the narrative is different, more eloquent, more urgent. One reader whose appreciation reached beyond a general sense into a specific perception of differences in language and style was the German philologist Eduard Sievers. In 1875, struck by features of idiom and prosody more resembling Old Saxon than Old English (Anglo-Saxon), he formed the hypothesis that *Genesis B* was an Anglo-Saxon recension of a continental original, a poem on the Genesis theme by the author of the Old Saxon *Heliand*.[48] Nearly twenty years later this conjecture was triumphantly confirmed, when among some manuscript fragments discovered in the Vatican library, three turned out to be parts of an Old Saxon poem on the book of Genesis and a fourth a part of the *Heliand*. Comparison showed the text of the Anglo-Saxon *Genesis B* to be a close rendering of the Old Saxon in one of the Vatican fragments. Rarely has the scholar's curious craft of taking pains been so happily justified.

Genesis B breaks into, or overlaps onto, on the "host" narrative to take up the theme of the rebellion against God's authority, and the onset of the war in which the rebels, under Lucifer's command, are repulsed. Lucifer - God's favourite, aspiring to stand higher than God - chafes at the demands of service which make him an underling:

> "Why should I toil?", he said
> "No need at all for me to have one higher.
> I with my hands can work as many wonders,
> great power I have to make a goodlier throne,
> higher in heaven - why serve at his command,
> bow to him in such service? I can be God
> as well as he. Staunch friends I have,
> comrades who will not fail me in the fight,

---

[48] E.Sievers, "Der *Heliand* und der angelsachsischen *Genesis*". Halle, 1875

> stern-tempered heroes. They have chosen me
> to be their lord, those valiant warriors.
> with such support at hand one might make plans,
> take counsel with such brave comrades-in-arms.
> Keen friends they are of mine, loyal in heart,
> and I may be their lord, rule in this Kingdom.
> It does not then seem right to me that I
> should flatter God, for any favour's sake.
> I will no longer be his underling." *lines 280-91 Genesis*

God hears of this overweening pride, and is gebolgen - "enraged", literally "swollen", a physiological response more appropriate, perhaps, to a tribal chieftain than the King of Heaven. (Beowulf about to confront a monster is said to be torne gebolgen, "swollen with rage"). The insurrection is suppressed before it is well begun, and the rebels are put to literally headlong flight:

> Then down from Heaven, the Fiend and all his folk,
> three days, three long nights, fell -
> angels from Heaven to Hell falling -
> and God changed all into devils.
> Because they would not honour His acts and words,
> therefore the Almighty set them down
> in a place of little light, below the earth
> sent them, vanquished, into the black of Hell.
> There in that everlasting night
> each one of them endures continual fire;
> then comes at dawn a wind out of the east,
> and frost, burning cold, like a flame or a lance. *lines 306-16 Genesis (B)*

Genesis B, it sometimes seems, has Miltonic "pre-echoes". The lines describing the sensation of intense cold as something painful as burning or cutting anticipate the description of cold Hell in the second book of Paradise Lost (lines 594-5): the parching air / burns frore, and cold performs the effect of fire. [49]

---

[49] The connecting link between *The Later Genesis* and *Paradise Lost* is the Gallo-Roman Avitus, Bishop of Vienne (Alcimus Ecdicius Avitus, AD 490-c:a 518, latterly St.Avitus), whose numerous writings included a poem of 2552 Latin hexameters, in 5 books, on the Origin of Sin (with the revolt of the angels), Expulsion from Paradise, the Deluge, the Crossing of the Red Sea. The Old Saxon poet evidently had access to it, and Milton is thought to have used the earlier books in drafting parts of *Paradise Lost*. Historians and theologians will find an introduction to the writings of Avitus in *Avitus of Vienne, Letters and Selected Prose,* ed. and transl. Danuta R.Shanzer and Ian Wood, Univ. Penn Press/ Liverpool Univ. Press, 2002. As far as I know, the poem is only accessible to those with ready access to the Abbé Migne's *Patrologia Latinae Completus Cursus,* LIX, 191-398.

4   Rulers of the Darkness

The narrative goes on to describe the punishments and torments of the fallen angels. They endure unremitting toil in the ferocious weathers of Hell, and they do so, says the poet, *forþon hie þegnscipe Godes forgymdon* - "because they scorned the thaneship [service] of God". Their punishment is because they have betrayed the contract between *hláford* and *þegn*, which, as the poet presents it, exists in heaven as on earth. God punishes their *gal*, their *oferhygd*, their hygeléast, their *ofermetto*, words all signifying "arrogance", "folly", all that is involved in the Latin *superbia*, "pride", the first of the deadly sins. This is what happens when the servant considers himself his master's equal, or worse, his superior. As if in answer to the charge of betrayal, the Devil prepares to speak, and a long preparation it is, a stylistic tour de force. It elaborates something as simple as the business of reporting speech with an introductory tag, eg. "he spoke", "he declared", or "X proclaimed, lifting his shield", or "Y announced, weary at heart"- the ordinary devices of narrative. This is no ordinary device. It is almost an exercise in the baroque. It begins thus:

> Then spoke that proud king, lately the brightest angel,
> whitest in Heaven, beloved of his Lord,
> dear to his Prince - until to folly they turned,
> and for that folly the great God himself
> grown wrathful in mind, cast him into the pit
> down to that bed of death, and named him anew.
> He should be called, by the All-highest decree,
> Satan thenceforth, and live there in dark Hell,
> hold to the depths, no longer war with God.
> *lines 338-44 Genesis (B)*

The way is thus prepared, and more than prepared, for the expected speech; but the expected speech is not yet delivered. What immediately follows is a reprise, a reworking of what has already been said. "Then spoke that proud king" is resumed, with the "proud king's" new name, Satan. "Satan spoke...":

> Satan raised his voice - in sorrow he spoke,
> who thenceforth must remain confined in Hell,
> hold to the depths. God's angel once he was,
> white, in Heaven, until his pride undid him,
> and, above all else, one arrogant thought,
> that he would nevermore revere the Word
> of the Lord of Hosts. Within him, pride
> welled hot round his heart. Without, was heat,
> dire punishment. He spoke these words:
> *lines 345-55 Genesis (B)*

And there at last is the point at which the words may be spoken, after 18 lines of introduction. Recursion (repetition, with variants) is a common enough feature - indeed an essential element - of Anglo-Saxon poetics, at the level of phrases and lines; but a progressively recapitulated paragraph, as here in this passage from Genesis B is not so usual. It is a sample of the sophistication of this poet and his boldness in the handling of banal conventions; unless we assume an alternative explanation, that the writer at this point, musing over his text, somehow forgot

4 Rulers of the Darkness

his place in the train of his meditations.[50] It is in any event a testimony to the power of the scribal culture, the potential of composition when the verse can be written down and the structure supervised as it develops. We may think that no ordinary *gliwman*, no recitalist in the oral tradition, working "by ear" and by memory, picking up cues from phrase to phrase, could easily have kept that elaborated construction under control.

This intricate preliminary introduces a long speech, of huge dramatic intensity. Satan looks mournfully round the scenes of his new inheritance. Again, the language has "pre-Miltonic" echoes:

> "This is a narrow place, how different from
> that other we once viewed from Heaven's height,
> which my Lord gave to me,
> though by the Almighty's will we may not own
> nor occupy our kingdom. Justice, though,
> He has not done, who casts us into flame,
> down to the very depth of hottest Hell,
> exiled from Heaven. That land He sets aside
> to be a dwelling-place for humankind.
> Such grief it is to me
> that Adam, who was moulded from the clay,
> should take my lordly throne, and live in joy
> while we endure penance and pain in Hell."   *lines 356-68 Genesis (B)*

The shifting reference of personal pronouns, between plural (we) and singular (me) is marked. It can be read as vacillating between the collective reference (to all the rebels) and the individual (to their leader); though arguably, the deixis does not change, pointing always to Satan himself, as personal "I" and lordly "we".[51] His counter-accusation to the charge of neglected thaneship is that God has not been just to his thane, in rescinding a gift of land (a gift of grace and favour, like the *ár* of the earthly lord, the *sincgifa*) and presenting it to a new favourite, and an unworthy one, a mere clayborn ceorl. The thought of it goads him to a passionate outburst:

> "Alas! had I but the power of my hands,
> and could but for one hour - one winter hour -
> escape this place, then I, with all my host...!
> But bands of iron hold me fast,

---

[50] I do not ignore the possibility that in this instance the *Genesis* poet's "baroque" recital may owe something to the style of his source text – which, however, I have been unable to consult at the time of writing this. See my general note on Avitus at Postscripts p.75

[51] This is perhaps too bold a speculation, since the "royal we" is not generally evident in Anglo-Saxon. But here again, the shadowing of a Latin text (Avitus') in the background may explain the usage.

> and cruel chains. I have no kingdom now.
> Bondage of Hell imprisons me.
> Here is all fire, above, beneath,
> landscape more loathsome I never saw,
> through all of Hell the blaze never abates.
> Clasping links in a savage chain detain me,
> restrain my power to move. Bound are my feet,
> my hands manacled. Through these doors of hell
> all ways are barred, by no means may I slip
> the bonds that clasp my limbs.
> Hard irons forged in great heat lie about me,
> great fetters God has fastened round my throat.
> I know now that he saw my secret thought,
> and also that He knew, the Lord of Hosts,
> what strife might come, as between Adam and me,
> about that paradise...Had I the power of my hands!
> *lines 368-88 Genesis (B)*

Again, the poet's designing touch appears, in spanning a long verse-structure with one repeated phrase - *ahte ic mínra handa geweald*, "had I the power of my hands". Satan now lies helpless in the frustrated condition of "if", "if only". And thus prostrate in "if", the leader is obliged to make desperate appeal to his thanes. (His "host", or as he calls them, in traditional warlike style, his *werod*). They must plan revenge, he says, and heaven being lost beyond hope of recovery, they must consider how to strike at earth, by corrupting Adam and Eve and bringing them down to Hell to be slaves to the fallen angels. "Now begin to think about the campaign", he urges his followers, and the word he uses, here rendered as "campaign", is *fyrd*, familiar from the chronicles of war in the sense of "army", "levy".[52] Here is the disabled commander, exhorting his troops:

> If, in time past, to any thane of mine
> lordly treasure I gave, when blest we sat
> in the good Kingdom, ruling from our thrones,
> he could not in a better hour repay me -
> make recompense - that thane, any one of you,
> if he would pledge himself, to rise from hence,
> up through the darkness, and by craft of wings
> wheeling through cloud, to come to where they stand,
> Adam and Eve, created there on earth,
> in goodness ringed, while we are cast down here
> in these deep vales.
> *lines 409-21*

The tone of fretful anger, verging on pathos, is unmistakable. This is no heroic Satan, but a Devil writhing in the chagrin of frustrated devilry. "If...if..." he says,

---

[52] On *fyrd*, see Postscripts p.143

but the subordinate clauses make no principal conclusion. "If some thane - any thane - would find a way of getting to Adam and Eve..."; "if"... and..what then? He feels only jealous rage against the pair who have basely usurped the paradise that is rightfully his. "If...", he says again (the verse-rhythms quickening in lengthened sequences, as though in reflection of agitated speech):

> If any of you can find any way to make them neglect God's lore,
> the loathlier they will be to Him.
> If they break His command, then He will be enraged;
> and after, their wealth will be taken away, and punishment prepared,
> some torment dire.
>
> *lines 427-32 Genesis (B)*

Satan's view of the Almighty verges almost on the demeaning: God is made to appear as an irascible paterfamilias given to violent loss of temper. Then His creatures must at all costs be made to provoke Him with their disobedience:

> Give thought to this, all of you,
> how you might betray them. Then I will take my ease,
> rest sweetly in these chains, if their kingdom is lost.
> Whoever achieves this - for him reward is assured
> for evermore, since we, in this Hell fire
> confined, thenceforward may advance our cause.
>
> *lines 432-37*

Thus the Fiend promises - but nothing is assured "for evermore". There is no *ár*, no bestowal of property, no *þéodenmaðm*, "lordly treasure" in store for the deserving thane; and for the moment no thane at hand, eager, without prompting, to make his *béot*, his vow. Satan is not the proud figure of a *þéoden* exhorting his *werod* in hall, among the jubilant benches. He is at this point utterly powerless to do, or promise, anything. He is not like his Miltonic counterpart in Hell, free to act, alert, immediately dangerous, a commanding figure among his counsellors, ready himself to undertake the mission he proposes. Milton's Satan is heroic, perversely maybe, but heroic nonetheless. The Satan of The Later Genesis is vividly pathetic - pathetic in the strict sense that he can feel, all too passionately, but cannot act. His one possibility of action is to make anguished appeal to others who are able to act. This chieftain's *giefstól* is a fettered couch from which he cannot rise; his allotted province is gyman þæs grundes, "to preside over the abyss". God has put him ineluctably in his place, and the danger of this Devil must rest with the missionary devils, if they will accept their charge. He is not quite a chieftain in the old Teutonic style. "In the line of battle", says Tacitus, "shame befalls the prince who is surpassed in valour by his companions, and the companions whose valour does not equal that of the prince"[53] But the Satan of the Saxon Genesis cannot enter the line of battle; if he is to subdue mankind, it must be by proxy.

---

[53] Tacitus, *Germania*, 14: *cum ventum in aciem, turpi principe virtutis vince, comitatui virtutem principis non adaeqare*, "in the line of battle, shame befalls the prince who is surpassed in valour by his companions, and the companions whose valour does not equal that of the prince."

Because of a break in the manuscript at this point, we miss the entry of a volunteer, a thane willing to undertake the temptation of Adam and Eve. We meet him first as he prepares for his mission; he is described in a heroic style touched with ironic "asides", here represented in parentheses:

> God's adversary then for war prepared,
> eager in splendid armour (sly in soul),
> put on his warrior-helm, fastened it firm,
> with buckles clasped. Much eloquence he had,
> many words of deceit. Aloft he wheeled,
> through hell-doors made his way (ruthless in heart),
> and dancing on the air, the evildoer
> parted the fire at a stroke, by the craft of the fiend,
> and sought then secretly to betray God's servants,
> with wicked deeds to tempt and lead them astray,
> until they should be loathed by God.
>
> *lines 442-452 Genesis (B)*

This is the Tempter, Satan's emissary. The account of his actions imitates a feature of the traditional heroic style - the arming of the warrior before an exploit, noting his name, the splendour of his armour or weaponry, and the temper of his soul (or in military language, his morale). In Beowulf, for example, lines 1441-42:

> gyrede hine Beowulf
> eorlgewædum, nalles for ealdre mearn
>
> Beowulf made ready
> in princely armour, cared nothing for his life

Compare that with the present instance:

> Angan hine þa gyrwan godes ansaca,
> fus on frætwum (hæfde fæcne hyge)
>
> God's adversary then for war prepared,
> eager in splendid armour (sly in soul)

The prominent verb in those two instances is *gyrwan* (past tense, *gyrede*), to prepare, make ready, "gird up". It is the hero's preparation for the fight; it can also mean to "decorate", or "bedeck". Beowulf makes ready *eorlgewáedum*, "in noble array", meaning armour; the Adversary in *frætwum*, "in his trappings", similarly suggesting high rank or noble status.[54] It is in the note of morale,

---

[54] This might almost be called the "arming" trope. It is used for saviours, heroes, devils, also for saints; thus Guthlac preparing for an ordeal: *Gyrede hine georne mid gastlicum waepnum,* , "Swiftly he armed himself with spiritual weapons". (*Guthlac*, 177-78)

however, that the two passages markedly differ; for Beowulf, the hero upright, the people's champion, faced with peril "cares nothing for his life", whereas the Adversary, though apparently fús, "eager (for the fray)" is "sly in soul", an expert in underhand methods.

He prepares to fight with unheroic weapons, for at that place where in epic description we might expect to hear of a keen-edged blade or a file-tempered spear we read "much eloquence he had," deceitful words. The Adversary's weapon in the fight to enslave Adam and Eve is rhetoric, and he has an armoury of insinuating styles. The assault on Adam begins in a cajoling style, disturbingly suggestive of a representative sent down by head office to check on customer satisfaction and deal with any outstanding problems. "Is there anything you need?" he says. "Don't be afraid to tell me, I was with the Almighty recently, he speaks well of you":

"Up there, in His bright World, I heard Him cherish
your deeds and words, as he spoke about your life.
And you can cherish orders He sends by me,
coming down here. This whole wide world is full
of green gardens, and see, up there God sits,
the Almighty, up above all in the height of Heaven.
It could not be for Him, the Lord of Hosts
to run this errand here; rather, he sends
me, His officer, to speak with you." *lines 507-17 Genesis (B)*

God wants you to eat this fruit, he says, it is good, it will make you healthy, build your strength, increase your brain-power, help you lose weight, give you the body beautiful, but Adam is at first too wise or too sturdy to be taken in by the sales pitch; selfsceafte guma, the text calls him, a man made, not begotten - and hence not born yesterday. He repudiates the Adversary's claim to be an angelic representative bearing offers of additional benefits. "You don't look like one of His angels to me", he says - perhaps with heavy irony, and not surprisingly, since by this time the Adversary is in full serpentine mode, curled round a tree. Adam robustly insists that he takes orders from God alone, that he has been warned against false claims, and that this scaly newcomer is a person of very dubious character, whom he will not on any account obey. At this the Tempter is enraged, but quickly shifts the attack to Eve, complaining to her, inviting her collaboration, denouncing Adam for his incivility to an angel, his shocking mistrust, and his prideful disobedience to God, foretelling pain and sorrow to come should these impieties be reported to the Almighty. Talk to Adam, he says, bring him round, make him see sense, get him to eat the fruit, for his own good, and we'll forget the insults. He all but tells her that wives know best.

4 Rulers of the Darkness

The poet's representation of Eve's character is poetic, rather than sternly homiletic. She is a beautiful creature. Repeatedly he calls her *idesa scenost, wif wlitegost*, "of ladies the fairest, woman most comely", and particularly, as the critical moment of the temptation approaches:

> of ladies the fairest, of women the comeliest
> ever to be in the world,
> for she was the handiwork of heaven's King   *lines 626-28 Genesis (B)*

God made her beautiful, as God made her vulnerable, having, as the poet expresses it, "designed for her a weaker mind" (presumably so that she would obey Adam). The Tempter plays on her own awareness that she is not very clever. He offers her, with the forbidden apple, the gift of enhanced perception and understanding, of "enlightenment" in the literal sense of being able to view everything in a stronger light. The argument here turns on a primitive concept of vision, in which the eye itself is the projector of light, rather than the receptor.

As she tastes the fruit and looks about her, she sees from earth to heaven and everything is shining clear, including the credentials of the strange messenger her mate has so rudely offended. She goes to Adam, bearing a piece of the fruit for him to taste:

> "Adam, my lord, this fruit - it is so sweet,
> so blithe in the breast - and this fair messenger
> a true angel of God. From his habit I see
> he is for sure the herald of our Lord,
> the King of Heaven. Better by far for us
> to earn his favour than his enmity.
> If you have done him some offence just now
> he forgives that, but we two in his service
> must now obey him. Why this hateful strife
> against your Lord's envoy? We need his favour,
> to be our go-between with the Almighty,
> the King of Heaven. From this place I can see
> where He Himself is seated (south and east) [55]
> in glory enfolded - He who made the world.
> I see His angel-guard move all about him,
> winged, a great band, truly a joyful host.
> Now who would grant me such intelligence
> were it not sent directly by our God,
> Ruler of Heaven?"   *lines 655-74 Genesis (B)*

---

[55] "south and east" : in the cosmology of the poem, Earth and Eden lie to the north and west of Paradise, which Eve therefore sees as lying "south and east".

4 Rulers of the Darkness

So, having been tempted, she tempts her husband. "She did it with a sincere thought", the poet says, "not knowing what ills, what vast sorrows would follow for mankind". But as Adam by and by yields to her persuasion and takes the fruit, judgement on the fairest lady, the comeliest woman, is pronounced:

> He from the woman's hand
> took Hell and Death, though it was not so called,
> being known then only by the name of "apple";
> but it was Sleep-of-Death and Devil's-Clutch
> Exile and Hell and Heroes-forever-Lost,
> with Murder-of-Mankind, they made their meat.   *lines 717-23 Genesis (B)*

The immediate consequence is a terrible self-awareness, expressed in the perception that they are naked, and no longer in protected Paradise but in the vast hostile Predicament of the world as we all know it, and doomed.

Adam turns on his partner, passionately bewailing their state and denouncing her for bringing him to it:

> How shall we live now, we two - stay in this place
> if the wind blows from west, east, south or north?
> Menacing darkness looms, a hailstorm comes
> burdening heaven, then betweentimes frost,
> achingly cold. And then from heaven in heat
> the bright sun blazes, and we two stand here
> with never a clout to shield us. We've no roof
> to shelter from storms, no coin to buy us food,
> but God the Almighty rages against us.
> What will become of us now?
> Now I may rue I begged the God of Heaven,
> good Master, for my sake to fashion you
> out of my limbs - now you have led me astray
> into His hatred. Now well may I rue
> as long as I live, that I ever set eyes on you   *lines 806-21*

Eve's response to this almost hysterical cry is measured and submissive, and in its great dignity and acceptance of guilt arguably a mark of the poet's sympathy. She is, after all, a creature of feeling; how can she comprehend Adam's moral revulsion, his sense of an intellectual commitment broken?

> Then Eve replied, fairest of ladies,
> of women most comely, though by the devil's craft
> betrayed: "Blame me you may with your words,
> Adam, my friend; and yet this cannot pain you
> worse in your mind than it does me in my heart".   *lines 821-25*

It is a touching appeal, almost a reproof, but Adam is not to be mollified. He continues in his vein of outraged conscience:

> If I might know God's will,
> what punishment I ought to have from Him,
> no sooner said but you should see it done;
> should Heaven's God command me
> to walk into the sea, into the flood to wade,
> then were it never so deep, the ocean stream,
> never so great, I'd sound it to the depths -
> if I might do God's will.
>
> *lines 828-35 Genesis (B)*

He knows that it is too late to do God's will. By one act he has alienated himself from God, forfeited his rights in the earthly paradise, and condemned himself to the fate of the wanderer, the outcast:

> I look for no more service in this world,
> now I have forfeited my Master's grace
> and may not have it.
>
> *lines 835-37*

"May not have it" - may not have the service, may not have the grace, may not have the world. It is the voice of the renegade thane, now doomed to trudge the wilderness, knowing, like the Wanderer in the poem of that name, that he must long forgo his dear lord's cherished counsel. His mood settles into one of dull resignation. At last he turns to Eve and says, "Let us go into the forest here, and the shelter of this wood".

They are naked and aware of their nakedness. They go into the forest to find clothing among the leaves. It is the beginning of the long exile.

Here the enveloping poem, the so-called *Genesis A*, resumes its course and continues for a further 2000 lines, telling the Genesis story down to the episode of Abraham and Isaac. It is a competent recital, efficiently but not impressively versified, with none of the virtuoso feats, the dramatic gestures, the sinuous accumulations of syntax, the capacity to surprise, that mark the 616 lines of the *Later Genesis*. It is, indeed, paraphrase, where the poet of *Genesis B* gives us drama, and drama's content of character, passion, and psychological insight.into the angry lust for power, into human weakness, into temptation, into the presence of evil in all its banality and tarnished pride.

The nature of the beast

As the Tempter corrupts paradise, so the Adversary in many forms infects the physical world - or such was the medieval view, reflected in the bestiaries, those books of animal lore whose origin can be traced back to Aristotle and Pliny the Elder in classical times, and in the Christian era to a fourth-century treatise called the *Physiologus*. The classical writers might have claimed to be disinterested observers of nature, with some help from hearsay, but Christian homiletic had its own programme for alternative zoology. There, the whole of non-human nature could be read as a paradigm of God's will and purpose on earth, an image of His teaching, to be interpreted by the pious; and also as an exemplar of the Devil in action to subvert God's will and tempt careless humanity away from God. In the medieval bestiaries, factual observation is at a premium and fanciful report - or travellers' tales, perhaps - a useful currency. We read in them of bird called the pelican, one so concerned for the welfare of her young that she would wound her own breast to feed them with her blood: a prefiguring of Christ's self-sacrifice for mankind. (And so "the pelican in her piety" becomes the badge of the Guild of Corpus Christi). The elephant, we are assured, had no knee-joints and could only sleep standing up, leaning against a tree; then the cunning hunter, having dug a great pit on the other side, would chop the tree down, and the elephant would fall helpless into the pit, from which it could only be rescued by the action of a strong young elephant that would bend down, and with its trunk lift up the fallen beast. It is not too difficult to perceive in this the image of proud man, who will not kneel before his God, but falls to the wiles of the Devil and can only be redeemed by the intervention of a Saviour. The myth of the "inarticulate" elephant persisted for centuries; it is one of the vulgar errors dismissed by Sir Thomas Browne in his *Pseudodoxia Epidemica* (1646), by which time, however, its theological purport had also been discredited [56]

Anglo-Saxon has a version of the *Physiologus*, in the form of three linked poems, each about an animal and each with a moral-religious application. One concerns the panther, a second the whale, and the third, in a fragmentary text, the partridge. The whale, we are told, is a bad beast, evil of intention and a sheer menace to shipping:

> I'll make a tale now of the fishy kind.
> I mean to choose my words with poet's art,
> and speak my mind concerning the Great Whale.
> Often encountered, though by no man's will,
> a savage menace to the seafarer -
> as to all men - this ocean voyager
> is called Fastitocalon.

(He is called Aspidochelone in the ancient accounts, where the baleful sea-beast is a Great Turtle). [57] By another name – but he has many - he might be Leviathan, as described by Milton in *Paradise Lost, Bk.I, 200-208*:

---

[56] Sir Thomas Browne, *Pseudodoxia Epidemica, or Vulgar Errors*, London 1646, Book III; Browne makes no reference to theological interpretations of bestiary lore; his book is a massively learned assault on superstitions, old wive's tales, and pseudo-science. He makes reference, incidentally to the whale's "sweet breath", which he attributes to the presence of ambergris in the sperm whale's stomach.

[57] Aspidochelone, in Greek *aspido* + *khelon* The name means "shield turtle", from *aspis* (shield), whence *aspido*- (shield-shaped), and *chelone* (turtle). By a false etymology, deriving from

> That Sea-Beast
> Leviathan, which God of all his works
> Created hugest that swim th'Ocean stream:
> Him haply slumbring on the Norway foam
> The Pilot of some small night-founder'd Skiff,
> Deeming some Island, oft, as Sea-men tell,
> With fixed Anchor in his skaly rind
> Moors by his side under the Lee, while Night
> Invests the Sea, and wished Morn delays.

This, indeed, is the very Sea-Beast that the Anglo-Saxon preacher-poet pictures for us:

> His semblance has the colouring of rocks,
> well worn, it seems, and overgrown with plants,
> with sandhills set about, all marram-grass, [58]
> so that when sailors catch a sight of him
> they fancy him an island, and they moor
> their high-prowed ships, putting out anchor-ropes
> to the false land, hitching their sea-steeds there
> at journey's end. Then up ashore they go,
> all the bold boys, leaving behind their boats
> moored at the staithe, riding the ocean tide.
> And so they make their camp, the seafarers,
> weary, unaware of any threat,
> and on that island build a fire, a blaze
> towering up high. Happy the heroes then,
> the weary voyagers, as they sink to rest.
> But when he is aware, the guileful beast,

---

another (Latin) sense of *aspis*, as "asp", this mythological monster is called by some the "Asp-turtle". Its ill repute, under diverse names – for example Zaratan - is ancient; some of Alexander the Great's men are said to have come upon a huge shield-turtle, big as an island, in the Indian Ocean, and to have landed on it, in expectation of finding the hoard of a dead king; whereupon the treacherous beast sank beneath them. Something of the sort is narrated of Sindbad the Sailor, who barely escaped with his life after an encounter with the beast. The Anglo-Saxon form, Fastitocalon, is as Tolkien has pointed out, essentially "astitocalon" (close enough to "aspidochelon") with an "F" to satisfy the demands of alliteration., in the line *fyrnstreama geflotan, Fastitocalon.* Tolkien employs Fastitocalon as a cautionary name in one of the songs of his character Tom Bombadil; whence the monster has taken on a new life in the conventicle seminars of modern Middle Earthers. There are several websites, eg. that of The Tolkien Wiki Community. See www.thetolkienwiki.org/wiki.cgi?Fastitocalon.

[58] "marram grass" freely translates the text's *sáerýric*, apparently a *hapax legomenon*, or unique reading. In structure it divides into the elements *sáe*, "sea", and ? *rýric?*, meaning, at a guess, "reed". This corresponds to the formation in Old Norse of *marr*, "sea", and *halmr*, "straw", in the compound *marrhalmr*, "sea-straw", modern *marram*, a tough grass often found in sand-dunes.

that strangers have a foothold in his fort,
keeping a watch there while the weather holds,
all of a sudden through the salt sea-wave
downward the monster plunges with his prize,
And holds them drowning in the hall of death,
the craft and all their crews.
lines 8-31 The Whale

This description resembles an element of medieval pulpit rhetoric, a part of the sermon called the *exemplum*, a story or anecdote designed to engage the congregation's interest and assent. It is followed by a *significatio*, the moral application, in which the religious analogy is worked out in some detail:

Such is the phantom's craft,
and devil's guile, that they, pretending good,
by hidden powers deceive the best of men
with goodly showing - harmfully persuade,
mislead them, so that in distress they look
for comfort to the Fiend, then straight away
they make their dwelling place with the Deceiver.
When he, the wily, the importunate,
knows, from his house of pain, that any one
of noble kind is circled in his snare,
he through his cruel guile becomes the bane
of high or low, too prompt to do his will;
then he, in helm of sightlessness concealed,
makes haste for Hell, barren of all things good,
bottomless sea-surge under the misty gloom.
Thus the Great Whale, who drowns the seafarers,
captains and ships and all.
lines 31-49

Here, "the best of men" translates the original duguð, familiar from the vocabulary of heroic poems in the meaning "seasoned warriors". The phrase "of noble kind" renders *hæleþa cynnes*, the word *hæleð* signifying primarily "hero", "fighter", though in some contexts - as indeed here - it is hardly more than an honorific for "man". Another word of heroic colouring is *eorlas*, here translated "captains", though *eorl* suggests a person of greater consequence than a seafaring skipper. The preacher - if we may think of him in that role - exhorts his audience by dignifying them; sinners they may be, but as *duguðe* and *hæleþas* and *eorlas* they are decent folk, respectable, "good people all"[59]

---

[59] "good people all": on this theme, cp Chapter 3, note 40, p.66

He goes on to amplify his theme with a second *exemplum* and a consequent *significatio*. The talents of the Great Whale are not confined to the impersonation of islands:

> Another way he has,
> this mighty Whale, and one more wondrous still.
> When on the ocean hunger troubles him
> and prompts the monster with desire of food,
> then the sea-keeper opens up his mouth,
> sets wide the jaws, and from his inward parts
> comes a delightful odour; other fish,
> deceived by that, then make all speed to swim
> to where the fragrance issues forth, and there,
> a heedless company, they enter in,
> filling that gape - then on his plunder straight
> the monster clamps his cruel chops together.   *lines 49-62 The Whale*

Thus the *exemplum*; the moral follows:

> And so it is for every man, so often
> heedless to ward his life in these sad times.
> He lets himself be fooled - so weak of will -
> by pleasant fragrance, so that he becomes
> guilty of sins against the King of Glory.
> For those who in this life
> preferred the empty pleasures of the flesh
> to service of the soul, after their death
> the Accursed opens Hell. When, treacherous,
> crafty in evil, he has brought them down
> to the whirlpool fire, sullied with all their sins -
> all who in life were pleased to do his will -
> then, after death, his cruel jaws he fastens -
> Hell's lattice-gate. For those who enter there
> there is no turning back and no way out,
> for them is no escape and no retreat,
> they can no more avoid it than the fish
> can swim away out of the whale's wide mouth.   *lines 62-81*

The sermon is ended. It remains only to dismiss the hæleþas, the good folk, with an exhortation and the echo of a doxology:.

> Therefore it is indeed
> to the one Lord of Lords, the Glorious King,
> that we most look, as we renounce the Devil
> in all his works and words. So let us pray

>in this our transient life to have from Him
>peace and prosperity, and that we may know
>in this life to be, the love of Him, the praise,
>the glory everlasting.

lines 82-88 The Whale

The sentence-structure and word-order of this poem are in more places than one curiously un-Anglo-Saxon, involved, laboriously wrought into discursive shape. This cleric is no scop, skilled in the traditional music and rhythms of poetic performance. The effort of versifying some quite long sentences forces him into odd patterns of phrasing, here and there reminiscent of Latin. *The Whale*, dating from the 10th century, hardly suggests a poem composed for performance, as though to the sound of the harp; it suggests, rather a poem made scribally, to be read, and conceivably to be read aloud, in religious company. The *duguð* and the *hæleþas* would then be as a band of respectful parishioners, or clerical "thanes", companions in chapel or refectory, hearing of man's fight against the Devil.

The strong impression of sermonising, of exhortation of the most earnest and heartfelt kind, curbs any inclination on the modern reader's part to take this beast-fable as a naively amusing notion. For the anonymous poet, this is serious; indeed, this is war. We for our part are privileged by our superior science. We are acquainted with catastrophe, and we do not need peculiar monsters to explain why things go wrong. Fantasy fiction entertains us with horrors we can comfortably discard, partly because they have no counterpart in the truths of real science, but also because belief in the supernatural is itself widely discarded and discredited. We have a hard time actually believing in God, are reluctant to believe in the Devil, and are not at all inclined to give credence to malignant cetaceans dedicated to the service of infernal powers. To look back 1000 years, however, is to retrieve a time when God and the Devil were the objects of unconditional belief, when they were assumed to exist in a state of desperate and unremitting conflict, and when monsters were needed, to emphasize the point. This was serious, beyond curious and entertaining circumstance. So the author of *The Whale*, for all his ambition to speak *wóðcræfte*, "poetically", yet makes clear his corollary intent to preach *þurh módgemynd*, to "speak his mind", or "tell his thought" about the Great Whale: one might say, "to tell the plain truth"

The sleep of reason...

In the literature of Northern Europe in the early Middle Ages, monsters are simply a part - an essential part, it might be said - of the belief system. They are elementals of air and fire, earth and water. They are giants, or trolls, or dragons, or sea-beasts, and their imputed existence serves, in pagan times, to explain catastrophes of nature and the inscrutable ways of Wyrd; and then, with the advent of Christianity, as an apparatus to represent the tremendous conflict of God and the Adversary. These creatures have their particular fields and functions. Dragons, for example, those of the fire-breathing kind, are portents. Thus the Anglo-Saxon Chronicle for the year 793 portends (retrospectively) the coming of the rapacious Northmen: *wæron geseowene fyrene dracan on þam lyfte fleogende* - "fiery dragons were seen flying in the air" Possibly any abrupt brightening of the night sky could be attributed to a fire-dragon. The opening lines of the so-called *Finnesburh Fragment*, or *The Fight at Finnsburh* have the young hero-king Hnaef, woken at night when he and his werod are surrounded in their quarters and attacked by their treacherous Frisian hosts, exclaiming at the sudden flashes of brightness:

> Then he cried out, the king young in battle -
> "No dawn in the east is this, nor dragon flying here,
> nor the gables of this hall ablaze, but here
> come warriors, armed! *lines 2-5 The Fight at Finnsburh*

It is significant of a wholly different way of reading the world that the "young king" should consider the advent of a dragon as a plausible alternative explanation - along with daybreak and a house fire - of the sudden lighting of the hall. Whatever is not explicable as an act of God or an accident of man can be attributed to the access of monsters.

The dragon has another, more important capacity, as a guardian of burials; where men have been interred with some pomp of treasure, he appropriates the hoard for his own and sits forbiddingly on the tomb. The Maxims of MS Cotton Tiberius briefly note this as his proper function:

> draca sceal on hlæwe,
> frod, frætwum wlanc
>
> a dragon must guard the grave-mound,
> old watchman, proud of his treasures *lines 26-7 Cotton Maxims*

This is the function of the dragon in Beowulf, the last of the monsters the hero is called upon to slay, the slumbering creature having been provoked to malignant, retributive action by the intrusion of a thief, who has made off with a precious cup. One man's criminal deed brings on a whole people a disaster that only one other man, the people's king, can repel.

Beowulf in age is the saviour of his people, in a fight against a monster; in youth, too, he wins fame with his rescue of another people from another sort of monster, a pair of giants, or huge amphibious beasts, living in the watery depths of a marsh, from which they make attacks by night on the occupants of a noble king's hall. The *Cotton Maxims*, which briefly define the proper character of dragons, also tell us where giants live:

> þyrs sceal on fenne gewunian
> ana innan londe
>
> a giant belongs in the fen,
> under the marsh, alone. *lines 42-3*

That is precisely the condition of the first of Beowulf's monstrous adversaries, a malignant marsh-giant:

> "Grendel" their name for him, this grievous guest,
> stalking among the marches and the moors
> and fenland fastnesses...
>
> *lines 102-4 Beowulf*

Ancient superstition figures here; Jordanes, the sixth-century historian of the Ostrogoths, alludes to a tradition among them that witches and evil spirits have their home among the fens, and in the pagan legends of Scandinavia and Iceland, fierce mountain trolls haunt waterfalls and the pools below them. Every landscape hides a peril. On such beliefs, however, the Beowulf poet puts a doctrinal gloss, assigning to Grendel and his kind a biblical descent:

> The accursed being
> dwelt in the realm of monsters a long age
> after the Lord Creator had proscribed him.
> Thus on the kin of Cain the eternal God
> wrought vengeance for the crime of killing Abel.
> The killer had no profit from that feud;
> for that he was cast out
> by God, far from the company of men.
> And thence sprang all the progeny of evil,
> the monstrous fiends and elves and devil-birds
> and all the giants that made war on God
> long ages gone. He gave them their reward.
>
> *lines 104-15*

This is one important instance of the "christianising" revision of an old tale by a poet with doctrinal errands to run. The existence of evil in the world, the weakness of humanity before its power, its frustration of God's benign purposes, are explained, or "glossed" in the emblem of the beast that monstrously infects Creation; and the beast is the emblem of the Adversary, forever exiled from God for disobedience to the immutable Law.

Beowulf as we know it from its 10th century manuscript is a Christian poem with pre-Christian origins, an exquisitely-patterned, unifying mosaic of diverse elements: the chronicled fortunes of Teutonic peoples in the early centuries of the first millennium, the legends of popular heroes, the tales of the supernatural ("unnatural/natural history"), are all worked with sophisticated artistry into what becomes at length a celebration of Christian kingship in savage times. Its main narrative, however, its load-bearing span, is a tale of monsters, whom the hero fights, at first in pursuit of glory, and at the last in responsible defence of a hapless people, knowing himself a doomed man. The rest is commentary. Not the dark histories of tribes, or the high deeds of a Sigemund or a Hengest, can displace in the reader's mind the terrible fame of the monster Grendel, or Grendel's more wicked mother, the "merewife", the *grundwyrgen*, "wolf of the deeps", slain in her firelit cave a day's dive down beneath the surface of the serpent-haunted mere; or the dragon fatally awoken, against whose incandescent fury Beowulf's iron shield is a poor defence. The monsters possess the imagination because, through their power as symbols that generate symbols ("those images that yet fresh images beget") we know them more immediately than we know Hygelac or Ongentheow; they are always with us, in whatever form we acknowledge them, in whatever significance we assign to them. "To live", as Henrik Ibsen puts it, "is a fight with trolls in the halls of the heart and the brain".

Beowulf himself, before his ultimate habilitation as a wise and devout ruler - *mildost, monþwærust*, "mildest, most gentle" - is, dare one say it?, not wholly human. His name literally signifies "Bee-wolf", suggesting "bear", and the details of his story reflect those of diverse folk-legends from Germany and Scandinavia His enormous strength is bear-like, as is his preference for wrestling over other forms of combat (he has bad luck with swords). He is a creature ferocious on land and fearless at sea, an incredibly strong swimmer This appears in one of the poem's bravura passages, the account of a swimming match with one Breca the Bronding when, fully armoured, and all the time fighting with sea monsters - and slaying nine of them - he swims for five nights before fetching up on Finna land, "in the land of the Finns"[60] It is seen again in his pursuit of the mere-wife, when his plunge into the haunted pool takes him down, down, down, *hwil dæges* - "the space of a day" - *ær he þone grundwong ongytan meahte* - "before he could see the bottom". (Holding his breath, it seems, presents no problem). And yet again in the poem's account of how, when his royal master Hygelac has been repulsed and killed in a disastrous expedition against the Franks in what is now the Netherlands, Beowulf escapes into the sea, carrying thirty pieces of armour, and swims all the way home to his countrymen the Geats, in the south of Sweden. This is no ordinary capacity - he is part man, part animal, and not far short of a troll; but maybe it takes a troll of the right sort, a godly monster, to defeat those of the wrong sort.

Only in his last encounter with a monster, the fire-dragon, is Beowulf less troll-like, less instinctive, more reflective, and this is the episode in which the Bear's Son, he of the overwhelming rages and the mighty grip, is powerless, and the King of the Geats, a king by elective chance, one who has seen his share of fights, and heard much talk of kings and battles, wins peculiar glory, as the shield and benefactor of the people who look to him for protection. The long passage describing the fight, in prospect and in its aftermath, is interspersed with the reminiscences of a hero who has seen the fall of princes, the ravages of the blood-feud, the betrayals of trust, the dispersal of clans. This aging king knows that the glory of the warrior is brittle, that

---

[60] "the land of the Finns" : commentators doubt that this could be the same as modern Finland, or even, as in some translations, Lappland. A location somewhere further south on the Baltic coast of Sweden is preferred (see the note on line 580 in the Wyatt/Chambers 1914, repr.1948 edn. of *Beowulf*). But this line should be read in the full context of the swimming match episode. The contest begins off Geatland, in the south and south-west of Sweden. At first the two champions swim together and cannot be separated. Then wind and turbulent current divide them and they are borne their separate ways - Breca along the Swedish west coast to "the Heathoræmas land", in the south of Norway, Beowulf along the east (Baltic) coast to "the land of the Finns". But there is perhaps little point in ransacking the text for topographical precision.

4 Rulers of the Darkness

- in the words of the Preacher - "time and chance happeneth to all"; knows that this fight is forced upon him; knows that this time he cannot hope to win by main strength; knows that he is fáeg, doomed, his time at hand; yet will take on the monster single-handed, to lift a curse from his people and bring them wealth and prosperity. When he has killed the beast, but sustained mortal wounds, he speaks to the young thane Wiglaf, who has come to his aid:

> Beowulf spoke, despite his grievous hurts,
> his pitiful deathly wounds, knowing full well
> his time on earth was drawing to an end,
> life's joys all gone and all its tally of days
> spilling away, death waiting hard at hand:
> "Now I would give to my son, if son I had -
> an heir of my own flesh to follow me
> after I am gone - my armour and war-gear.
> Fifty years over this people I ruled,
> and there was never chief of neighbouring race
> dared menace me with terror and the sword.
> In life I bore the fate allotted me,
> held what was mine for holding, laid no plots,
> and never gave my solemn word in vain.
> For all this now, though wounded to the death,
> I may rejoice, because the Lord of All
> shall find no cause to lay to my account
> the murder of my kin, when soul at last
> shakes off this body.
>
> *lines 2724-43 Beowulf*

This is the piety of the hero transcendent, the image of the virtuous Christian king. He rejoices now, not with savage exultation " rejoicing in his work" (the phrase used to describe how he deals the "mere-wife", Grendel's mother, a neck-shattering death-blow) but in the knowledge that he has accepted his station in life, with its duties, has never plotted against anyone, never taken a false oath, and never been guilty - like some leaders - of the murder of kin. For fifty years he has been an exemplary king. When he asks Wiglaf to go to the dead dragon's hoard and bring back some of the treasures for him to see, it is not - the poet makes clear - in the spirit of a man covetous even at death's door, but as a dying ruler anxious for tangible proof that his people will be provided for. So he prays:

> "I give my thanks to God, Ruler of all
> The King of Glory, the eternal Lord
> for all these treasures that I gaze upon,
> for he has granted me, before my death,
> the winning of such wealth, to feed my folk.
> I have laid down my old life for this hoard -
> I bid you now, look to the people's needs.
> I may no longer stay here."
>
> *lines 2794-2801*

4 Rulers of the Darkness

The good man's dying hope, that by his self-sacrifice he has won security of his people, is a pathetic illusion. His people want nothing to do with the gold. It is accursed, tainted with the monster's spite. It shall be burned on the funeral pyre, they say at first; but later, take some of the hoard to be interred with the warrior's remains and leave the rest in the ground, "as useless to men as it always had been".

By his death Beowulf has won nothing, except - in the words of the Seafarer, "the praise of the living, spoken after his death" His people praise him, but are full of forebodings for a future that for them is far from secure. The Geats are vulnerable to the enemies they have made among the surrounding peoples - the Swedes, the Frisians, the Franks. The closing pages of the poem are sombre in their foreshadowing of disasters to come. Among the crowd of mourners round the funeral pyre is an old woman, *bunden-heorde* - "with her hair bound up" whose grieving for the fallen king is mingled with deep dread of what the days to come will bring for her and her like, now the protector is dead: [61]

> And a widow-woman, her hair tied back,
> sang of her sorrow for Beowulf's death,
> crying again and again her dread
> of harm to befall in days to come,
> great bloodshed to be, the terrors of war,
> humiliation and captivity...
>
> The smoke rose into the sky.   *lines (conjectural) 3151-55 Beowulf*

Hers is the usual condition of woman when war is the invariable condition of man. *Vae victis* - the defenceless are plundered, violated, enslaved. The sleep of reason brings forth war; and that may be the greatest of the monsters, the one invincible troll.

---

[61] "a widow woman, her hair tied back". The mark of her widowhood is that she us *bundenheord*, with her hair worn short and close. This part of the MSS (some eight lines) has been so badly damaged as to be in places almost indecipherable. The 19th century critic, Sophus Bugge, made a conjectural restoration, in which the relevant words defining the "widow" are *séo géo-méowle / æfter Beowulfe,* "the former maiden (spouse) after Beowulf". More recently J.C.Pope, in his *The Rhythms of Beowulf* (Yale, 1942) deciphered the phrase as *sé géatisc méowle,* "the Geatish woman". The inference left to be drawn is that this is a woman twice-widowed, Hygd, who was widow of the Geatish king Hygelac, and who later married Beowulf. But the documentation misses the poetic point, the "objective correlative". An image of desolation: here is a widow-woman, here is a funeral pyre. The rest is commentary.

5 avenger and redeemer

After the dissolution of the monasteries in the 16th century, the MS of *Beowulf* came by and by into the possession of Sir Robert Cotton, the antiquary whose collections subsequently formed part of the library of the British Museum at its foundation in 1753. Cotton had an engagingly simple filing system; his library of manuscripts was housed in bookcases, each of which was topped by the bust of a Roman emperor, whose name, together with a classifying number, served to identify the texts stored below. Of these identities the most familiar - tip-of-the-tongue familiar - to students of Old English, is Cotton Vitellius A.XV, the "name" of the *Beowulf* manuscript. Or rather, of a codex, a compilation, containing various works in prose and verse, including *Beowulf* and another epic poem, called *Judith*.

These works have been the victims of a chance to which ancient manuscripts are peculiarly vulnerable, the chance of fire. In 1731, when the Cottonian collection had been moved to Ashburnham House, Westminster, a disastrous blaze consumed most of the printed books and a large number of manuscripts. The *Beowulf* was very seriously damaged, and subsequently suffered a progressive deterioration of the MS, halted or countered only by labours of preservation and scholarship. We still have, however, a complete epic poem of more than 3,000 lines. Not so with *Judith*, a text reportedly consisting of 12 cantos, or "fits", of which the fire left only the last three, 349 lines in all. The writing is so accomplished, so spirited, that we may well rue so great a loss; on the other hand we can take the view that if the three surviving cantos are truly representative of the whole, in style and narrative technique, the loss is not total, since we at least have access to the complete story from a different source. It would be catastrophic indeed if three-quarters of the text of *Beowulf* had been irrecoverably lost, for only by reading the whole poem do we learn, or form a critical opinion of, the scope and significance of the work. In *Judith*, by contrast, we have foreknowledge of theme, contents, and the purpose of the narrative. The matter of the Eastern story that inspired an English poet is supplied from scripture, by the book of Judith in the Apocrypha.

The Vulgate text tells the following story. Nebuchadnezzar, the Assyrian king, sends his general, Holofernes, to occupy Judaea. The campaign is ruthless, conducted with great cruelty, and when Holofernes besieges a walled city near Jerusalem, called Bethulia, the sufferings of the occupants are extreme. A plan to raise the siege is proposed by a virtuous young widow called Judith. Attended only by her maid, she is to seek out Holofernes at his headquarters and offer herself to him, if he will spare her countrymen. She goes, however, with the intention of killing him. Arrested by the besiegers' outposts, she is brought to Holofernes and held for questioning and observation. The general holds a drunken feast for his commanders, and afterwards orders Judith to be brought to his tent. As he lolls in a stupor she takes a sword and decapitates him. She and her maid then escape and return to Bethulia, bearing, in token of their success, the severed head of Holofernes. At this sign of their deliverance, the citizens are roused to arms; they march out of the besieged city and attack their besiegers, who are put to humiliating flight, or slaughtered. Thus God's providence for His people is made manifest.

This narrative, which a Catholic theologian might choose to regard as an *exemplum* of true faith in positive action, has had for others an appeal that is nothing if not sensational.[62] Its qualities are potentially cinematic - as indeed one director, the great D.W.Griffith, readily grasped. His film called *Judith of Bethulia*, made in 1914 (on what would have been, for its time, an ambitious budget), still invites the commendation of historians of the cinema, one of whom has remarked, in a recent appraisal, "This is a Biblical story with all the trappings of a soap opera. It's about the siege of the Israelite city of Bethulia by the Assyrians, complete with betrayal, loyalty, murder, Biblical characters, mass killings, decapitation, soldiers and weapons"[63] That it certainly is; but so is the Anglo-Saxon poem, a *coup de cinéma* indeed, that pre-dates the film by more than 900 years.

Judith is a poem of the tenth, possibly late tenth century; freedoms in language and style, in metre and mimetic sound-textures, suggest this late date. Its "modernity", however, is not signalled by any crucial departure from classic models of versification. Though the verse sentences are often quite long (another possible mark of "lateness"), with extended sequences of "run on" lines, there are few if any passages of involved syntax; it is comparatively easy for a translator to construe at sight. As an epic, and a story of violent events, it has not the tragic grandeur of *Beowulf*; it lacks that poem's anxious perception of a moral dilemma, as between the urge to glory (*dóm*) and the desolation of war. What it has, in abundance, is hectic action and a high verbal colouring - a tale told in gorgeous Colorama, with a huge sense of relish in the telling The action is displayed straightforwardly, scene by scene, "take by take", as in the following review.

Scenes from a popular script

The *Judith* fragment begins with a carousal. Judith has arrived, with her petition, on the fourth day of a debauch to which a triumphant Holofernus has summoned his veterans and senior commanders - in Saxon terms, his *duguð*, or his *heorðwerod*.[64] She is held captive - or held in reserve for his further pleasure - while he gets on with the business of drinking his captains under the table. The feast is a very noisy affair:

---

[62] Catholic theology, numbering *Judith* among the canonical books, is obliged to consider it as a history with a divine purpose. Thus, "The purpose of the book is to give an example of heroic virtue and to show God's loving providence and care for His people." - John E. Steinmueller, *A Companion to Scripture Studies, Vol.II, p. 133;* New York, Joseph F. Wagner Inc., 1942. There are good grounds, however, for regarding the history as unhistorical. It amounts to what modern irreverence might call "a rattling good yarn", like many good yarns, morally ambiguous as it rattles.

[63] John de Bartolo, reviewing D.W.Griffith's *Judith of Bethulia* in the film magazine Silents are Golden; online at http://www.silentsaregolden.com.features folder

[64] The Assyrian commander's name in the Vulgate text is spelt Holofernes; in the Anglo-Saxon, Holofernus.

5 Avenger and Redeemer

> Then to their feasting sat they down -
> proud host, grim henchmen, all together,
> the captains outrageous came to their wine.
> Deep were the bowls, the goblets, the tankards
> borne down the benches to the folk in hall
> Death-doomed they were, even as they drank,
> hard fighting men, though he could not have guessed it,
> their fearsome overlord. For Holofernus,
> bountiful, joyful as the wine poured out,
> so cackled, chuckled, ranted, canted,
> that from a good way off he might be heard,
> the hard man, at his bawling, bellowing,
> proud, wine-flushed, urging them all the while,
> drink up, drink deep.   *lines 15-27 Judith*

This goes on all day long, until the general has "drenched his companions with wine", so that they lie "in a swoon", "like men slain". Then he sends his servants to the guest chamber to fetch his next victim, "the blessed maiden". In the Anglo-Saxon version of the story she is not a "widow", though she is undoubtedly "pious". Insistently, with the nouns *mægð* and *meowle*, our poet presents her as a maiden, a beautiful virgin, *wundenlocc*, "with braided locks", who arouses Holofernus' lust .[65] His intention is to besmirch her "with shameful acts", but, the poem tells us, "God would not permit that", She is brought to his chamber, and to the privacy of a bed meshed around with gilded hangings, but by the time he joins her there he can do no more than collapse into a drunken stupor. "There", the text announces, perhaps even with a pinch of irony, "he was to lose his renown, utterly, within one night". Then Judith, now called *nergendes þeowen,* "the Saviour's handmaiden", sets about her appalling task. She grasps the hilt of her sword and draws the sharp blade, "shower-tempered",[66] from its sheath - but then, before the awful act, appeals to the Almighty in prayer:

---

[65] "braided locks" here translates *wundenlocc* compare this with the translation of *wunden gold* as "braided gold", see Postscripts p.144. But is it altogether certain that "braided" properly describes Judith's seductive *coiffure*? The Vulgate account describes her transformation, before her exploit, from the severe habit of the widow to the opulence of the total charmer. She bathes, anoints herself with "the finest myrrh", dresses lavishly, picks out a pair of sandals, puts on her jewels and her earrings, and - the Latin says - *discriminavit caput eius*, meaning, possibly, "braided" (or "plaited") her hair (*discriminare* = "to separate"), or perhaps "combed out" her hair, or even "let down" her hair. As a widow she would have worn her hair tied back close. Her aim is to deceive Holofernus by presenting herself as a maiden footloose and fancy-free; perhaps her tresses, like those of a lass in an old song, "hung down in ringlets". Was it a curly-haired seductress, not a braided belle, who chopped off Holofernus' head?

[66] Tempering a sword. The blade is described as *scurum heard*, here literally translated as "shower-tempered". A first impulse, guided by the reminiscence of Othello's "sword of Spain, the ice-brook's temper", is to read this as meaning "tempered by plunging the forged blade into cold water". That would certainly indicate the swordsmith's practice of hardening the edge of a blade in the process of "annealing" . Note, however, that the epithet *scurheard* (according to Clark Hall) means "made hard by blows" - the "shower" being the repeated hammer-strokes on the anvil.

5 Avenger and Redeemer

> "Creation's Lord, Comforter, Mighty Son,
> to Thee, O threefold majesty, I pray:
> grant mercy to me in my hour of need.
> Cruelly my heart is inflamed, my mind oppressed,
> gravely oppressed, by sorrows. Grant, Heaven's Lord
> victory and true faith, that with this sword
> I may cut down this death-dealer. Pardon my sins,
> stern Lord of All; never had I more need
> of mercy and grace. Avenge now, mighty God,
> giver of glory, wrongs in my mind raging,
> hot in my breast." Straightway the All-High Judge
> inspired her with great courage, as he does
> all humankind who turn to him for help,
> with counsel and with true belief. Her mind
> was eased then, and her sacred hope renewed
>
> *lines 84-98 Judith*

When a Hebrew maiden adjures the Trinity, we may perhaps suspect some doctrinal ambition on the part of the Christian poet who speaks for her. Her orisons are dense with the names of God. He is *frymða god*, "Lord of Creation", *frófre gáest*, "Spirit of Comfort" (Holy Ghost), *bearn alwaldan*, "Son of the Almighty" (Christ), together in *ðrynesse ðrym* ("Glory of the Trinity"). Further, he is *swegles ealdor*, "Lord of Heaven", *þearlmód þéoden gumena*, ("stern Lord of men"), *mihtig dryhten* ("mighty Lord"), *torhtmód tíres brytta*, ("noble giver of glory" - or "source of honour"). In his prompt response to her appeal, this manifold God appears as *se héhsta déma* ("the highest judge"), and that is perhaps the most significant, in this pious context, of the catalogue of divine names.

Judith's prayer is an argument for justifiable homicide, based on her appeal for "*victory and true faith*" (or "*true belief*"). She is full of passionate hatred for her victim, and nothing else but "victory" will appease her - but do her wrongs, and those of her people, justify the act of murder? The dilemma is less hers than that of the Christian poet, who makes her appeal for "true faith" somewhat ambiguous. She is pleading, perhaps, for the strength and the conviction to carry her through her ordeal. Or she may be asking for doctrinal revelation, the theological teaching on killing in an acceptable cause ("give me assurance that I am doing the right thing for the right reasons"). The phrase "in true faith" is repeated by the poet in his comment on the value of prayer, that God "inspires all humankind who turn to him for help, with counsel (*mid ráede*) and with true belief." God is asked to sanctify the dubious act.

This lingering in theological anguish has artfully suspended the action. Holofernus lolls, drunken and comatose, on his bed. Judith pauses, sword in hand; prays; and then -

> She clutched the heathen's hair, to haul him close,
> the loathed man, with hatred and contempt,
> positioned him where she might readily
> do the grim deed, and then, bright-braided one,
> struck with her glittering sword the malignant foe,
> so that, his neck half-severed, he fell back,
> unconscious, drunken, wounded mortally.
>
> *lines 98-107 Judith*

Not only in a swoon, then, but in a drunken swoon, and more than that, a semi-decapitated drunken swoon. Enough, one might think, is enough, but our zealous poet makes a second scene of her second attempt:

> Nor yet, though, was he dead, the life gone out.
> Fiercely she struck the heathen dog again,
> the valiant lady, so that now his head
> spun to the floor, and the foul trunk of him
> lay behind, dead.
>
> *lines 107-112*

And at length the deed is accomplished; but Heaven's justice has not yet finished with Holofernus. His body being dead, his spirit wanders into a terrible exile, like that prescribed for Satan and his followers in the poem of *The Later Genesis*:

> His spirit strayed elsewhere,
> under a huge cliff, and lay there condemned,
> for ever sealed in pain, by serpents wound,
> in torments bound, imprisoned and held fast
> in the pit of hell, after his going hence.
> Whelmed in darkness, never a hope he had
> that he might leave the snakepit, but must dwell
> for ever and ever there, world without end,
> in that house of shadows, reft of all joyful hope.
>
> *lines 112-21*

This is a picture of Hell as conceived by the medieval Christian: the forbidding terrain, the darkness, the imprisonment and bondage, the unceasing pain, the hopelessness. Here lies Holofernus, given the reward his life has deserved.

Judith - now called *se snotere mægð,* "the wise maiden", and *ides ellenróf,* "courageous lady" - prepares, with her maid, an attendant figure in the drama, to return to Bethulia and announce a mission accomplished. Gathering up their belongings (which include Holofernus' head, carried in the maid's knapsack) they make their way back to the city. Good news, the inhabitants are told, see now, your troubles are over. At that, the citizens come running from all quarters to meet and hear Judith, their eager bustle imitated in the skipping of the verse:

5 Avenger and Redeemer

> The folk came running, women and men together,
> in groups, bands, clusters, troops, throngs,
> pressed, pushed, in thousands to the gate,
> old and young, to meet the maid of God.
> In that fair city the spirits of one and all
> soared, when they saw that Judith had returned
> home to her own, and so they brought her in,
> rejoicing, in all haste.   *lines 162-70 Judith*

Judith orders her maid to show to the delighted people the proof of their deliverance: Holofernus' bloodstained head, in token of "how she had fared in the battle". She urges them then to take up arms and march out to destroy an enemy whose fate, thanks to God, by her agency, is already sealed. Then as the Hebrews go forth to war, the familiar theme is couched in the rhetoric of Germanic battle:

> Out they marched, proud kinsmen and companions,
> marching out to fight in a righteous cause,
> bearing victorious banners, helmeted heroes,
> out of the holy city, in that same dawn.
> Shields resounded, echoing loud, delighting
> the lank wolf in the wood and the black raven,
> corpse-greedy bird. Both sensed how the people meant
> to have their fill of the doomed; and behind them flew
> the eagle, keen for carrion, dewy-feathered,
> dark-plumed, horn-beaked, and made its battle-song.   *lines 200-212*

The cast of animal characters is familiar; the wolf, the raven, the vocal eagle suggest the landscapes of Brunanburh or Maldon, though here the scene is the country round Bethulia, a fictive city not far from Jerusalem.

Then the warriors reach the enemy camp, and the Israelites begin a ruthless slaughter of opponents hardly wakened from the previous night's carousing:

> Then swiftly they let fly
> from their curved bows, their arrows shot in showers,
> snake-biting shafts, the points hard anvil-tempered.[67]
> Loud they stormed, the furious warriors,
> flinging their spears into the foe's grim pack,
> heroes, patriots, hating that loathsome breed.
> Grimly forward they pressed, stout-hearted ones,

---

[67] "snakebiting shafts" – for *hildenáeddran*, "battle vipers", a kenning for "arrows". On "anvil-tempered" and "shower-tempered", see further Postscript p.150

> ungently rousing a mortal enemy
> still muddled with mead. Fighters drew from the sheath
> the well-tried blade, the ornamented sword,
> and fierce, ruthless, scythed the Assyrian flower.
> None of that host they spared, the mean or the great;
> left none alive where they could overtake them.
>
> *lines 220-35 Judith*

This manages to convey on the one hand, random impressions of confused fighting, and on the other a reminder of the procedures for assault, Saxon-style: first the winnowing storm of arrows then, as the attackers press forward, the battle-yell, then the spearmen thrusting into the body of the enemy, then the fighting at close quarters with the sword. It is elaborate, almost voluptuous, in comparison with account of the onset at *Maldon*, but the rhetorical kinship is apparent.[68]

There follows a progressive collapse of morale among the Assyrians. The front-line fighters, seeing that they are being pushed back, wake the senior officers to report the advancing menace; they in their turn go to rouse Holofernus - and here it is a terrified respect for the chain of command that seals their fate. They dare not take control of the situation on their own authority, and they dare not go into the general's tent to wake him from what they assume to have been his lustful pleasures. It is an irony that does not escape the poet's attention, that they wait in limp anxiety outside the dead general's chamber, none of them daring to pass the gilded curtains while their enemy is pressing closer and closer and their situation becomes hopeless. At length, one of them plucks up courage to go into the bedroom, and there finds Holofernus' headless corpse. The general is their salvation, their sole hope; without him, the Assyrians are nothing. The intruder falls to the ground, tearing his hair and his garments; then calls to his fellows, waiting outside:

> "Here is our destiny spelt, our future betokened,
> our time is surely upon us, hard at hand;
> needs must we perish, in strife altogether destroyed.
> Here lies our general, put to death by the sword -
> beheaded."
>
> *lines 285-89*

Were this a tale of Northern chivalry, we might expect the general's *heorðwerod* to stand and fight to the death. (As with the steadfastness of the "old comrade", Byrhtwold, at Maldon: "Here lies our master, butchered, a goodly man, dead in

---

[68] The *Maldon* poet, describing the battle's first onset, says: *the time had come when doomed men must fall. A shout went up; ravens circled, and the eagle keen for carrion; there was uproar on earth. Then they let fly from their hands the file-hardened spears, the well-honed javelins; bows were busy; point struck shield; bitter was the storm of battle.* Behind its poetic rhetoric, this is a convincingly ordered account of what would happen in the opening moments of the battle.

the dirt; now may he who thinks to run from this battle rue it for ever"). No such resolution strengthens the Assyrian warriors; they promptly throw down their weapons and take to flight.

They are pursued, and like the fleeing Norse-Celtic army at Brunanburh, cut down where they run, "hewn down with swords for the pleasure of the wolf and the comfort of the birds of prey." The Hebrews cut through them in swathes, break any show of resistance. "Few came home to their kith", says the poet. Then the taking of the spoils begins:

> Back to the scene of the carnage, the reeking corpses,
> the noble pursuers wheeled; found space enough
> to strip, from lifeless bodies of a foe
> inveterate, deeply loathed, a gory plunder:
> bright armour, shield and broadsword, gleaming helm,
> and priceless jewels. On that battlefield
> the guardians of the homeland gloriously
> defeated their oppressors, hated of old,
> and put them to the sword.
>
> *lines 311-21 Judith*

The pillage, a whole month in the taking, is carried back in triumph to Bethulia:

> Helmets, daggers, old mailcoats, battle-gear
> studded with gold; more gems than the wise might tell -
> these things an armed people, bold under banners,
> had won, with glory on the battlefield,
> through the shrewd skill of Judith, the brave maiden.
> And in reward they brought her, from that fray,
> those spear-proud earls, the sword and bloodied helm
> of Holofernus, and his broad mailcoat
> with red gold studded - and all treasures, all
> the goods the haughty tyrant owned - rings, bright jewels
> they brought to the shining lady, to the wise one.
>
> *lines 327-41*

The listing of the spoils is in the typically grandiloquent style of this poet. The Vulgate text is - also typically - more restrained. Chapter 15, v.3,4:"And thirty days were scarce sufficient for the people of Israel to gather up the spoils of the Assyrians. But all those things that were proved to be the peculiar goods of Holofernes, they gave to Judith, in gold, and silver, and garments and precious stones, and all household stuff, and they were all delivered to her by the people".

The Vulgate story tells how Judith dedicates to God two trophies of her exploit: Holofernes' armour, and the canopy of his bed, taken down by her after the killing, a symbolic act of triumph. These details are not mentioned in the Anglo-Saxon text, which proceeds directly to the heroine's words of gratitude to the Creator:

> For which, to God be the glory, forever and ever,
> who made the wind, the sky, the stars, the great deeps
> and the tumbling streams besides, and the joys of heaven,
> through His benevolence.
> *lines 346-49 Judith*

Thus the Old English poem closes. The phrase *swegles dréamas*, "joys of heaven", might at a venture be read in another way, as *joys of song*. "Sky" or "sun" are the usual meanings of *swegl*, but there is another sense, "music", as in *swegldréam*, which is further reflected in compounds like *sweglrád* ("modulation"), *sweglhorn* (a kind of trumpet) and in the adjective *swéglic* ("sonorous"). But then why should one suppose that the poet chooses to end his poem by thanking God, not for the gift of heavenly joy, but for the gift of music - "for the tumbling streams and the joys of song"? Possibly because the source-narrative, the Apocryphal version, has Judith at the end raising a lengthy, sonorous *canticum* or *hymnus* to God the Creator; *hymnum cantemus Domino, hymnum novum cantemus Deo nostro*, "let us sing a song to the Lord, to our Lord let us sing a new song". If, as may seem reasonable, our pious poet had his source-text always before him, may not these words have licensed for him the ambiguity of *swegles dréamas* / *swegldréam*?[69]

The style and the message

In general description, it might serve to call *Judith* an *epic*, and yet the writing is of a different quality from the ancient severity of *Beowulf*, its manuscript companion. It is more akin to the later medieval narratives we call *romances*, those tales of derring-do in which fictional heroes survive figmented perils, overcome fictitious villains and reach a haven of factitious happiness. Its staging of big scenes is unblushing grandiose, in comparison with its Apocryphal source, the language of which is comparatively stringent. One outstanding example of this "romantic expansion" is the episode of Judith's prayer for God's help, followed by her execution of Holofernus, as quoted above. In the Vulgate original (cap.13.9-10) this is simpler, more compact, almost matter-of-fact: *cumque evaginasset illud apprehendit comam capitis eius et ait confirma me Domine Deus in haec ora et percussit bis in cervicem eius et abscidit caput eius et abstulit canopeum eis a columnis et evolvit eius truncum,* "and when she had drawn it [the sword] from its sheath, she grasped the hair of his head and said 'Strengthen me, Lord God of Israel, in this hour'

---

[69] An apposite instance of *swegl* in the sense of "music of heaven" is *Genesis B*, line 675. Having eaten the forbidden fruit, the deluded Eve tells Adam *ic mæg swegles gomen gehyran on heofenum*, I can hear the mirth of music in heaven"

and struck his neck twice and cut off his head and took down the canopy from the columns of his bed and rolled his body away." This has a narrative rigour hardly to be found in the voluptuous detail of *Judith*. The treatment of this episode invites further reflection on the style of the Old English poem. It is exciting, and excited; it is heated; it disturbs; it is supercharged with violence, sensuality - and triumphal zeal The feverish episodic progression of these cantos - from the debauched feast to the beheading of Holofernus to the ruthless slaughter of the Assyrians to the plundering of the routed enemy suggests an *animus* far beyond the feeling projected by the biblical tale. Is the cause of this to be traced to the circumstances of the author's origin? He is thought by some to have lived in Mercia in the early 10th century, when the warrior queen Æthelfleda led her people in battle against the occupying Danes and recovered from them the five boroughs of Stamford, Leicester, Derby, Nottingham and Lincoln, the fortresses of the Danelaw. Is it then patriotic fervour, and detestation of the entrenched enemy, as well as burning religious zeal, that for this poet informs the analogous tale of the Jewish warrior-maiden's fight against a ruthless pagan foe?

What can be said for certain is that the Anglo-Saxon poet manipulates his literary source and adjusts its emphases to suit his own doctrinal purposes. His principal, and pervading, act of manipulation is the changing of Judith's *widowhood*, in the Vulgate account, to her *maidenhood* in the Old English poem, where repeated reference is made to her as *méowle, mægð, nergendes mægð* ("the Saviour's maiden"), *mægða máerost* ("most excellent of maidens" - a style not inappropriate to the Virgin herself). Judith's virginity, it is implied, is the source of her strength in the hour of need; God will help the pure and innocent, when they turn to Him. This emphasis in the Old English text suggests something like the erotic mysticism of the Virgin cult in later centuries, though it is much more of a defence than a mystery - a defence of womanliness and a restoration of womanly honour. The first woman was weak, was foolish, was easily tempted, and brought about the suffering of humankind, the exile from God. Not so Judith, the warrior-maid. In her purity, her wisdom, her steadfastness, she comes as a saviour, a true soldier in the service of the Lord of Hosts. Piety might almost read her story as a tale of Eve the avenger.

A different kind of soldier, a different sort of war.

If *Judith* sometimes resembles a precursor to medieval romance, *The Dream of the Rood* anticipates another medieval convention, that of the vision vouchsafed to the poet in a dream. We have the title from the poem's nineteenth-century editors, and it is possibly a little confusing for anyone coming upon it for the first time, since it means "a dream about the Rood" (that is, the Holy Cross), and not "the Rood's dream". As previously noted, its manuscript form is the *Codex Vercellensis*, or "Vercelli Book", a 10th century collection of Old English manuscripts which "found its way" (the cliché circumvents the question 'how'?) to the Cathedral library at Vercelli in Italy, and lay there, all but unnoticed, until 1822, when it was in a proper sense discovered, revealing treasures of Anglo-Saxon poetry including the Cynewulfian *Elene* and *Fates of the Apostles*, the

5 Avenger and Redeemer

narrative *Andreas*, and, the greatest treasure of all, the poem to which we now turn. The Vercelli MS is not the earliest version of the poem in English. We have mentioned elsewhere (Chapter 1 p.19) a fragment of "text", from the late 7th or early 8th century, a "text" incised in runes round the shaft of a monumental cross at Ruthwell in Dumffriesshire. Decorative panels on the four sides of the stone cross contain quotations from a poem we recognise, but there is no way of knowing if the carver of these runes was working from a pre-existent oral tradition (words known by heart) or from a current version of a written text (words transcribed). In either event, the supposed date of composition is early, preceding by some three hundred years the manuscript form of the poem we know from the Vercelli book. It is hard to believe that no other manuscript form existed in the intervening period; some have posited the existence of a 9th century version of the Vercelli text.[70] But the history of this poem is a classic instance of the at times intractable problem of dating Anglo-Saxon poems, a question to be further addressed in the next chapter.

In Anglo-Saxon, the word *ród* has the primary significance of "gallows", "gibbet". It is used, in fact, no more than half a dozen times in the course of a poem which makes more use of other words, of literal or figurative import, to describe the structure on which Christ died - *tréow*, *béam*, (tree) *gealga* (gallows) *béacen* (beacon). In the course of the poem, however, the implied meaning of *ród* changes, from "method of torture and execution" to "means of salvation"; so from "cross" to "Cross", from "rood" to "Rood". That word no longer carries for us the emotional impact that must come from the merging of "gallows" into "Cross of salvation". We know it decoratively, or architecturally, as in "rood arch", "rood screen". As "Rood" it is now archaic, even genteel. We do not speak of "the Rood", but in church sing, rather, of "*the wondrous Cross* on which the Prince of Glory died." That line from an eighteenth-century hymn might be taken as concisely summarising the theme of one of our eighth-century poems

The traditional pattern of the dream-poem as we know it from medieval examples is A-B-A: *A*, the poet describes how he falls asleep and dreams, *B*, the events of the dream, *A*, the dreamer awakens, instructed and enlightened, perhaps changed by the vision in the dream. *The Dream of the Rood* is an expanded version of the pattern, in which *A1*, the poet tells how he has had a wonderful dream of the Cross that mingles the most sordid and the most splendid images; *B1*, the Cross itself speaks dramatically of its ordeal on Calvary, where it suffers as Christ's comrade; *B2*, the Cross preaches to the dreamer a sermon enjoining repentance and discipline; *A2*, the dreamer, awoken from his dream, takes the message to heart and resolves to follow the way of the Cross during the time that remains to him. The poem, as it opens, is immediately dramatic, with powerful images:

---

[70] The possibility of a text intermediate between Ruthwell and Vercelli, a "full northern text" dating from early in the eighth century, "with the flowering of the Cross cult in Northumbria" is discussed by Michael Swanton in his edition of *The Dream of the Rood*, University of Exeter Press, repr.2000, p.39

5 Avenger and Redeemer

> Hear now, while I tell a most wonderful dream
> that came upon me in the midnight hour
> when people around had gone to rest.
> It seemed that I saw a wondrous cross
> borne aloft in the air, enveloped in light,
> the brightest of trees, and that beacon was
> encrusted with gold; jewels there were,
> beautiful, round the base of the shaft,
> and five more such on the shoulder-span.
> Angels of God, forever fair,
> beheld it; that was no gibbet for rogues,
> for holy spirits gazed upon it,
> earth's people, and all Creation besides. *lines 1-12 The Dream of the Rood*

"People around", our translation says; but the original is a so-called "kenning", a kind of metonymy frequent in Old English verse. It says *reordberend*, meaning, in general, "human beings", but literally "speech-bearers". The kenning (on which term, see the next chapter, pp.132-33) invites both a general and a literal reading. It is not only that all the world is asleep. All the world around is silent, and the silence is not broken by human speech. What speech there is in the poem is speech heard in a dream, when the cross itself begins to speak. It is certainly a wonderful vision that comes to the dreamer, striking him with a hapless, terrified remorse for his own sins.

> Glorious that gallows, and I stained with sins,
> defiled with filth. I saw the wondrous cross
> with banners bedecked, shining in bliss,
> with gold adorned, and, fittingly,
> with jewels that graced the tree of God.
> Yet under that gold I could discern
> some terrible strife of old, when it had bled
> on its right side. I was stricken with grief,
> afraid for that fair vision, that beacon
> aloft in its hangings and hues. At times
> it was all drenched in sweat, soiled
> with the flow of blood, and then at times
> bedecked with gold and precious jewels.
> Still, I lay there for a long while,
> grieving, watching the Saviour's cross
> until I heard it utter human sounds.
> These words it spoke, that noblest of all trees: *lines 13-27*

5 Avenger and Redeemer

This concludes the first part of the dream-sequence, the *"A1"* section of the poem, with its descriptive language that shifts, or "morphs" - or, as in a film, "fades" - between images of the Cross, debased or exalted. Now, as the Cross begins to speak, the style assumes the tone of heroic discourse:

> Long years gone it was, and still I remember,
> I was cut down at the edge of the wood,
> hewn from my root. Fierce foemen took me,
> put on a show, said I should hang up their rogues;
> men shouldered me, then set me up on a hill,
> fiends enough fixed me there.
> I saw the Lord of Mankind
> hastening, eager to ascend me.
> There, I dared not, against the Lord's command,
> bend down or break, although I saw
> the whole earth shudder. I might have killed them,
> all of my enemies - but I stood fast
>
> *lines 28-38 The Dream of the Rood*

The "tree's" *foemen* are those who have taken it from its proper place in nature and forced upon it a repugnant office, as executioner of common criminals. This shameful task the "tree" is compelled to perform, until it recognizes the Lord of Mankind, coming eagerly, as though on a soldierly mission. From this point on, a note of military discipline is repeatedly sounded.[71] The "tree" is not allowed to act on its own impulse, against orders, to quit its station and attack the enemy. Trees in the wood may fall and kill the axe-man. This one must stand fast. It is a soldier in service. It goes on to speak of its Commander, and the dreadful battle they fight together:

> He girded himself for battle, the young hero
> who was God Almighty - brave and resolute
> came to the high gallows, masterly
> in the sight of many, come to redeem mankind.
>
> *lines 39-41*

---

[71] Is *The Dream of the Rood* a "heroic" poem? Michael Swanton (op.cit.) writes, " Heroic elements in the poem are largely allusive and a matter of mere vocabulary. The poet is concerned to illuminate aspects of the Redemption rather than to linger on the theme of the victor prince." That the *Dream of the Rood* is a "Redemption" poem is undeniable, but Swanton dismisses perhaps too readily the sustaining importance, through much of the poem, of battle language and the warrior ethic . The "heroic elements" are matters of *invocation*, rather than mere *allusion*.

5 Avenger and Redeemer

The phrase here translated "girded himself" - *ongyrede hine* - conventionally expresses a warrior's arming for battle. (See the discussion of this in chapter 4, p.80) Then:

> I trembled when the warrior clasped me,
> yet dared not bow to earth,
> fall flat to the ground. I must stand fast.
> As the Rood I was raised up
> I carried the great King, Lord of the Heavens.
> I dared not fall down.
> Black nails they drove through me. The wounds
> you may still see - terrible, open scars.
> I dared not hurt any one of them
> Together they shamed us. I was drenched in blood
> poured from the man's side when he gave up the ghost.
>
> Such torment I endured there on that hill.
> I saw the Lord of Hosts in cruel thaneship.
> A shroud of darkness wrapped the Master's corpse,
> that shining ray. Shadow reached out,
> blackened the sky. All Creation wept,
> bewailing the King's fall. Christ was on the Cross.
>
> *lines 42-56 The Dream of the Rood*

In the original of this passage, the verse-rhythms are disturbed, anxious, in a way not easily reflected in translation, expressive of great emotional turmoil. This intensity culminates in the words "Christ was on the Cross"; what follows is a retreat towards calm, and the Rood's anguished narrative settles to a steadier pulse:

> But still there came keen warriors, come from afar
> to the Prince who fought alone. I saw it all.
> Heavy with grief I was, yet I bowed down
> into the hands of those men, gladly, humbly.
> Almighty God they received, from his grievous pain
> they took him down; and me, those warriors
> left standing, drenched in blood, with arrows pierced.
> They laid Him there, exhausted, and stood by him,
> gazing on Heaven's King, as He, for a while
> rested, weary from His war. Then they began
> to build Him a tomb, in the sight of His enemies;
> the warriors fashioned it from shining stone,
> and laid in it the Lord of Victories.
> And in that evening, wretched, they began
> a lamentation, when they took their leave,
> weary, from their King. He lay there, all alone.
>
> *lines 57-69*

5 Avenger and Redeemer

This "burial" is in the Germanic warrior-style - a little reminiscent of the scene at the end of Beowulf, when twelve thanes ride round the hero's burial mound, making their lament for the fallen. As to "all alone", the text says *mæte werode*, literally "with a small guard" "lightly guarded", using that military word, *werod*. It may be recalled that when Cynewulf rode to his tryst in Merton (see chapter 2, page 22) he went *lýtle werode*, "with a small company". Some commentators accordingly choose to regard Christ's "small guard" as the company of the angels; however, *máete werode* = "with a small guard" = "all alone" makes convincing sense as a type of understatement not uncommon in Anglo-Saxon literary usage [72] Then, while this is happening, and the "thanes" (disciples) are taking their last leave of their lord, the three crosses stand, awaiting their destiny:

> We, though, stood, a long time, mourning,
> keeping our place while the cry went up
> from the warriors. The body cooled,
> the fair house of life. And then they felled us,
> all, to the ground. What a dreadful fate!
> In a deep pit they buried us,
> but there the Lord's thanes, friends, found me
> and made me fair with gold and silver.
>
> *lines 70-77 The Dream of the Rood*

By this the narrative has passed from "tree" to "cross", from "cross" to "Rood", to the splendoured sanctity of the vision the dreamer has glimpsed in sleep. Now the Rood, having related a passionate account of its ardours and endurances on Calvary (section *B1* of the poetic structure) turns (*B2*) to homiletic. It addresses the dreamer as *hæleð mín se léofa*, in the manner of a priest addressing his congregation with "dearly beloved":

> Now you may hear, dearly beloved,
> what cruel torments I endured,
> what bitter griefs. Now the time is come
> when men throughout the world, and all creation,
> will pray to this Light. On me, the Son of God
> suffered awhile. Therefore I, glorious now,
> tower under the heavens, and I may heal
> anyone who shows reverence to me.
> Once I was deemed the cruellest of torments,
> abhorrent to all, until I showed

---

[72] Understating. The reading of the text's *máete werode* as "all alone" is confirmed by a line in the concluding section of the poem, where the poet describes himself, after his vision, as lying *þær ic wæs ana, mæte werode"*, "where I was alone, with little company" (ie "by myself"). For a comparable instance of "Anglo-Saxon understatement", see the poet's confession at the end, *Nah ic ricra feala freonda on foldan,* "I have not many rich and powerful friends on earth. By "not many" he means none at all - they have all passed away and are living in heaven.

> the one True Way of Life to humankind.
> For see, the Lord of Wonders honoured me,
> Heaven's master, over all trees in the wood!
> Just as he raised His mother, Mary herself,
> Almighty God, in the sight of all the world,
> honouring her above all womankind.
>
> *lines 78-94 The Dream of the Rood*

Here the connection of the Cult of the Virgin and the Cult of the Cross is explicitly established. In what follows, the Rood enjoins the "dearly beloved" to make his vision known by putting it into words. Initially, the sermon hints at the wording of the Creed:

> Now I command you, dearly beloved
> to make this vision known to men;
> let words tell, this is the Glorious Tree
> on which Almighty God endured,
> suffering for the many sins of man,
> and for the deeds of Adam of old.
> He was buried, but he arose again, the Lord,
> in all his power, to help mankind.
> He ascended into Heaven, and will come again
> upon this earth, to seek us out
> on Judgement Day, the Lord himself,
> Almighty God, and all His angels with Him.
> And He will judge, who has the power to judge,
> each one of us, by what he has deserved
> here in this life on earth.
> Nor then may anyone be unafraid
> of what the Master's words shall be.
> Of the many, he shall ask, where that man is
> who in the name of the Lord would suffer death
> and the bitterness of the grave, as He did on the Cross
> But then they will be afraid, and few will think
> of what reply they shall then make to Christ.
> Nor yet need anyone there be afraid
> who in his heart carries this beacon bright,
> but through the Rood shall every soul
> looking to live with God above
> make for the Kingdom beyond this earth."
>
> *line 95-121*

So the Rood's sermon ends, and the dreamer, wakening, addresses himself to prayer and to the resolution that, in what remains to him of life and in the isolation of old age, he will seek and follow the way of the Cross:

5 Avenger and Redeemer

> Then, glad at heart, I made my prayer to that cross,
> there, where I lay alone, and fervently.
> My soul had wandered, in much weariness,
> in exile driven. Now it is all my joy
> that I should seek to find the Glory Tree,
> and I, more often than all other men,
> should worship it. My will is set on that,
> firm in my mind, and for assurance I
> look to the Rood. Few powerful friends have I
> here on this earth; they are departed now,
> from this world's joys, to the King of Glory gone.
> They live in heaven with the Father on high,
> dwelling in splendour; and I look to when
> that day shall come to pass, that our Lord's Rood
> which I saw once, here in my time on earth,
> shall come to fetch me from this wretched life
> and bring me to a place of lasting bliss,
> great joy in heaven, where the Lord's folk are found,
> guests at a feast where happiness has no end,
> and set me there, where thenceforth I also
> shall live in glory, sharing with the saints
> their greatest joys.
>
> *lines 122-44 The Dream of the Rood*

The dreamer's confession, seemingly complete at this point, runs on into a brief coda, or cadenza - or at all events an afterthought. It alludes to the account, in the Apocryphal Gospel of Nicodemus, of the "harrowing of hell", describing how Christ, the victorious warrior still, invaded and conquered the underworld, liberating father Adam and king David and a multitude of the departed, and bringing them home to heaven. This is the final significance of the Rood; the Cross is for all humanity, past, present, future:

> God be my friend,
> who here on earth once suffered on the gallows
> for the sins of men. There he redeemed us all,
> gave us the gift of life, and a heavenly home.
> Joy was renewed, a flowering of bliss,
> for all the souls that suffered in hell's pit.
> Victorious was the Son in that campaign,
> mighty in conquest, when with a multitude,
> a host of spirits, into God's Kingdom he came,
> the almighty Captain, to the joy of angels
> and all the saints who waited there in heaven,
> waiting in glory for their King to come,
> almighty God, to his homeland returned.
>
> *lines 144-56*

5 Avenger and Redeemer

The language of the second half of this great poem - in our analysis, the sections *B2* and *A2* - is never so passionate and poetic as that of the introductory lines, and the Rood's tremendous description of the warfare on Calvary. It is, by comparison, sedate. It is not without emotion, certainly not without *pathos*, in the proper sense of that word, but it is the style of the sermon, of doctrinal exhortation, of confessional penitence. For this reason, no doubt, anthologies tend to omit the Rood's homiletic, and much of the penitent dreamer's confession at the close, fostering the impression that a poem which has come down to us in manuscript, complete and uncorrupted, is yet another of Anglo-Saxon's precious fragments, to which, in this case, some dispensable lines, perhaps of dubious authenticity, have been attached. It must be said, however, that the lines customarily omitted are essential to the structure, the "argument" of the poem, and to its message, which is that of one saying *repent ye, for the kingdom of heaven is at hand.* Let us insist that the principal in this "dream about the Cross" is, after all, the dreamer, not the Cross itself.

The fact remains, nevertheless, that for most readers the great image that lingers in the mind, as representative of the poem, after much of the text has faded, is that of the great fight on Calvary, where Christ is a chief deserted by his *heorðwerod* and supported by His one true *genéat*, that gallows-churl, the cross, by loyalty ennobled as the Rood. The vocabulary is heroic, but this is a strange heroism, not the fated, "fey" heroism of the warriors dying at Maldon, not the triumphal rage of the Hebrew fighters in *Judith*. Soldiers of a sort are here, but this is a different kind of soldier. And a different kind of war, with a different view of victory, which is redemption, not revenge; and the poet would surely not have us think otherwise.

6   tunes on a broken lyre

One of the chapters of Robert Graves' The Crowning Privilege (the published text of his Clark Lectures on Poetry, Cambridge 1956) is called "Harp, Anvil, Oar". The words convey, emblematically, Graves' impressions of metre in three ancient languages: classical Greek, Irish, and Anglo-Saxon. In the Greek lyric measures, with their patterns of short and long, essentially the steps of the dance, he perceives the music of the harp. Into early Irish poetry, strictly accentual, with alternations of heavy and lighter beats, he reads the image of the smith, hammering out his work on the anvil. But Anglo-Saxon verse, as he construes it, will fit neither of these interpretations. Long and short syllables it has, with strong and weak accents, but its steps are not for dancing, and its pulses are seemingly irregular. For a working image, Graves ingeniously compares the dynamic effect of Old English verse with the effort of pulling an oar in a heavy sea. This engaging and not wholly uninstructive perception he then mars by taking a perceptual figure as literal fact. When the minstrel played and chanted, he suggests, the warriors on their mead-benches in hall would recognise in his rhythms an imitation of their labours on the rowers' benches of their seagoing boats, heaving and ho-ing until voyage's end; and so back and forth over their beer they would rock together, in grunting sympathy.[1] This is stretching an amusing impression into a stark absurdity that undervalues both the virtuosity of the poet and the appreciative capacities of his audience, some of whom, at least, must have had an ear for the rhythms and progressions of a sophisticated verse form which is now indeed a departed music.

The general sense of Anglo-Saxon prosody, or what we are able to recover of it, is concisely summarised by J.R.R.Tolkien, in his *On Translating Beowulf*.[2] He observes that as we read Old English verse, trying to recreate its metre, we will find "no single rhythmical pattern progressing from the beginning of a line to the end, and repeated with variations in other lines. The lines do not go to a tune. They are founded on a balance, an opposition between two halves of roughly equivalent weight, and significant content, which are more often rhythmically contrasted than similar. They are more like masonry than music" The allusion to

---

[1] Robert Graves, The Crowning Privilege (The Clark Lectures, 1954-1955). London: Cassell & Company. Graves elaborates his notion of the maritime origins of Germanic metre: "The function of the Nordic *scop* seems to have been twofold. Not only was he originally a "shaper" of charms, to protect the person of the king and so maintain prosperity in the realm; but he had a subsidiary task, of persuading the ship's crew to pull rhythmically and uncomplainingly on their oars against the rough winds of the North Sea, by singing them ballads in time to the beat. When they returned from a successful foray, and dumped their spoil of gold collars, shields, casques and monastic chalices on the rush-strewn floor of the beer-hall, then the *scop* resumed his song. The drunken earls and churls straddled the benches and rocked to the tune: "Over the whale's way, fared we unfearful...." To this, Graves adds the assurance that "Anglo-Saxon poetry is unrhymed because the noise of rowlocks does not suggest rhyme." (!)

[2] See the Introduction, pp viii – xli, of Beowulf and the Finnesburg Fragment, A Translation into Modern English Prose, J.R.Clark-Hall, rev. C.L. Wrenn, London 1940

masonry occurs, perhaps, because Tolkien is writing about Beowulf, and conceives of that great poem as an edifice, built stone by stone, course by course, to the glory of God and the heroic heart. Anglo-Saxon lines certainly do not go to a tune that we can hear, but intonation, with its ups and downs, is implicit in them; they have their onsets and their cadences, their suspensions and resolutions; and while each half-line is undoubtedly a block in a developing structure, frequent references to the lyre or harp argue that music, or a sense of music, played some part in the shaping and regulation of the structure. In the traditional representation, the poet sits at his lord's feet, playing the harp and taking pleasure in his skill as a music maker.[3]

Tolkien's description of how Anglo-Saxon metre works is nevertheless persuasive, particularly in the assertion that there is "no single rhythmical pattern progressing from the beginning of a line to the end, and repeated with variations in other lines." This is the heart of the matter, concisely reflecting the fact that since the later middle ages, English poets and their audience have sung, danced, or wagged their heads to tunes with a defined metre and a variable rhythm. Metre is a constant; it is like the time-signature in music, stipulating how the regular beat should fall, or be felt. It is a silent count. Rhythm is a variable contained within the count; in music, the heard pattern of accents and note-values making up the bar. So there is a prescription, of "timing" and a performance, a mode of "telling", and these things are recognised in verse, from epics down to nursery rhymes:

> Humpty Dumpty sat on a wall,
> Humpty Dumpty had a great fall.
> All the king's horses and all the king's men
> Couldn't put Humpty Dumpty together again.

In that well-known text the prescribed metre is tetrameter - with four "beats", or four so-called "feet", to a line. The contained rhythms vary between the so-called trochaic (/ x) and dactylic (/ x x) in the first three lines, then the fourth line breaks into a free variation, reversing the rhythm, turning the dactyls into anapaests (x x /):

> "couldn't PUT Humpty DUMPTY toGETHer aGAIN"- "x x / x x / x x / x x /.

Though the rhythms may thus vary from line to line, or even within a line, there is one overriding constraint, the timing of line after line. It is isochronic, meaning that the "beats" are equidistant, falling regularly, whatever the number of intervening weak syllables.

---

[3] "Sits at his lord's feet" - like the happy harpist of *Be monna wyrdum*, cited in Chapter 1, p .1

This corresponds to Tolkien's "single rhythmical pattern progressing from the beginning of the line to the end, and repeated with variations in other lines" No comparable interplay of implied beat and actual rhythm, no such complementary or implementary signature is apparent in Anglo-Saxon verse. It has no ascribed "metre" like the tetrameter (or the trimeter, or the pentameter, etc). It does not scan in quite that way. To convey an idea of Old English scansion, we might attempt a pastiche of Humpty Dumpty's tale. He falls down phrase by phrase, like this:

> Humpty who was Dumpty   down from a walltop
> headlong was hurled,   - that was hard falling -
> then the king's cavalry,   and his keen footsoldiers,
> never could unshatter   the shards of the earl

(The shards of the earl being the pieces of the noble gentleman's "shell", or body armour). This pastiche represents the line of "Anglo-Saxon" verse as divided at the middle into two phrases, each with its own rhythm, the pair connected in sense and bonded by alliteration. The relationship between half-lines <u>a</u> and <u>b</u>, the on-verse and the off-verse, is essentially one of balance between equivalently weighted phrases; not isochronic, equally timed, but isotonic, equally flexed, or poised. It is a swaying, shifty sort of balance, adjusted and readjusted from line to line; here Graves' fanciful description of "pulling an oar in a heavy sea" makes something akin to sense. The oarsman makes adjustments from stroke to stroke, keeping time for the time being. The *scop* likewise adjusts the beat and balance, correcting the trim of the verse, keeping time as time goes by. Coming into the on-verse, he anticipates the counterpoise of the off-verse; or perhaps he does not feel so far ahead, but deals with the off-verse as it comes. In either event, the outcome is not the predictable beat of accentual verse, and certainly not the brawny yo-heave-ho-ing of Graves's boating bravos. The verse is not "metred" as we now understand metre, as an arithmetical signature. Nevertheless it is "measured" or "meted out". It has what the Elizabethan writer George Puttenham called "stirre"; and it is this "stirring", from half-line to half-line, that makes up the measure.[4]

The unit of movement, then, is the half-line, a rhythmical phrase conjoined with other such phrases in a varying pattern of rhythms. The patterns are characterised by relationships between syllables at varying levels of stress and (by implication) vocal pitch; "lifts" for the weightier syllables, and "dips" for the weaker, are terms often used in metrical analysis. These relationships already

---

[4] George Puttenham, *The Arte of English Poesie*, London, 1589: George Puttenham on "stirre"; this is his name for the variable tempo which he perceive in quantity-based classical metres. The poetry of his own time ("our vulgar running verse", he calls it) he regards as strictly syllabic; it keeps a count ("time"), but it lacks any fluctuation of movement, or "stirre". Puttenham ascribes this to the monosyllabic base of common spoken English, which he regards as "Saxon". He knew nothing of Anglo-Saxon poetry, however, or the fact that "stirre", a fluctuating tempo, is implied in its metrical techniques – as Eduard Sievers first demonstrated in the late 19th century.

exist in the perceived rhythms of prose or in the common tongue; what the poet apparently does is take them and tailor them, as it were, to his own discursive purpose. The poet in the scop tradition often appears to be working with ready-made phrases; and that may be because he is dependent on ready-made rhythms. To know what these were, we must go directly to the study of Anglo-Saxon poetry, but we have some access to them through the rhythms of modern English, as we hear it on the radio and TV news, or read it in newspaper reports or advertisement copy. Such sources yield examples of rhythmic patterns recurrent in our spoken language, in its habitual accentuation of words and phrases contained in clauses and sentences. Call these patterns types; then take note of five, here lettered A-E. The mark / indicates a full stress, \ a reduced or secondary stress, and x an unstressed syllable:

A. Type, "bright and breezy", "bunch of bananas", "promised upon marriage".
Rhythm: / x / x ...../ x x / x..../ x x x / x The phrase has two strongly stressed syllables, or "lifts" (/), evenly "timed", spaced by one or more weakly accented syllables (x). A strong accent leads the phrase - like a downbeat.

B. Type, "a stroke of luck", "the kindest of men", "of a questionable sort"
Rhythm: x / x / ... x / x x / ... x x / x x x /. The phrase has two "lifts", as above, separated, as above, by weak syllables; but here a weak syllable, a "dip" leads the phrase - like an upbeat

C. Type, "the next morning", "in a brief letter".
Rhythm: x / / x.....x x / / x . The phrase has two adjoining "lifts", bounded by "dips". In a variant, the second lift may take a lighter, "secondary" stress: "a rail journey", x / \ x, where (\) denotes a "half-lift" with a falling pitch (ie the voice drops)

D. Type, i) "Queen's godchildren", "few firefighters"; ii) "next market day",
Rhythm: i) / / \ x , or ii) / / x \ . This is a more complex type than A, B and C. In them, the phrase divides into symmetrically balanced pulses - or call them "feet":
A / x | / x   B x / | x /   C x / | / x

Type D is asymmetrical, with a "foot" consisting of a single "lift" ("Queen's", "next"), then a foot with a "lift", a "half-lift" and a "dip" ("god-child-ren") or else a "lift", a "dip", and a "half-lift" ("mark-et-day"): D / | / \ x or / | / x \

E. Type, "headlong in flight", "God help the poor"
Rhythm: / \ x | / Another asymmetric pattern. The foot-division is between a longer foot, with a "lift" followed by a half-lift and a dip ("headlong in", "God help the") and a foot consisting of a single "lift" ("flight", "poor").

Those examples were collected, with little effort of seeking, from the weekly colour supplement of a broadsheet newspaper. They do not include, under each type, variants and modifications due to changing word-accent or sentence-connection (the way that pronunciation and stress are affected in the contextual flow of the sentence). The latter, if examined in detail, would point to distinctive features in the phonology and prosody of modern English that emphasise its differences from Anglo-Saxon. Nevertheless, Old and Modern English are of one family in prosodic structure; they are alike in being "stress-timed" languages (like German or Swedish – "RUM-ti-TUM-ti TUM"), as opposed to "syllable-timed" (like French or Greek – "ta-ta-ta-ta-ta-ta" The phrase patterns lettered A-E above, existed in Anglo-Saxon speech as in ours, and indeed virtually dictated the rhythmic system of its verse. The perception of that system, however was lost for so long that it was not until the late 19th century that scholars began to recapture it with anything like a sense of a consistent, unified account. The pioneer of these studies was the great German philologist Edward Sievers (that same Sievers who solved the problem of the *Later Genesis*), who proposed and elaborated the basic system of the five rhythmic types, A-E, imitated above. Ever since that time the study of Old English and early Germanic metres has been promoted, dominated, at times obstructed by that groundbreaking work.[5]

It is a cumbersome task to present even in simple outline a prosody which, in the fulness of poetic practice, was complex in its particular effects, becoming increasingly so throughout the history and development of Old English verse. To try to follow that development is to become aware of the creative scope becoming broader and the craft becoming craftier, even while the technical foundations remain. Between Widsith and Judith (as possible extremes-in-time of the poems reviewed in this book), the stylistic differences are great; but they are alike the work of poets taking certain things as given. Eduard Sievers perceived the "given". His studies then embraced the variants of his primary model, drawing on a profound knowledge of the general principles of phonology (the study of speech-sounds in discourse), and a close acquaintance with the early Germanic languages and their literatures. The result was a consistently plausible, detailed account of the workings of Anglo-Saxon verse, put at the service of the reader in search of that departed music.

The intricacy of Sievers' exposition is impressive When his work became generally known to British scholars, Henry Sweet records, there were those who responded testily that this was impossible. They doubted that any poet could hold such an elaborate set of prescripts in his head. Sweet's reply was that Sievers' prosody was simple enough in comparison with the many forms and complications of form a modern poet bears in mind, subconsciously, and can draw on at will.[6] That is a telling point; but also one that, oddly enough, questions Sievers even as it supports him. The endless creation of poetic forms eludes finite systems. Sievers' analyses are based on the grammar of

---

[5] E.Sievers, *Altgermanische Metrik*, Halle, 1893.

[6] Sweet on Sievers. Henry Sweet, *An Anglo-Saxon Reader,* 7th edn: Oxford, 1894. "I have tried to give a clear abstract of Sievers' views" - views which, with demure irony, he professes himself "obliged to accept in spite of the adverse criticism of some English critics....These critics seem to forget that Sievers' classification of the Old English metrical forms into types is not a theory but a statement of facts, and that the complexity and irregularity to which they object is a fact, not a theory." Sweet then adds an observation that deserves red letter status: "The truth is that we know very little of the details of the versification of most languages; and it is possible that if our modern English metres...were analysed in the same thorough way in which Sievers has analysed the Old English metres, we should have difficulty in realising that a modern poet should carry such a complicated scheme in his head." (Preface, pp. xi-xii)

phrases in clauses building up sentences, which is a satisfactory guide to much Anglo-Saxon verse, but not a total guide. (Nor is it a wholly satisfactory guide to the metres and prosodic forms of some poets on the Germanic fringe - the skalds of medieval Norway and Iceland). There are poems - among those quoted in this book, the charm *Wið færstice* ("Against a sudden stitch") and that enigmatic lyric called *Wulf and Eadwacer* - that have their own poetic grammar, a dimension of feeling that eludes prosaic analysis. There are indications of strophic composition - more than an indication in the case of *Deor*. There are not a few instances in major poems of an emotional/psychological emphasis felt by the reader but apparently excluded or diminished by metrical law. Sievers provides an apparatus that is almost complete, but there remains a differential of unanswered questions, as there always must when poetic metres are the theme. Since Sievers' time, scholars have followed in pursuit of the facts and phantoms of an exasperatingly fugitive topic, modifying, amplifying, disputing the the theory of Anglo-Saxon metrics (see the Bibliography); but the end of it is, that after much study one may acquire a serviceable idea of it, and still not get the hang of it entirely. At length, the true measure of the verse has to be the conviction it stirs in readers who do their best to sound the verse aloud, or think it aloud, following the stresses, and feeling for the balance of the line.[7]

The scripting of the song

Caedmon sang his song to the bookmen, and the bookmen wrote it down; our Chapter 1 (pp.19-21) describes a transition from oral patterns to written lines. But "lines" is hardly correct, for the scribes filled the precious manuscript page with a continuous line of text, as though they were transcribing prose. This, for example, follows a facsimile of the opening lines of *The Wanderer*, as at folio 76v.of the Exeter Book:

---

[7] Apart from Sievers. What is offered in this chapter is a very general account of Siever's "five type" model of Old English poetic rhythms. Andreas Heusler's *Deutsche Versgeschichte*, 1925 and J.C.Pope's *The Rhythm of Beowulf*, 1940, criticise Sievers' phrase-based, speech-based, method, and offer something more closely resembling the traditional concept of metre, ie a kind of musical "barring", foot by foot, the "bars" being isochronic (equal in time, just as in music), irrespective of the number of syllables each contains, and with one strong "beat" on the first syllable in the foot = note in the bar. The problems of metre in Old English continue to engage the attentions of scholars and break the wits of students. For some fairly recent discussions, see the Bibliography. Then adopt the counsel of Kemp Malone, to follow "the natural rhythm of the lines, with due heed given to the lift-patterns and in particular to those syllables which the poets by alliteration and rhyme mark for heightening." (In "The Old English Period", Book I Part I of A.C.Baugh (ed) *A Literary History of England*. London: Routledge & Kegan Paul Ltd, 1950, p.25.)

> OFT him anhaga are gebideð metudes miltse þeahþe
> he mod cearig geond lagu lade longe sceolde hreran
> mid hondum hrim cealde sæ wadan wræc lastas wyrd
> bið ful ared · [8]

The text so written has a margin to the left, but runs to the right-hand edge of a page some 18cm. wide. Its only marks of punctuation, it may be noted, are capital letters, large and small, at the beginning of the sentence, and a raised point, like a decimal point, at the end.

Now here is the text of that opening, presented in verse-form by modern editors:

> OFT him anhaga   are gebideð,
> Metudes miltse, þeah þe he modcearig
> geond lagulade   longe sceolde
> hreran mid hondum   hrimcealde sæ,
> wadan wræclastas: wyrd bið ful aræd![9]

This makes considerable adaptations to the text of the MS, for the reader's comfort and in the editors' interest. It emends a dubious reading (*ared*); it links the separated elements of compound words (*módcearig, laguláld, hrímceald, wrædást*), it displays the half-lines and by spacing observes the caesura between them; and more than all these, it introduces a punctuation expressive of the editors' perceptions of emphasis and implied sense, whether in the capital M that exalts metud into Metud, or, more strikingly, in the rhetorical colon and exclamation mark of the last line, implying a delivery, or "tone of voice".

For a reminder, here is the translation of these lines provided on p.59 of this book.

> Often the outcast yearns for God's grace,
> the Maker's mercy, though sick at heart
> his lot is to wander the ocean way
> and thresh with his hands the ice-cold sea
> in the voyage of exile. Fate is resolved.

The translator brings his own idea of what the text means, of its scheme of cohesion, its points of necessary emphasis, creating his own rhythms endorsed by his own punctuation. This brings us farther yet from the text the clerk transcribed, which was itself a mere concept of the tunes the poet may have sung.

---

[8] For the facsimile transcribed here, I am indebted to an eccentric source – Tim Romano's "E-edition" of *The Wanderer*: http:/www.aimsdata.com.tim/anhaga/edition.htm The edition is useful and interesting in many respects, though least, unfortunately, for its attempt to reject orthodox prosody (ie Sievers) in favour of a metrical theory of "chiasms" - segments of text sequenced on the pattern of the rhetorical figure of *chiasmus*.

[9] *The Wanderer*, ed. T.P.Dunning & A.J.Bliss, London, Methuen, 1969, repr.1973.

For the scribe of *The Wanderer*, the marks of punctuation guiding the reader to the structure of the text were two only: the capital letter (usually a small capital) announcing a distinct segment, ie sentence or paragraph, and the "decimal point", as noted above, which marked the end of a section, but which was also used to mark out parallel or coordinate constructions, or to resolve potential confusions of syntax - to indicate the phrasing, as it were. It was an economical and not inefficient system; it did a job without gesturing, leaving to reader to make a sense and perceive a feeling. It has been remarked, in the preface to one of the best editions of *The Wanderer*, that "If editors had paid more attention to the punctuation in the manuscript, the syntax might less often have been misconstrued"[10]. That is the kind of judgement that only extensive knowledge can make, but it does underline the possibility that modern punctuation, with its subtler apparatus of stops - comma, semi-colon, colon, full point - and its marks of expression, may misrepresent a text even as it attempts to illuminate it

What the manuscript punctuation does not purport to do, other than coincidentally, is to communicate the structure of the poem in its procession of rhythmically-patterned half-lines and lines. The punctuation, in other words, is for syntax, or for rhetoric, but not for prosody. With that observation, we may return to Sievers in his empire, and with his guidance try to follow the beat of the first five lines - or ten half-lines - of *The Wanderer*. They are set out below, in phrase-book or Berlitz phonetics, with the metrical pattern noted and labelled to the right of each half-line.   Only the essential pattern is represented. Weak introductory syllables external to the pattern, so-called anacruses, are shown in brackets. "Lifts" are shown thus / , and in underlined heavy type. "Half-lifts" are shown thus \ , and in heavy type. The symbol -/- represents a "resolution", that is, the treatment of two adjacent short syllables as a long syllable, creating a "lift":

<u>Oft-him</u> **ahn**-ha-ga	-/- | / \ x	D(i)
ah-reh ye-**beed**-eth	/ x x | / x	A
metud-es **meelts**-eh	-/- x | / x	A
(thyah-theh)		
hay **moodchair**-y	x / | \ x	C
yond **laoolah**-deh	x -/- | \ x	C
long-eh **shold**-eh	/ x | / x	A
hrair-an mid **hond**-um	/ x x | / x	A
hreemchald-eh **sae**	/ \ x | /	E
wadan wretchlast-as	-/- | / \ x	D(i)
wyrd-bith ful ah-**raed**	-/- | / x \	D(ii)

The Anglo-Saxon original of these lines presents metrical questions that will persist until the student of this exotic language can hold the sounds and rhythms in his head, without recourse to such an uncouth key as this.[11] The clerk who

---

[10] Dunning & Bliss, ed.cit, Introduction, p.11.
[11] See Postscript p.152 "Matters of metre"

transcribed the linear text, however, being a native speaker, needed no theoretical acquaintance with Sievers' five types to inform him of the progression of rhythmic patterns. The necessary information lay before him in one recurrent feature: alliteration.

Alliteration: art and artifice

Alliteration was involved with metre as a structural feature - the poem is "pegged", as it were, on alliterating syllables which mark the beat and define the shape of the verse-line. From the printed page in college "readers", where the staves are often marked in italics, or underlined, a student may perceive the outlines of alliterative patterning. One perception may be of a "full" line, with three alliterating staves, two in the first half-line, one in the second; in the off-verse the alliterating stave must be the first "beat" in the pattern:

on lyft laedan . leohte bewunden,   x / / x . / x x / x, (C - A)

"aloft leading, in light enfolded", the 5th line of *The Dream of the Rood*. However, a glance at this or any other poem is enough to reveal that this "full" prescription is not realised in line after line. The first four lines of *The Dream*, for example, each have only two alliterating staves, in the on-verse placed either on the first or second "beat" of the phrase-pattern, in the off-verse always on the first beat. The alliterative dominant, or key, is then the first stave of the second half-line. This might be called the "default" or "standard" scheme, the basic requirement in any poem. There may be a rhetorical purpose in the variations of the "fuller" line and the "standard" line (for example, the two alliterating words in the on-verse of a "full" line may be yoked in equal significance, and require parallel emphasis - as in "broad and bright-edged", "grim and greedy") or the "default" line may simply reflect the difficulty of finding alliterations again and again through a long recital. These are indeed mere matters of "may", open to intuition or guesswork in this case or that.

The Anglo-Saxon poet, if we imagine him in his minstrel persona, working impromptu, framing his verses as he found them, may well have had occasional difficulty in finding a sensible alliteration, much as a modern lyric poet or songwriter will be stumped now and then for a feasible rhyme. The problem of rhyme makes an instructive comparison. Not all themes are promptly or plentifully suggestive of rhyme, and any casual versifier is well aware that some rhymes come more readily than others. (So, if the word to be rhymed is "seen", the prospects are wide open; but for "glimpsed", the shutters are pretty well down). Rhymes in oral poetic recital may be mnemonic, helping the performer to remember the verse, or heuristic, prompting the discovery of a word, a phrase, an "idea", or mainly structural, marking out form (eg the "scheme" of a lyric stanza) So also, we shall suppose, the *scop's* practice of alliteration may have been mnemonic or heuristic or structural. Or else a quick fix for an instant problem. This last suggestion might explain why, in *Beowulf line 383*, the Danes are the West Danes, while at *392* they are the East Danes, at *463* the South Danes, and at *783* the North Danes. "In allusion to their wide distribution", says a distinguished commentator.[84] But all these references are to Danes gathered at one place, Heorot, the *héah hús* of Hroðgar, the beloved lord of the *Hring-Dene* (the Ring Danes, "in allusion to their warlike character"). Rather than argue their allusive value, may it not be conjectured that these variants occur because they fit the metre and fill the alliterative pattern of particular lines? It is surely no insult to a poet who shows his greatness in so many intricate passages, to suggest that he sometimes made use of allowed conventions.

The modern rhymer looks for escape in half-rhymes, consonances, assonances - devices permitted through their recurrence in poetic practice, developed over generations. The alliterating poet had comparable resort to licences allowed by the traditions of his practice Vowel-alliterations evidently presented problems, essentially of a statistical origin, because, as Henry Sweet puts it, "initial vowels are not frequent enough in OE to allow each vowel to alliterate only with itself."[85] Consequently, the maker in a quandary had the licence to "alliterate" any vowel with any other vowel or diphthong. See *Beowulf, line 33*, describing a ship: *i̲sig ond u̲tfus, æþelinges fær*, "i̲ce-covered, o̲utward-bound, a craft for an e̲arl" Does that suggest great poetic license? Would the audience find an artistry in the "ee"- "oo" - "ah" of those circuiting vowels? Or would they (the vowels) be no more than acceptable markers of the beat?

Modern readers, however, almost inevitably think of Anglo-Saxon alliteration as principally a linking by letter, a token of a text more than the vestige of a voice. The sounds that the letters represent are muffled for us, their distinctiveness and subtlety somehow blurred, as a glance at a particular instance may show. In our edited texts, the letters c and g represent sounds of Old English in each case differing in the place and manner of their articulation; as to place being either "palatal" or "guttural", and as to manner, "stop" or "spirant". Now these sounds, when represented as single, word-initial consonants, had the following properties "Palatals" occurred before " "front" vowels (i long or short, e long or short, æ long or short), "gutturals" before "back" vowels (long or short a, o, u, and y when the latter was a mutation of an earlier u). Historically, the guttural spirant ġ became the guttural stop, ġ , as in *gold*, *guma* (man) *gylden* (golden). Palatal spirant ğ, a sound approximating to "zh", in, for example, geolu, *giet*, became at some point a semi-vowel, / j /, like the y in modern English *yellow* or *yet* The palatal spirant ç was at first a sound resembling the ch of German *Ich*, and then developed into something like the ch of modern English *church*. In brief, these two representative letters, plain and simple on the page, represent

---

[84] The (indeed) distinguished commentator being R.W.Chambers, in his revised edition of A.J.Wyatt's *Beowulf and the Finnsburg Fragment*, Cambridge, 1914.; see there p.166, and his note on *Dene*

[85] See Sweet's remarks on metre in *An Anglo-Saxon Reader*, 9th reprint ed. C.T.Onions, 1921, p.lxxxv, para 35.

points in the phonetic history of an old language we can read but never be wholly confident of "hearing".[86]

So it is that the full acoustic character of this line or that can elude us. Lines *205b-206a* of *Beowulf* are an interesting example:

    Hæfde se goda   geata leoda
cempan gecorone, þara þe he cenoste
findan mihte

"The hero had chosen from among the people of the Geats the boldest warriors he might find" - the lines are quite commonplace, an ordinary transition in the narrative. Their interest lies in a texture not apparent to the eye, a texture of sounds, woven by alternations of guttural and spirant. Here g represents a guttural stop in *goda*, and a palatal spirant in *geata*; c is a guttural stop in *gecorone* (past participle of ceosan), but a palatal spirant, ç, in *cempan* and *cenoste*. The alliterating words, in order, are *goda, geata, cempan, [ge]corone, cenost*; and in the acoustic "weave" of the verse, the order is:

guttural	palatal	palatal	guttural	palatal
stop	spirant	stop	spirant	spirant

Presented thus, the progression of sounds implied in these ordinary lines appears subtler, more discreetly modulated than an ordinary reading-with-the-ear-switched-off might suggest. The sceptic will object: "but how can we know that poet intended anything of the kind?" And of course we cannot know; we can only resort to an intuitive sense of the psychology of composition, in which the choice of words, the elected placing and sequence of phrases, can follow acoustic prompts, the sounds whispering from the back of the mind Any living writer will confirm this; but whether it was so in the 10th century - well, of course we cannot know.[87]

---

[86] This is of necessity a crude and cursory account of the spirant/stop, palatal/guttural variants of the consonants c and g, in word-initial positions, ie as relating to the practice of alliteration. A much fuller consideration of these sounds, in word-medial and word-final contexts, as well as in consonant groups, in Primitive Germanic and after, would lure the student away from mere verse and into the dense Teutonic boscage of the *Lautlehre* - an expedition well worth making for its own disciplinary interest, though perhaps not as an adjunct to literary criticism.

[87] On the question of intention: the sceptic might possibly wish to rebut the idea of the intentional or instinctive opposition of sounds in a phonetic/stylistic texture, as suggested here, with the argument that the opposition of spirant and stop is in any case "structural" - embedded in the forms of the grammar and the lexicon. Example, from verb conjugation: the verb *céosan* (choose) has palatal ç in the infinitive and guttural stop c in the past participle, *gecoren*. From lexical relationship (word formation): the verb *gadrian*, (to gather), guttural stop g, and the adverbial phrase *on geador*, (together), palatal spirant g > semivowel /j/, "on yador". Many such instances could be adduced, without suppressing altogether the intuition that in some poetic contexts, the opposition becomes a feature of style.

The state of the art

The account of Anglo-Saxon versification briefly outlined above conveniently assumes an unchanging state of the art throughout the whole history of Old English poetry. That is indeed a false convenience. The "whole history" means several centuries of script, with the assumed precedent of an oral "foreshadowing", the old habit of the gleeman, subsequently adapted and transmuted by the scribes - in all, too long a period, through eras of cultural change and upheaval, to have passed without significant development, even revolution, in the craft of verse-making. Innovations there certainly were, expansions of technique that persuade the modern reader to adjudge the style of a given poem or passage as "early" or "later" - but meaning what? - "early" as what? - "later" than what? Anything later than the late 9th century is late enough, and anything earlier than the early 8th is seriously early, but to assign a poem to a date anywhere in that long period is not so confidently done on the basis of language and style alone. The history of the manuscript stock is a complicating factor. Most of the poetic manuscripts were written in West Saxon scriptoria in the 9th and 10th centuries, and have survived in one copy only. The effect of this is to foster an illusion that the bulk of poetic production, in something called "late West Saxon", or even "Indeterminate Saxon", (a category favoured by the Labyrinth Library) was compressed into a period around the year 1000. The *Beowulf* MS, for example, dates from the late 10th century, but scholars place the origin of the poem around the year 700. *Deor* is one of the poems in the Exeter Book, a 10th century compilation; but its content turns on pagan legend lightly "christianised", in such a way as to suggest (but on this, see Chapter 1, p. 16-17) a precedent, an older version in the background. *Widsith*, also from the Exeter Book, may have been composed in the early 8th century. The Vercelli Book, from the late 10th century, contains the full text of The *Dream of the Rood*, but we know of that poem's existence, if only in fragmentary form, in the late 7th / early 8th. In short, questions of "early" and "late" are difficult to settle when a work exists in one manuscript only, but points to antecedents in theme, language and style.

Scholars, confronted with a text in a manuscript of known date, and facing the problem of defining something not quite the same, the date of composition of a poem, are often trapped in an anguish of adverbial uncertainties, of "arguably", "relatively", and "comparatively", of conjectural attribution and putative location, subject to ongoing revisions. Some authoritative comments on Judith, from various sources, are typical. It was, declares one, "composed during the second decade of the "tenth century"; it has features that according to another "seem to point to a comparatively late date, nearer 900 than 700"; a third says "we take him" (the poet) "to have been an Angle of the ninth century, *but he may have lived later*" (my italics); a literary historian, observing that "its use of rhyme and the character of its language has led some critics to place the poem comparatively late", adds, "the use of rhyme, however, is no conclusive argument"; another mentions "the assumption of Ten Brink and others that it was composed in the early part of the ninth century" (that is, at the time of Cynewulf) then adds that "a close investigation of its diction by Gregory Foster has led him to place it a century later", concluding however, with the assertion that "nothing can be said with certainty on the subject". Anyone bemused by these vagaries might consider Dr Johnson's advice to readers of Shakespeare, to put enjoyment first and only then attempt accuracy, and read the commentators.

6 Tunes on a Broken Lyre

In some ways Anglo-Saxon poetics, as observed in works taken to be "late", is boldly innovative; by the end of the period, poets were evidently pushing at the limits of metrical experiment, exploring the uses of rhyme and phonaesthetic device, extending the range and power of the lexicon, discovering ambiguity, word-play, refining the language of perception and feeling. In other ways poetic practice is conservative; the basic structures never wholly change, are not extended out of existence, and the poetic lexicon, the "diction", may be extended but is never superseded. There are features of style, seen to be prominent in what are recognised as late works, that are in themselves not especially "late" additions to the poetic resources of Anglo-Saxon

One such feature is "hypermetric" verse, passages of which occur in *The Dream of the Rood*, *The Later Genesis*, *The Wanderer*, and *Judith*, among the poems examined in this book. These are all late texts, of poems in which passages of hypermetric verse have an obvious rhetorical intent; but hypermeter is not a necessary mark of lateness. Anglo-Saxon verse is deemed hypermetric when the half-line measure contains three full "lifts" instead of the usual two - in effect, an extra beat. Thus, from *The Dream*, line 32:

/ x x   x   / x x / x   x x x x x   /   / \ x
bæron me þær beornas on eaxlum   oððæt hi me on beorg ásetton

"There men carried me on their shoulders, until they set me down on a hill". The first half-line is essentially an A-type (/ x / x), but with three beats (/ x / x / x); the second is of the type D, with a long "prelude" of weak syllables. Discernible in this line is an interlacing pattern of regular alliteration and incidental "chime"; principally on the *b* of *bæron*, *beornas*, *beorg*, and incidentally on the vowels in *eaxlum*, *ásetton*. In another instance from *The Dream*, both half-lines are clearly hypermetric:

/   x   x   x   / x   x / x   /   x   x x x   /   x   x / x
Sare ic wæs mid sorgum gedrefed   hnag ic hwæþre þam secgum to handa [88]

"I was sorely oppressed with sorrows, yet I sank down into the men's hands". Both half lines are expansions of type A, and here again the line suggests a dual concord, the formal alliteration on the *s* of *sare*, *sorgum*, *secgum*, and the internal echo on the hn - h of *hnag*, *handa*. It is not unusual in hypermetric verse for the sound-pattern to be enriched in this way; indeed, it may be in the enriching as much as in the metrical expansion that the poetic significance lies.

---

[88] This line, or most of it – the on-verse and two words of the off-verse – appears in runic inscription on the Ruthwell monument (for a transliteration, see Michael Swanton, ed.cit., p.48). Proof, no doubt, that hypermeter is not a "late" development, though it is used quite extensively in "later" poems like *Genesis B*, *Judith*, and the Vercelli *Dream*.

Hypermetric verses occur in Anglo-Saxon poetry both early and late; it is in the later poetry, however, that passages of hypermeter become substantial and significant. The significance is a matter for interpretation. Why has the poet "changed step", a reader might ask, changed register and tempo? "Because that's the way it happened", may be the answer by default, but it is natural to look for a dramatic or psychological intention One of the editors of *The Dream of the Rood* comments on the style of the poem, describing it as "composed almost entirely of rapidly moving short inverted clauses, the sense contained within the line", but adding "against this are set blocks of hypermetric verse used contrapuntally to accommodate significantly more complex thematic material."[89] In the *Dream*, for example, the "contrapuntally used" blocks of hypermetric lines dwell on the iconic details of the crucifixion, presenting, in effect "stations" of the Cross - the image of the Cross as it first appears to the dreamer, the picture of Calvary hill, Christ ascending the Cross, the driving of "dark" nails, the taking down from the Cross, and in all of these the agony and humiliation of the crucified is represented as the Cross's own humiliation and agony.

In the music of the *Dream*, the hypermetric lines, so interpreted, read like a shift in tempo - to adagio - or in register, to a minor key, muted. (Sweet's comment on "lengthened or three-wave verses", in his *Anglo-Saxon Reader*, 7th edn, 1894, p.xciv, is that they "are introduced only occasionally, in solemn, lyrical passages". This, for once, is wide of the mark). In *Judith*, by contrast, the long lines break into swells of sound, a triumphal tone, maestoso. This, for example:

> then was the brute in his heart
> blithe, the master of men, and the bright lady he meant
> to smirch with shame, and sully - nor so would the Saviour in heaven
> allow it, Guardian of glory, for His was the grace that guided,
> Lord, Leader of Hosts.
>
> *lines 58-62 Judith*

This is a rendering of lines 58-62 of the original text, lines describing Holofernus' exultant, braggart mood after Judith is brought to his headquarters. The translation is somewhat artificial - or "artful" - with the intention of reflecting the artifice of the original, in the bouncing triple beat, the alliterative patterns, and the free-wheeling turn-over of the metre, eg in the run-on lines "in his heart / blithe" (in the original *on mode / bliðe*), "would the Saviour in heaven / allow it (the original has *wolde þæt wuldres dema / geþafian*). There are also features not represented in this translation. In line 61, for example, where the translation has "guardian of glory"...."the grace that guided", the original has *þrymmes hyrde....þaes ðinges gestyrde*, an internal rhyme on *hyrde / gestyrde* linking the two half-lines in addition to the alliteration on þ (= th) in *þrymmes...þinges*. In line 59 the original reads *bliðe, burga ealdor, þohte ða beorhtan idese*, with the b-alliteration on <u>b</u>liðe, <u>b</u>urga, <u>b</u>eorhtan, and on the "third beats", *ealdor, idese*, a vowel-chime, <u>ea</u> ("iya"- "iyaldor") and <u>i</u> ("ee"- "eedeh-seh"). In the translation this is imitated with a

---

[89] Michael Swanton, ed.cit., p.61

consonance, "master of men", "lady he meant". But imitation can never be ingenious enough to capture the pervasive textural richness of Judith. It has a colouring, a complexion, sanguine in comparison with the passionate austerity of *The Dream of the Rood*. In its style it is manifestly a late poem; but then it can also be said that the *Dream* is a late poem, though we know it to have been elaborated out of a much earlier version, or possibly more than one version

The textual history of the *Dream* illustrates the difficulty of dating Anglo-Saxon poems. the difficulty, even, of deciding "earlier than" or "later than". The problem has been outlined in the preceding chapter. That the *Dream* probably existed by the end of the 7th century, or the early 8th century, whether in oral tradition or in written form, we know from those quotations in runic writing inscribed round the decorative panels of the shaft of the monumental Ruthwell Cross. They are hardly enough to constitute a "text", but they are enough for us to recognize the text they quote. Our recognition is based on the text scribal tradition has given us, the text of the Vercelli Book, in a manuscript dating, at a fairly conservative estimate, from the mid-to-late 10th century. There are, then, three centuries between our "first sight" of the *Dream* and our final view of it. And in the time between? No texts are extant from the intervening centuries, but the Vercelli MS, ostensibly written in the standard West Saxon literary dialect of the 10th century, contains, beside some non-standard West Saxon forms, a number of readings which are definably "Anglian", ie of Northumbrian origin, suggesting the possibility that the Vercelli text is a transcript of an older text dating from a time before the the Viking wars all but demolished Northumbrian literary culture. We know that in the Anglo-Saxon England of the 8th and 9th centuries, a Cult of the True Cross flourished, intensively, perhaps more intensively than anywhere else in Europe, and may conjecture that the fervour of the cult could have included a scripting, or re-scripting, of the old poem on the Rood theme. Editors supporting this conjecture have noted a Chronicle entry for the year 885, recording the presentation, by Pope Marinus, of a fragment of the True Cross to King Alfred.[90] This can hardly count as firm evidence for a lost text, an "Anglian precursor", but it suggests at least a plausible context of composition, or transcription.

Then what can be said about the history and dating of a poem like the *Dream*? What constitutes "earlier than" and "later than"? How much is real evidence and how much passes for reliable, or at least plausible conjecture? The dating of a text may be based on the "internal evidence" of language and style - a task reserved for the erudite grammarian and philologist. A manuscript may be dated from palaeographical evidence - the type of MS hand, the script conventions, the association of the handwriting with the practice of certain scribes or the usages of particular scriptoria. This can give quite accurate information about script and manuscripts, not necessarily telling us a great deal about the poem so transmitted. There remains the possibility of "external evidence", in the form of cultural references, historical allusions, etc., more or

---

[90] See Bruce Dickins & A.S.C.Ross, *The Dream of the Rood*, London, Methueb, 1954, repr.1963.

less easily dated. It is easy to establish from "external evidence" that the *Battle of Maldon* must have been composed not long after the year 991, or that the *Battle of Brunanburh* is assignable to the year 937, because Chronicle entries supply us with dates. In other instances the external evidence is not quite so firm, because it includes an element of speculation, or most-likelihood. We take the Ruthwell Cross itself as solid evidence for the date of the incised text; but the dating of the Cross, from the evidence of its art, its lettering, its place in ecclesiastical history, also involves some conjecture of the "it is more than probable" kind. The art historian's dating of the Ruthwell decorative panels implies a dating for the surrounding runic text; or a date for the inscription of the runic text; but the text so inscribed could be rather older than the fabric of the memorial.

Amid all these twinings of fact and conjecture, all the modal musings that scholars so love, what becomes of our view of the scop? What has happened to that romantic-tragic-heroic figure, singer of ancient songs, praiser of chiefs and the glories of tribes, grateful recipient of grace and favour, sad, proud exile turned out of office, wanderer, maker and shaker of the world? He has been overtaken by religion and writing; his music is departed into literature, his vocal emphases and taut turns of phrase are an imagined echo in the quiet of the cloister What has come down to us, through the centuries after the Conquest, is the impression of a noble eloquence in which we can perceive, as in a simulation, the passionate speech-music of the scop:

> Where is the steed? Where the rider? Where the giver of gold?
> Where the places at the feast? Where the joys of the hall?
> O, the burnished cup, O, the man-at-arms, O, the prince's fame!
> How time has gone, grown dark under night's helm
> As though it had never been. *lines 92-96 The Wanderer*

It is an imitation of the minstrel's voice, in tribute to a lost minstrelsy. But even that voice of mourning, in these fine lines, has become literature, and the sentiments gather to a topos that in the later middle ages will become a literary commonplace - the theme called ubi sunt.[91]

Compositional styles

To read Old English verse with an ear for its music is to become aware of shifts in compositional style, as from presumably early to supposedly late. These changes are both progressive and cumulative, in that the "later" makers can adapt, in creative mimesis, "earlier" features of style. In its developing artifice, the language of poetry becomes compendious and self-informing. To illustrate this from original texts would make a book in itself: then for economy´s sake let us resort once again to pastiche, imitating the most basic elements of compositional growth.

---

[91] On *ubi sunt*, see Postscripts, p.147

The styles to be imitated are called end-stopped, run-on and for want of a better term, overrunning. Put these into a modern setting. Imagine, for example, our *scop*, our oracy man, the chanter, the roll-caller of chiefs and tribes, translated into the person of a sports commentator summarising the results of a day's matches in the English FA Cup:

Arsenal won against Aston Villa,
Wolves were at West Ham winning one-nil,
Charlton had Chelsea chasing a late goal,
Man.United missed a penalty,
Liverpool lost in the last minute,
Everton were awesome after injuries,
Spurs were successful, but Sheffield went down.
So fortunes fared in the FA Cup.

Here is a passage of verse-discourse in principle resembling the "catalogue" sections of *Widsith* (see Chapter 1, pp.10-12), or some parts of the *Maxims*. This is the "end-stopped" style. The principle is, to build the verse line by discrete line, each line making sense in itself. It is occasionally put to use in narrative sequences in some poems, but as a rule the classic recital practice is more complicated. For this we have to imagine our *scop* intoning the exemplary tale of Jack and Jill:

Jack and Jill   jogged up the hill,
strove up the slope   sister and brother,
peerless pair   a pail to fetch,
bucket brimming   with bright water,
delightful drink   but down went Jack,
he crashed, crumpled   his crown broken,
joined by Jilly   gentlest of maidens
in turn tumbling   trusty companion.

In this kind of construction, the discourse turns on the caesura, the point of division between the half lines. It is the so-called "run-on" style. It can proceed by couplets, or, characteristically, can develop in units of a line-and-a-half. In this style, a half-line may supplement the sense of a predecessor, sometimes repeating it, sometimes expanding it, presenting it in a different aspect. So "strove up the slope" expands "jogged up the hill", "sister and brother" become "a peerless pair", a "pail" reappears as "bucket brimming", "bright water" extends to "delightful drink", Jack's "down went" expands to "crashed, crumpled", and Jill, as "gentlest of maidens" is further called a "trusty companion". It is easy to see how such a mode of composition might have evolved from the earlier, end-stopped style of the oral tradition. There are no lengthy propositions, no involutions of syntax. The recitalist can work his way from phrase to phrase, conceivably with a little business from the accompanying harp. The alliterating patterns are partly mnemonic, helping the memory along, and partly heuristic, prompting the maker to discover elusive meanings. At a pinch, if the inspiration of the moment lapses, he can fall back on some well-tried filler-phrase, eg "gentlest of maidens". (It is a point occasionally made but seldom stressed, that cliché has a useful part to play in Anglo-Saxon versifications, even the loftiest; even the noble *Beowulf* has its share of "fillers", or formulaic progressions).

The phrases that make up such a compositional structure are put together in a way a carpenter might call "butt-jointed", short blocks of material set end to end in a loose coordination. The run-on construction still reflects an oral style. But sit the poet at his table in a quiet place, furnish him with writing materials, allow him books to read and time to meditate his compositions before, not while, he delivers them and there appears a different style of discourse, with different demands on the author and the audience. So let us imagine our Anglo-Saxon poet-scribe writing in honour of a nursery saint:

> To the cupboard she came   the kindly mother,
> helpful hostess, Hubbard her dameship
> foraged for food for Fido her dog
> (no mongrel he   but a mastiff of pure
> British breeding) yet bare was the shelf,
> and Wyrd the wayward   willing no comfort,
> the hound hungry   at hearthside lay down

That celebration of Old Mother Hubbard is in a style that goes beyond the method of the classic "run-on". This is a developed run-on, for which there is no simple term, unless we venture to call it "overrunning". The example presents a single sentence, a sequence of phrases and clauses in a progressively subordinating or "dependent" relationship, and containing a parenthetical clause. At two points the lines are allowed to overrun, or "enjamb" (dameship / foraged, of pure / British breeding). In comparison with the structure mimicked in "Jack and Jill", this is something more like prose, even like prose imitated from the Latin. The grammarian's word for this stylistic method is hypotaxis, meaning "subordinating". In the poem of *The Whale* (see chapter 4 , Samples p.184) much of the syntax is hypotactic; so, in a more refined and skilful way, is the language of the characters' speeches in *Genesis B* (chapter 4 pp.76-87); it is also characteristic of this passage in *The Wanderer*, previously quoted (chapter 3 p.61):

> So I, often wretched, exiled from home,
> far from my kin, have had to fetter my heart
> since that day long ago, when the darkness of earth
> enfolded my dear lord, and I, sad wretch,
> wintry-heart, wandered over the frozen waves,
> seeking the high hall of a giver of gifts,
> searched the world, near and far, in hope to find
> a master who would know my deepest thought,
> or would befriend me in my friendlessness,
> receive me kindly.   *lines 19-29 The Wanderer*

Here the style clearly points to "scripting" rather than "saying". Give the *Wanderer* poet his due, call him *scop* by all means - he is the minstrel of those elegiac lines quoted earlier - but on the evidence of this passage call him also clerk, reader, scholar. *The Wanderer* as a whole is, in fact, the most remarkable mixture of styles, each appropriate to its place in the work's unfolding theme. It can be studied with profit as a compendium of the varieties of Old English versification. All the developments described above appear in one poem.

Words, words, words

As to the Anglo-Saxon poetic vocabulary, at first hearing so quaint and stiff-syllabled, and then so exotic in its inventions, and then, as studies proceed, so opaque, so diffuse, even abstract, this also reflects a story of growth and change, over several centuries; though to document that story in any detail would be almost as long and complex a labour as to tell, say, the story of diction in English poetry over the last four centuries.[92] Anglo-Saxon poetry indeed has its "diction", in the sense of words that poets create, or make over, or establish in poetic senses conventional or special. (Example: *secg*, [pron. "sedge"], a reed, or "flag" > poetically (perhaps from the shape) "sword"; then from "sword", by metonymy, "warrior"). It also uses a lexicon of words and expressions drawn from the common tongue, or else from its "book language", with reference to the institutions, preoccupations, presuppositions, etc, of life in English days before the Conquest. (Example: *wer*, "man" > *werod*, "band of men, company, army"> *heorðwerod*, "hearth company", a chieftain's household retainers, an expression which not only "denotes" fact, but also "connotes" the feelings associated with the fact). It has a "morphology", a system of word-building, quite freely, from simple elements into derivatives or compounds. (Example: *cumbol*, "sign, standard, banner" + *hnáest*, "collision" > *cumbolgehnáest*, "collision of banners" = "battle") Comparable principles of growth and structure might be discerned in any poetic period. Out of what he has, a poet makes more, intuitively, instinctively; it is hardly to be supposed that poets, singing or writing, reciting or scripting, inventing or imitating, do so with a highly raised sense of lexical structure, any more than that they fashion their verses on a rigorously articulated theory of prosody. Poetry, as a way of happening, is not analysed or pre-planned by the poet; though it is possible, to return to our distinction between *scopcræft* and *wóðcræft*, that the poet who scripted his eloquence chose his words with a more calculating sense of how language is structured and how it "reads".

---

[92] For a general treatment of the literary vocabulary of Anglo-Saxon, see Stephen A.Barney's *Word-Hoard, an Introduction to Old English Vocabulary,* 2nd edn, New Haven 1985. An excellent short introduction to the heroic vocabulary is J.R.R. Tolkien's essay "On translation and words", pp. ix - xxvii of his Prefatory Remarks to J.R.Clark Hall's *Beowulf and the Finnesburg Fragment, A translation into modern English prose,* revised edn. by C.L.Wrenn, London: George Allen & Unwin, 1950. "Kennings" in Old Norse and Anglo Saxon are concisely and informatively discussed in G.Turville-Petre's *Origins of Icelandic Literature*, OUP 1953, pp.27-31.

For the older minstrel, the primary drive to vary and expand the vocabulary came undoubtedly from the half-line alliterative structure of his verse. Its aesthetic committed him to sequences of repetitions and variations, the piecework of the poem calling for synonyms, synonymic variants, metaphor, metonym, synechdoche, for diverse ways of calling a spade a spade, or a shovel, or a trenching tool, or an agricultural implement, or an inland navigator's tiller. This diversity can be illustrated from the repeated naming of common themes - men, their weapons, their kings, their horses, their gold, their ships. Here are some of the Anglo-Saxon words for "ship": *scip, bát, flota, naca, cnearr, stefna, wundenstefna* (also *bundenstefna*, also *hringedstefna*, also *hringnaca*), *ýðhengest, merehengest, wǽghengest, lagumearg*. Among these, *bát, scip, flota* - "boat", "ship", "vessel" represent a primary vocabulary, the words used when there is no compulsion to elaborate or refine the notion of "ship"; *naca* has the sense of "bark", a ship of some size, and *cnearr* a different, shorter type of seagoing vessel, like those used by the Vikings (Old Norse *knorr*) designed for stability and seaworthiness. (The compound *nægledcnearr*, "nailed ship" indicates a method of construction with rivets or possibly with hardwood plugs - in fact, clinker building). The word *stefna* is a case of synechdoche, the part for the whole; it means "stem", "prow". At the beginning of the poem of the *Seafarer* the narrator bewails his many nights of keeping watch *æt nacan stefna* - "at the prow of the long ship"; there, however, we may fairly guess at an implicit metaphor, the *naca* being the navis, the nave, the "long ship" of the church, and the *stefna* the chancel or altar. *Wundenstefna, hringedstefna, bundenstefna* are descriptive compounds, "curved prow", "ornate prow"; similarly hringnaca "round-stemmed longship". Another type of compound is represented by *merehengest, wǽghengest, ýðhengest*, all meaning "stallion of the sea/ waves/billows, and *lagumearg* signifying "mare of the ocean"

These are compact images, one-word riddles, and the usual name for them is"kennings", from the Norse *kenningr*, pl. *kenningar*. The essence of the kenning as a compound is that at least one of its components should be figurative in a literal context. A modern English compound like "penholder", for example, would have no status as a kenning. But call it "pen's holster", and you attempt a kenning; call it "thought-sword's sheath" and you have managed something like an Icelandic riddle. The verses of the Norwegian and Icelandic court-poets, the "skalds", are laden with kennings, so densely that a single strophe might seem to call for genius alike in rapid composition and speedy comprehension.[93] The Anglo-Saxon kennings, or quasi-kennings, do not pack the composition in anything like the same way, and as descriptive expressions are often conventional to the point of cliché.

---

[93] Egil Skallagrimsson's Brunanburh poem (Chapter 2, p.44) typifies the complexity of skaldic verse-composition. The impromptu poem made by Egil in honour of Æthelstan is a strophe of 8 lines, divided into two half-strophes, each syntactically complete; each line containing six syllables; each line ending with a trochee; in each line two alliterating staves, in each line two fully rhyming or half-rhyming syllables; the whole package called the *Dróttkvætt*. There is nothing so intricate in Old English. The plain sense of Egill's strophe is "Æthelstan causes a gold bracelet to hang on my wrist; the warrior (thereby) wins greater glory." A series of kennings, some interlinked, conveys this simple sentiment: "hawk's tree" (wrist), "tinkling halter" (bracelet), "red flour" (gold), "hawk of battle" (raven), "feeder of ravens" (warrior, ie Æthelstan), "spear storm" (battle), "fish of battle" (sword), "gallows of the sword" (wrist).

Frequently they occur as phrases, or phrasal compounds: the sea may be called *swanrád*, "swan-road", but also *hwæles éðel*, "home of the whale", or, for a variant, *mæwes éðel*, "home of the gull", and further, *ganotes bæþ*, gannet's bath". Many of the Old English kennings are little nature-poems, small riddles not too difficult to unravel: the cuckoo, for instance, is *sumeres weard*, "keeper of summer", and a wing is *fugles wynn*, "bird's joy". Not unexpectedly, kennings on warfare and weapons are common. "Battle" is *aesca ðrýþ*, "press of spears", or *cumbolgehnáest*, "clash of banners"; a hero's sword is *beaduléoma*, "flash of battle"; arrows are *hildenáeddran*, "battle vipers". Almost as common are the kennings that speak of body and soul: *bánhus*, *báncofa* - "bone house", "bone casket" - the body, together with *líchama*, "dress of flesh", and *feorhbold*, "castle of life"; then, for the inner being, the places of thought and feeling, *bánhuses weard*, "the body's keeper" = "the mind", and for the heart, *hreðerloca*, "bosom fortress", *breostcofa* "chamber of the breast", *hordcofa*, "treasure chamber", variants serving to express different nuances in context (or maybe to provide alliterations at need). The context of such words is often one of mourning for loss, of discretion in suffering, of silent endurance, themes that appear alike in heroic or religious verse. Religious poetry has it own stock of "creation kennings", as they might be called, celebrating God's power and presence throughout the universe; these may be elaborated as phrases, bringing them closer to the modern notion of visual imagery, eg. *Godes candel beorht*, "God's bright candle" = "the sun".

This is essentially an art of naming things, or the functions of things, or actions connected with things. "A man's a man for a' that", says Burns, and we know what he means; but in Anglo Saxon poetry a man may be plain man, or *wer*; or be called by a more elevated name, eg *hæleð*, "hero", *eorl*, "earl"; or be called *beorn*, *guma*, *secg*, all meaning "warrior"; or be designated by the specific functions or trappings of a warrior, eg *gárwiggend*, *helmberend*, "spear-fighter", "helm-bearer"; or be wrapped up in a kenning, eg *wælwulf*, "slaughter-wolf" = "warrior", *reordberend*, "speech-bearer" = "human being". So with this and with other words of common import. The poet presents a verbal map of the known world, to be recognized or, perhaps, if the naming were highly original, pleasurably guessed at. No doubt poetic inspiration settled into scribal imitation as compositional time went by. No doubt many compounds and kennings lapsed into cliché, so that this "compounding" aspect of Old English poetics can seem laboured, and at length even a little tedious, to a modern reader. Yet almost any poetic compound in Anglo-Saxon has something of the allure of a language we know superficially at best, as an inventory of written words, not as a living thing in the barter and banter of usage. Take, for example, the meanings of *wunden-*, literally "wound" in such compounds as *wundenfeax*, "with plaited mane", *wundenlocc*, "with hair braided", or "in ringlets", *wundenhals*, "with curved prow", *wundenmáel*, "damascened", ie with a sinuous motif, as on a sword-blade. To which add the sense of the participial adjective *wunden* in the phrase *wunden gold*, "corded gold", a gold rope made by the torsion of strands of gold wire.[94]

---

[94] The aesthetic import of *wunden* - that "curves are beautiful" - appears not only in references to ships' prows and the damascening of swords, but even in architectural decoration and jewellery design. The Wanderer's *weall wyrmlicum fáh* - "wall adorned with serpentine shapes" suggests something like the intertwinings of the Byzantine vine-motif (seen in the panels of the Ruthwell Cross). An example from jewellery is the Sutton Hoo gold buckle, with its sinuous, endless ribbon-pattern.

Here is a field of related senses attached to that one word, *wunden*: "twisted", "braided", "corded", "curved", "sinuous". It is also evident that *wunden* expresses an aesthetic, positive value; things so "wound" or "winding" are beautiful, or decorative, or at the very least, shapely. The horse saddled and bridled for King Hrothgar in Beowulf is a *wicg wundenfeax*, "a steed with plaited mane" - the poet makes a point of mentioning this stylish detail. The heroine Judith is called *wundenlocc*, "the lady with braided tresses" - blonde tresses, the poet may well have imagined, put up in ropes of plaited gold;[95] with this word he reminds us of her pure beauty, in the very moment of her frenzied assault on the drunken Holofernus - *Sloh ða wundenlocc / þone feondsceaðan fagum mece / heteþoncolne, þæt heo healfne forcearf / þone sweoran him* - "Then she of the braided locks smote with her gleaming sword the foul brigand, the oppressor, hacking through half of his neck" The poetic value of *wundenlocc* at this point is not simply descriptive; it is not merely a synonymic or "synechdochic" variant of "lady"; it is affective, emotive, in its juxtaposition of the agent, the purely beautiful, and the act, wholly sordid, stirring in us revulsion, and also a sense of what it has cost Judith to stoop to this, a humiliation worse, almost, than being the victim of her captor's lust.

To know the poetic value - the sense-in-depth - of simple words is even harder than the task of deconstructing the sense-in-spread of poetic compounds; the latter are always in some degree "transparent" - we have at least a superficial notion of what the poet is getting at - whereas the former are frequently "opaque", hiding from us the sense of some interior meaning. Words denoting nuances of colour, light, and shade often provide examples of senses that seem vague to the modern reader while they are apparently precise to the Saxon poet (and presumably to his audience). A typical instance is the word *fealu* - "fallow" - which a dictionary (Clark-Hall) defines as "fallow, yellow, tawny, dun-coloured, grey, dusky, dark", as though the poetic eye viewed the world shiftily, in grisaille or a pale sepia. Sea-waves are *fealwe* (grey? or inshore sandy?) Horses (or specifically, mares) are *fealwe* (grey? or dun-coloured?) Colour words are relatively infrequent; the Anglo-Saxon palette includes the primary colours, red, blue, green, yellow, and secondary colours such as brown and purple. Here, however, it is not so much a question of what colours are named, as of how colours are seen. A case in point is the word *brún*, "brown". How did the Anglo-Saxon visualise brown? As something roseate, a sub-species of red? As something more akin to bronze? Or yet again, did "brown" imply, not a colour as such, but a peculiar and distinctive sheen? In the poem of *Maldon*, Byrhtnoth's sword is described as *brád ond brúnecg* - not "broad(-bladed) and brown-edged", which makes uncertain sense, but rather "broad-bladed and bright-edged", the cutting edge of the sword having been honed until it gleamed.[96] That is a particular

---

[95] But on Judith's "braided hair", see further at Postscripts p.150.
[96] "broad and brown-edged" The construction of the sword involved what is now called "pattern welding", with separate stages in the forging of the blade and the edge. The blade was created by taking iron rods, twisting them together, then hammering them flat. The edge, of metal made hard by a technically critical process known as annealing, was then added. The edge was then burnished with a file, which would give it the dull sheen the poets may have meant by "brown". This phrase, cited here from *Maldon*, has a previous history, in *Beowulf* .line 1548.

example of how intensity of light rather than density of pigment governs the Old English poet's descriptive perceptions. And his "affective", or emotional perceptions also, for *léoht* ("light") is a master-term, the token of all things bright and beautiful, of all things holy, of life itself. Whatever radiates light is *scír* ("sheer") - the glitter of light on the water is *scír*, the radiance of Christ is *scír*; his body is *scíma*, a ray of light. An attractive woman is *scíene*, or *scéne* - which means both bright ("sheen") and beautiful ("schön"). Eve, in the *Later Genesis*, is called *ides(e) scénost*, "lady most bright" The virtuous Judith is called by her poet *(ða) beorht(an) ides(e)*, "bright lady", and also, with no apparent sense of a debt to pagandom, *ides ælfscín*, "lady elf-bright".

All things shining exist in counterpoint with all things dark, dusky, shadowed, gloomy obscure. One of the most striking examples of this poetic chiaroscuro is the account of the Crucifixion in *The Dream of the Rood*. The Rood declares, *þurhdrifan hi me mid deorcan næglum*, "they pierced me with dark nails" - a fine example of a complex word, in which a literal/descriptive meaning is shadowed by a figurative/affective meaning. Commentators assume that *deorc* indeed means "dark" or "black", possibly with reference to the dark red of the blood staining the nails; some have argued that *deorc* has a secondary meaning, "hideous, horrible", invoking Celtic parallels[97]; it remains to say that *deorc* in Old English can surely bear the figurative sense it has attracted throughout the history of our language, that is, "dismal, "cheerless", "hopeless" Such a sense would reflect the subjective state of the viewer rather than the character of the thing viewed. The heart of the reader/hearer at this dramatic moment in the recital is "darkened". Then we read how shadows envelop Christ's body, the *scír scíma*, "brilliant ray", and how the radiance leaves it and a shadow goes forth, *wann under wolcnum*, "dark under the clouds" In that "wan" darkness, all Creation weeps.

There is a form of imagery called "phonaesthetic" - meaning that it conveys pictures in sound; and Old English poetry is not without it. Its moments of sound-symbolism are brought into focus very often by the rhythmic/alliterative patterning of the verse. A line from the *Battle of Maldon*, for example, evokes the slap of an arrow against the shield raised to deflect it:

bogan wæron bysige   bord ord onfeng

Literally, this reads "bows were busy, shield point received", but that laboured rendering obscures the effect, which is the rhyming of *bord* and *ord*, adjacent accents in an `D-type' half-line (/ | / x \). It is more than likely that the frequent alliteration of "plosives", or "stops" (consonants like p, b, `hard' c, `hard' g) and "fricatives", or "sibilants" (like s, sh), facilitated some types of sound-portrayal. Here are some lines from the poem *Guthlac*,[98] describing a ship at the end of a voyage, running ashore into the sand and shingle. First the Old English text, with the alliterating staves and the "lifts" marked:

---

[97] See Michael Swanton, *The Dream of the Rood,* cited edn., p120, commenting on line 46
[98] *Guthlac*, lines 1332-35, (ASPR text)

6   Tunes on a Broken Lyre

```
             -/-  x    / x
            Lagumearg snyrede                A

       [x]  / x x / x x x /  \x
       gehlæsted to hyðe þæt se hærnflota    A - C

        x x  /  \ x  /  \  x  /
       æfter sundplegan sondlond gespearn    C - E

              /   x  /  x
            grund wiþ greote                 A
```

Rhythm and sound here are impossible to translate, other than in lumpish mimicry:

> The sea-horse hastened
> laden to landward, till the long ship then
> after sea-prancing sand-land spurned,
> gripped and grounded

Two images are entwined, of the galloping horse and the ship tossing on the sea; but the phonaesthetic image at the close is of a boat hard-driven, grinding into a sandy beach. It is the image Robert Browning evokes, from similar resources of sound, in his poem Meeting at Night:

> As I gain the cove with pushing prow,
> And quench its speed i' the slushy sand.

Browning's pushing prow, "quenching" its speed i' the slushy sand represents a faculty of auditory imagination expressed no less powerfully in the Anglo-Saxon poet's *sond-lond spearn, grund wiþ greote*. And where Browning "embeds" into his sound-symbolism an additional metaphor, "quench", giving focus to the moment of the boat's grounding, the Guthlac poet similarly embeds in his lines a focusing metaphor, with "spurn". In the craft of poetry there is nothing too old to be new.

"Extended imagery", as we know it from Elizabethans or Romantics, an elaborate design often sustained throughout a dramatic speech, or protracted through a whole poem with the consistency of an argument, is rarely to be found in Anglo-Saxon, which nevertheless has some striking passages of visual imagery. The visual impulse of Old English poetry is usually one of rapid impressions rather than extended representation, but a passage like the following, from *Beowulf* (lines 217-224) shows how well an Anglo-Saxon poet could build a sequential image, picturing event and scene as they unfold:

> Over the waves, before the wind,
> the ship, foam-throated, bird-like, rode,
> till at the turn of the second day
> the ring-prowed craft had sailed so far

that the seamen had first sight of land,
with gleam of cliffs, steep mountain-sides,
broad headlands; so the sound was crossed,
the voyage done. *lines 217-224 Beowulf*

As always, the attempt to regulate the pulse of the original, here with a translation into a form of unrhymed tetrameter, reduces the sharp emphases, smooths the pointed moments. This passage begins with a vivid kenning, in conjunction with a striking simile: *flota fámiheals fugle gelícost* - "the foamy-throated vessel" [the ship] "most like a bird". There could hardly be a more powerful visual impression of a ship under sail, running before the wind (*winde gefýsed*). It is not "rather like" a bird, or "somewhat like"; with the spread of sail, it is "most like" - no hesitant comparison will serve. As it breasts the sea it makes a bow-wave. Nineteenth century sailors might have said "it has a bone in its teeth", but the Saxon poet calls it "foamy-throated", describing the plumage of white water spreading out under the stem of the hard driven vessel. This is powerfully "visual"; but so in an equally imaginative way are the lines describing landfall, the approach to land on first sighting. First comes the glint of the cliffs (the verb is *blícan*, to "shine", "glitter", "flash") Then follows the perception of hills rising up from the land behind the coastline (*beorgas stéape*), and then the sense of solid encompassing ground - *síde sáenæssas*, "broad headlands" - as the boat runs in towards the beach. This is beautifully conceived and faithfully imagined, a true account of the experience of being in a ship as it makes landfall. If it were ever necessary to confute the idea that poetic descriptions in Anglo-Saxon are generated out of old and well-worn verbal conventions, never direct observation or keen imagination, this passage alone would serve.

At the close

The departed music is, after all, still with us - but as manuscript, as printed edition, as a notation to be laboriously deciphered by the scholar brooding over the page. The living voice has gone out of it; it is just a little too far away to hear properly. We might more easily attempt to recapture in imagination the sound of Chaucer reading his work aloud, than we can begin to reconstruct notionally the sound of Caedmon or Cynewulf reciting, still less the ancient echo of the gleeman at his "scoffing". This is in large part - and yet not only - because the sounds and grammar of our language have undergone profound changes; in large part - and yet not only - because intonations and rhythms escape us; and in still larger part - yet not only - because we no longer think of the forms, the techniques, the materials of verse in ways that came naturally to the Saxon poet. The music is departed also because the pragmatic claims of the music have gone, its purposes, its designs on a given audience, its social meaning in the life of clan and class and nation, its automatic assumption of commitment to certain beliefs and codes. What those purposes were has been the theme of much of this book; they are defined rather less wordily by this short poem - a riddle, number 28 in the Exeter Book collection:

6 Tunes on a Broken Lyre

Out of the earth it comes, to be beautified
by the toughest, roughest, harshest of human crafts -
carved, swarfed, tried, dried,
bound, wound, bleached, leached,
embellished, garnished, then brought from afar
to everyman's door. It bears the joys
of living men; and while they live, so long
it clings, haunts, grants their desires, gainsays nothing;
but then, after their death, begins to judge,
at times to accuse. Let wise men give it thought -
what is this thing?   *Riddle 28 Exeter Book*

The poem (see p.166) demonstrates the technical flair often found in the Riddles, but also the riddler's enigmatic way with a vocabulary of possible, "at-a-stretch" meanings. It is generally agreed, however, that "this thing" is the Harp, the minstrel's *gléobeam*, the instrument that Caedmon the Cowherd had never learned to play. It comes "out of the earth" when a tree is chopped down (*biþ foldan dǽl* says the original, "it is a part of the land"). Then this product of nature is industrially maltreated - carved, swarfed, tried, dried, etc - to make a thing of beauty for the pleasure of humankind. It makes dearly-loved music. People are rapt by it, it tells them about their feelings, about their experience, it withholds no pleasure. But then comes the riddle within the riddle - "after death", the Harp "begins to judge, at times to accuse" (*deman onginneð, meldan mislíce* - the sense of *mislíce* being "in various ways, diversely"). What is this talk of judgement and accusation? It does not concern *lof*, "praise", praise for the chief in his high seat, praise for the honoured guest, praise for the comrades on the benches, praise for the homestead and the land, for everything that tells of pleasure and desire, of life's favours granted. It concerns *dóm*, the unalterable judgement after death, the final truth. The music tells of the king's honour and lasting fame; it also tells of cruel and unjust kings, and of thanes who betray their pledges to their tribal lord, of wretches who tread the paths of exile, of apostates who turn from God. In the long tale of Anglo-Saxon poetics, this is the note to which, early and late, all the harps are tuned. The poet's business was to tell of success and failure, in worlds natural or supernatural, in actions and beliefs in which he and his audience were unquestioningly united, to which they were as unquestioningly committed. We investigate this societal art as from a distance, uncertainly, with an effort; though there are moments of insight and reward, moments when the inner ear is tuned to the paean or lament of a voice that sings of joy beyond telling, or love, or grief for loss. Then we acknowledge our human fellowship with the past, and for the labour of study we are recompensed and consoled.

Postscripts

This is an aftermath, a gathering of comments already made as footnotes in the main text. My first intention was that because of their bulk, going beyond a footnote's normal requirement for brief reference or explanation, they should appear only as end-notes. I believe, however, that many readers find it irritating to have to interrupt the flow of their reading in order to go in search of information which they might or might not find useful. Better to discover this by merely glancing at the bottom of the page. The notes are replicated here for supplementary reference, and for indulgent browsing.

Scop – "scoff"

Etymologies: *skeubh* related to "scoff", etc. This is the etymology suggested by the OED and Webster's New World (which defines *scop* as "a maker of taunting verses") . It is conceivable that a thread of inner sense runs from "scoff" to "mock", in the sense of "imitate", "mime" (as in `mocking bird'). Then part of the scop's business could be seen as *mimesis*, imitation; the craft of original invention being *poesis*, "making".
Chapter 1. p.9

The happy harpist's "sounding nail"

The text reads *naegl neomegende*, "sweet-sounding nail" - a transferred epithet, for of course it is the harpstring, not the plectrum, that makes the sweet sound. The "nail" here is a fingernail, or something resembling one. The Old English word for plectrum is *sceacol*, "shackle", suggesting a device in some way fixed (bound, tied) to a finger's end. The MS of the Vespasian Psalter has an illustration of David playing a harp - a lyre of the six- or seven-string type found among the treasures of the Sutton Hoo ship burial. The illustration shows clearly the function of the two hands in playing the Saxon lyre, the right hand to pluck the strings, the left to "stop" or "fret" the sounds. This illustration is copied and enlarged in http://www.cs.vassar.edu/~priestdo/lyre.html. See at that source an informative paper, "The Saxon Lyre: History, Construction and Playing Techniques", by Dofinn Hallr-Morrisson and Thora Sharptooth.
Chapter 1. p.9

Rings and things

The text says "a ring worth six hundred 'sceatts', reckoned in shillings". A 'sceatt' was a twentieth part of a shilling , six hundred "sceatts" being therefore equivalent to thirty shillings This costly *beag* was probably of the variety known as a *torc*. Torcs, or "torques" were artefacts made of thin strands of precious metal, twisted or "braided" into short pliable lengths, with at each end a solid gold terminal or clasp. For a fine example see, among the treasures of the British Museum, the Snettisham Great Torc. (See online at http:www.thebritishmuseum.ac.uk/compass) Tacitus (*Germania, cap.14)* mentions *torqui* among the customary gifts and barter payments of the Germanic chiefs, adding, with Roman irony, "we have now got them to take cash". On *wunden gold* - "wound gold" - and related matters, see further Chapter 2, note 21
Chapter 1. p.11

Snorri Sturluson, c.1179-1241

His *Heimskringla* (so called from the opening phrase of its preface, "Kringla heimsins...", "The circle of the world") is quoted here from the text of Samuel Laing's (1844) translation, published in 1907 by the Norroena. Society. Electronic edition at http:sunsite.berkeley.edu/OMACL/Heimskringla The most recent (excellent) translation is that of Lee M. Hollander. See Bibliography, Section 4.
Chapter 1. p.12

About Maeringaburg

It seems, from learned commentary, that the Maeringas were the Ostrogoths. A runic inscription from 10th century Sweden calls Theodoric *skati marika*, "Lord of the Maeringas". In that same inscription the Adriatic is called "the Gothic sea" Towards the end of the fifth century Italy had been under the control of the Germans under Odoacer; but in 493 Theodoric, at the command of the Byzantine emperor Zeno, led an Ostrogothic invasion and took the city of Ravenna. It is possible that Ravenna is "Maeringaburg". Theodoric "held" it, and all Italy, for 33 years, until his death, still in exile from his homeland, in 526. Perhaps these are the "thirty winters" the poem refers to - but only perhaps. The text is too laconic to allow of more certain conjecture.
Chapter 1. p.16

The dating of Deor

The question, "Is this a real person, or a poetic fiction, or a scribe's invention of the myth of a *scop*?" is asked in passing, but raises a substantial point about the dating of this text, and a few others which might be called "personations", because in them the author adopts a *persona*, conceived in an appropriate style. There are two possible views of *Deor*: one, that it is indeed an old poem, somehow surviving from the 7th century, originally composed by a poet calling himself *Deor*; the other, that it is a fiction, composed in the 9th or 10th century, by a Christian writer impersonating the character and style of a pre-Christian *scop*. Choose either way, or both ways at once; it typifies the difficulty of settling the OE literary calendar.
Chapter 1. p.16

The meaning of wóðbora

The glosses here are supplied by Clark-Hall, John R, and Herbert D. Merritt, *A Concise Anglo-Saxon Dictionary*, 4th edn., Cambridge 1960. As to a resemblance to the Welsh *hwyl*, my conjecture is that *wóð-* is from a Germanic root signifying "out of one's mind", "impassioned" (as in Middle English "wod", "wood"). It is related to Latin *vates* ("seer", "poet"). It is also related to the *od-* of Odin, the god of war and eloquence whose Anglo-Saxon name is Woden.
Chapter 1. p.18

Fuþark

Fuþark - from the first six symbols of a runic alphabet, representing the sounds of f, u, th, a, r, k. The "Common Germanic" or "Elder" futhark dates from the 2nd century AD, and is the form used in inscriptions from Low Germany and Scandinavia. The Anglo-Saxon runic alphabet, adapting to sound changes, is a futhorc and includes symbols not in the older versions. "Alphabet" poems on runic letters - along the lines of "A is an archer who has a big bow" - are extant from Norway, Iceland and Britain.
Chapter 1. p.19

A representative Common Germanic futhark

f	u	th	a	r	k	g	w
h	n	i	y	ǣ	z	p	s
t	b	e	m	l	ng	d	o

A representative Anglo-Saxon futhorc

f	u	þ	o	r	c	g	w
h	n	i	(j)	(ih)	p	(x)	s
t	b	e	m	l	ŋ(ng)	œ	d
a	æ	y	ia	ea	st	k	

On Christ and Ingeld

Alcuini Epistula 124. (in *Monumenta Alcuiniana*, ed. Jaffé, Wattenbach & Dummler, Berlin 1873; published in the *Bibilotheca Rerum Germanicarum*) Alcuin of York, 735-804, in his day among the most eminent of European scholars and teachers, was master of the Cathedral School in York, and later head of Charlemagne's Palace School in Aachen. He wrote, in Latin, devotional verses of a sort more dutiful than inspired. The anger expressed in Letter 124 was apparently excited by reports of young clerics´ enthusiasm for heroic narratives.
Chapter 1. p.21

Re the bearlike Beowulf

In 1910 the German philologist and folklorist Frederick Panzer published a study of more than 200 folk-tales with elements akin to the fantastic or supernatural parts of *Beowulf,* notably in the Grendel episodes. These stories came to be know collectively as "The Tale of the Bear's Son." F.Panzer, *Studien zur germanischen Sagengeschichte: I, Beowulf.* Munich 1910. For a brief discussion of this material, see the Introduction (pp xxii-xxiii) to C.W.Kennedy's *Beowulf: the Oldest English Epic*, OUP 1940; further, *R.W.Chambers, Beowulf: An Introduction to the Study of the Poem,* 2nd edn, Cambridge UP, 1932
Chapter 1. p.22

Ship design and Frisian seamen

The long Chronicle entry for the year 826 describes King Alfred's attempts to create a fleet to fight the Danes. The ships he designed were "very nearly twice as long" as the Vikings' ships, and also "faster, more manoeuvrable and of deeper draught". They were constructed "neither on the Danish model nor the Frisian, but as he himself considered most apt for their purpose" Serving in the squadron that first encountered the Danes off the Dorset coast (conjecturally, round Poole Harbour) were Frisian seamen, some of them mentioned in despatches: Wulfheard Friesa, Æbbe Friesa, and Æþelhere Friesa. These three were all killed in the battle, and never came home to their wives.
Chapter 1. p.23

Monastic Riddle

The pioneer of the monastic riddle was Aldhelm of Malmesbury, Bishop of Sherborne, d. 709. He wrote his verses in Latin, and encouraged others to do so; his riddles were based on those of the 5th century poet Symphosius. After Aldhelm, Archbishop Tatwine (d.737) was the author of 40 riddles; then Eusebius (Hwaetberct, Abbot of Wearmouth and Jarrow from 716) increased the total to 100. For further information, see M.R.James´ review of "Latin Writings in England to the Time of Alfred", Chapter V of Vol.1 of *The Cambridge History of English Literature.*
Chapter 1. p.25

ealdormon

On the word *ealdormon*, also *aldormon, aldor*. This is the ancestor of modern "alderman", but the cousin of ancient "earl". The Old English word *eorl* is cognate with the Norse *jarl*, and in the Anglo-Saxon Chronicles of the 9th and 10th centuries invariably signifies a "Danish" chieftain or field commander. The Old English equivalent is *[e]aldormon*, a deputy of the king, in effect a "lord lieutenant". The distinction between English and Danish terms is strictly kept in historical accounts, until the late 10th century and after, when *ealdormon* and *eorl* are sometimes used indifferently, or "equivalently", eg. The AS Chronicle for the year 992, "the king entrusted the leadership of the *fyrd* (the English army) to the ealdormon Ælfric and the eorl Thorod." In the Peterborough Chronicle for the year 1048, *eorl* is used consistently, in reference to people whose names clearly indicate Saxon origin - *Leofric, Godwine* - as well as to others with Scandinavian names - *Swegen, Siward*. But in poetic usage *eorl* is established early, whether as an indicator of rank, or more generally in the meaning "nobleman, noble warrior" - an expression of *caste*. Beowulf has *eorl* repeatedly, and rather less often, *aldor*. In the poem of *The Battle of Brunanburh,* the Saxon king, Æthelstan, is called *eorla drihten*, "overlord of earls", and his ancestors *eorlas árhwate*, "earls eager for glory." In *The Battle of Maldon,* the English commander, Byrhtnoth, designated *ealdormon* in the Chronicle for the year 992, is throughout called *sé eorl*, "the earl".
Chapter 2. p.30

Did they know this was Tryggvason?

But it was hardly the poet's wish, or business, to know the Viking commander's name. There is evidence that even the Viking's own men were not wholly aware of his identity at the time of his raids on Britain; he had his reasons for keeping it secret. According to a distinguished source, Snorri Sturluson's *Heimskringla* (see Chapter 1, p.12, his crews at first knew him only as Ole (familiar = "Olly"), and thought he was Russian. For details, see *Heimskringla*, Life of Olaf Tryggvason, caps. 32, 33.
Chapter 2. p.34

On armies, ours and theirs

The two armies, "home" and "away", Saxon and Viking, are consistently distinguished by the words *fyrd* and *here* (the latter eytmologically related to *hergian*, "harry, ravage, plunder") A campaign by the native army, called a *fyrding*, could on occasion be as oppressive to the home population as the operations of the *here*. Thus the Chronicle for the year 1005: "Then the king ordered the call-up of all the forces of Wessex and Mercia; and during all the harvest time they were out campaigning against the Vikings. But it was of no more use then that it ever had been, for during all that time the Vikings came and went as they pleased. And the campaign did all kinds of harm to the country folk, so that for them there was no choosing between one army and the other." The words the writer uses here are *innhere* ("in-" for the home army) and *úthere* ("out-" for the invaders)
Chapter 2. p.34

More about "wound gold"

The *béagas* were only one form of tribute, salary or reward (others being weapons, jewels, horses, grants of land) but they are most frequently mentioned in poetry. They were apparently made of "wound gold". The exile in *The Wanderer* (see Chapter 3) complains that his lot is "the way of the outcast", *nalaes wunden gold*, "not the wound (braided, or twisted) gold". In *Beowulf* (lines 1380-83) as the hero is about to combat a monster, King Hrothgar promises to reward him *wundini golde / gyf þu in weg cymest* - "with the wound gold, should you come out alive". So again in the Old High German *Hildebrand*, the central character, facing single combat with his own son, who does not recognise him, offers him *bouga*, "ring", in earnest of his good faith: *Want do ar arme wuntane bouga / cheisurungu gitan so imo se der chuning gap / Huneo truhtin,* "Then he slipped from his arm the twisted ring of imperial gold which the king, the lord of the Huns himself, had given to him." The importance of the *béag* as an emblem of service, honour, and fealty is evident from these instances.
Chapter 2. p.35

"Sister's son"

In his *Germania*, dating from AD 98, the Roman historian Tacitus notes the importance of the "sister's son" relationship among the continental tribes. "The sons of sisters are as highly honoured by their uncles as by their own fathers. Some even go so far as to regard this tie of blood as peculiarly close and sacred, and, in taking hostages, insist on having them of this class; they think that this gives them a firmer grip on men's hearts and a wider hold on the family" (*Germania*, transl. H.Mattingly, cap.20; see Bibliography, section 4)
Chapter 2. p.38

The meaning of ceorl

Dunnere is described as *unorne ceorl*, "a simple peasant". "Churl" here has none of the pejorative overtones it has in modern English; it is an indication of social status - the poet's intention being to show that men from all ranks and regions fought on the English side. A note of aristocratic disdain , however, is sounded in the line describing Byrhtnoth's onset with one of the Vikings: *eode swa anræd eorl to þam ceorle*, "as resolute came earl against churl."
Chapter 2. p.42

A ring-giving by firelight

Egil's Saga, attributed to Snorri Sturluson, date c:a 1230; chapter LV. For a serviceable online translation, see http://www.blackmask.com , *Egil's Saga, translated from the Icelandic*, by the Revd.W.C.Green. Other texts are *Egil's Saga*, transl with an introduction by Hermann Pálsson and Paul Edwards, Penguin Books, 1976; also *Egil's Saga,* Everman Library edn, ed. Christine Fell, transl.John Lucas; in Everman Paperback Classics . This may be fairly called an "idiosyncratic account", in that it was written nearly three hundred years later than the events it describes, and is written by a man with a flair for arresting narrative. We are not to take it as wholesale fiction, however. Medieval Iceland preserved its family sagas in oral tradition for many years before they were

written down; and to judge by his *Heimskringla,* Snorri was scrupulously respectful of ascertainable fact.
Chapter 2. p.45

Chiefs and followers

Tacitus: *principes pro victoria pugnant, comites pro principe. Germania.* Cap.14. See *Beowulf,* 2490-93 and 2497-9, as the dying hero talks of his relationship with his chief, Hygelac:

> In battle, with my bright sword, I repaid him,
> as I was able, for such favours given;
> land he gave, a home, a dear dwelling
>
> ....
>
> Always, in the host, I went before him,
> as vanguard, all alone - and always thus
> shall I do battle, while this sword shall last

Chapter 2. p.45

Demands and rewards

Tacitus: *exiguunt enim principis sui liberalitate bellatorum equum, illam cruentem frameam,* "from the liberality of their chiefs they demand that warhorse, that bloodstained spear" *Germania,* cap. 14. This picture of a clansman making peremptory demands on the "liberality" of his chief suggests a negotiation rather more aggressive than the courtly *máððumgifu* of the Anglo-Saxon poems. On the subject of spears, Tacitus notes that the *framea*, "fighting spear", is the Germans' principal weapon, ritually presented to their youths on their coming of age, together with a shield.
Chapter 2. p.47

A biblical note on dóm

Ecclesiaticus, 44.1, "Let us now praise famous men...such as have borne rule in their dominions, men of great power and endued with their wisdom" --- 44.9, "And there are some of whom there is no memorial: who are perished as if they had never been".--- 44.10, "But these were men of mercy whose godly deeds have not failed" - 44.14, "Their bodies are buried in peace, and their name liveth unto generation and generation." An Anglo-Saxon poet would have taken this as a text precisely on the theme of *dóm*. The "famous men", the powerful, the wise rulers, the merciful whose godly deeds have not failed, who rest in peace, whose names live for evermore, have *dóm*. Others, who have no memorial, and who have perished as though they had never been, are *dómleas*. The word *these* in 44.10 refers to the "famous men", not to those who have no memorial. 44.9 is a stern judgement; no pathos is intended.
Chapter 2. p.50

Hávamál, "The Words of the High One"

Hávamál, "The Words of the High One", strophe 77. It is a moot point whether *fé* (in old English *feoh*) should be translated as "cattle" (livestock, the principal evidence of bucolic wealth) or more generally rendered as "riches" (goods and chattels, property in general). For the text, most conveniently, see the Runeberg Project, http://lysator.liu.se/runeberg/eddais . (Or go to Google and ask for Hávamál – there are many websites to choose from). This is a much-edited, much-translated poem. Translations include a version in Esperanto, and also, in parody, a "Havamál for New Yawkas". One of the most attractive translations, as a poem in its own right, is that of W.H.Auden and P.B.Taylor. See http://members.iquest.net/~chaviland/Havamal. Their rendering of the last line of strophe 77, *dómr of dauþan hvern,* as "the glory of the great dead", is debatable, however. What is implied is "every one of the dead"; and though *dómr* in Old Norse can certainly mean "glory" (like *dóm* in Old English), the sense here is closer to that of "judgement"
Chapter 2. p.51

Conjectural readings in Wulf and Eadwacer

"As though they were offered a prize". In our reading, "prize" translates *lác*. A possible rendering of *lác* is "offering", or specifically "sacrificial offering". "They will take him for sure". "Take" renders the original's *áþecgan,* a rare word meaning "to take food, to consume". What is suggested here is something like the biblical sense of "devour"; eg Psalm 27 v.2, "When the wicked, even mine enemies and my foes, came upon me to eat up my flesh, they stumbled and fell."

Then - "It is different with us". In the original, *Ús is ungelíc,* (literally, "to us is unalike"), a laconic statement, meaning either "In our situation we are different [from other lovers]", or "Our positions, as individuals, are different" - "Our fates are separate". The same construction occurs in a line (612) of *Genesis B,* when the Tempter, flattering Eve, tells her: *þe is ungelíc / wlite and wæstmas, siððan þu mínum wordum getruwodest* - "Your figure and form are altogether changed since you trusted my words" Perhaps the tenor of *us is ungelíc* is not so much "it is different with us" as "for us, everything has changed".
Chapter 3. p.54

"Impersonations"

Not the least puzzling thing about *Wulf and Eadwacer* is its unique lyric form. It shares that distinctive quality as a lyric with *Deor*, and the two poems appear together in the Exeter Book, between devotional texts and the Riddles, as if the compilers of this codex themselves hardly knew how to classify these poems. Both poems are "personations": *Deor* the work of someone impersonating a *scop*, *Wulf and Eadwacer* the impersonation of a woman, so convincing in its intensity and open emotion as to persuade the reader that if this was not written by a woman, it was at least the work of a man with a poignant sense of womanliness.
Chapter 3. p.55

"Those who hope for name and fame"

In the text this is expressed by a single word, *dómgeorne*. The meaning of *dóm* in that compound is "repute" (in the world), rather than "judgement" (out of it). A man of noble caste who does not "seal up the dark thought in his soul" is vulnerable to his enemies and detractors, and will be seen as (in the modern phrase) "a loser". This rule of reticence - "shut up and be famous" – is expressed in folk-wisdoms, like the 14th-century *Proverbs of Hending*: "If thou hast a sorrow, tell it to thy saddle-bow, and ride forth singing". That would be the way of the *dómgeorn*.
Chapter 3. p.60

Ubi sunt - *"where are...?"*

Ubi sunt - "where are...?" (as in "Where are the heroes of old?", "Where are the snows of yesteryear?", "Where are Chaplin and Keaton?" - questions which require no answers, though the questioner may go on to supply them). This rhetorical device has had a long life in western literature. Its first occurrence is thought to be c:a 525 AD in Boethius' *De Consolatione Philosophiae*, eg Book II, metrum 7:"Where now lie the bones of the loyal Fabricius? What of Brutus or Cato the stern?". The passage in *The Wanderer* beginning "Where is the steed? Where is the rider?" is an early occurrence of the *ubi sunt?* trope in English poetry, and arguably the finest. It (the trope) has since been used by poets of all schools and periods. For a fine modern example, see Edgar Lee Masters' poem "The Hill", a section of his *Spoon River Anthology* (New York: Macmillan, 1915):

> Where are Elmer, Herman, Bert, Tom and Charley,
> The weak of will, the strong of arm, the clown, the boozer, the fighter?
> All, all are sleeping on the hill.
>
> One passed in a fever,
> One was burned in a mine,
> One was killed in a brawl,
> One died in a jail,
> One fell from a bridge, toiling for children and wife -
> All, all are sleeping, sleeping on the hill.

(Compare the lines in *The Wanderer* beginning "War seized on some, and led them out of life, this one a bird bore over the open sea, this one was marked for death by the grey wolf...&c")
Chapter 3. p.64

"There were giants on the earth"

The *entas* were not malevolent giants, like the inhuman *eotenas, þyrsas,* and *gigantas* , but rather "mighty men", in the biblical phrase, the revered ancestors of a dwindled race. In his translation of Orosius' *History of the World*, King Alfred names *Mimbrað sé ent* (Nimrod the giant) as the one "who began the building of Babylon", and *Ercol þone ent* (the giant Hercules) as a demigod summoned to help Europe and Asia in their fight against the Amazons.
Chapter 3. p.68

The identity of Cynewulf?

We know, from his runic signatures claiming the poems *Crist, Elene, Juliana,* and *The Fates of the Apostles,* how he spelled his name. Otherwise, all is conjecture. It has been suggested, not very convincingly, that he was a Bishop of Lindisfarne; the signature *Cynwulf* attached to the Decrees of the Council of Clovesho in 803 leads to the conjecture that he may have been a priest in the diocese of Dunwich. (On the coast of Suffolk; those who opt for Lindisfarne or Dunwich find circumstantial support in the vivid sea-imagery in parts of his poems). "Abbot of Peterborough" has been suggested. Some scholars have argued for a Mercian origin, some for a Northumbrian. A melancholy or penitential strain in his writing prompts the assumption that he had known the high life as a minstrel at court, and then, as a convert, turned to the monastic life of repentance. Is it likely? The options are discussed - and dismissed - in *The Cambridge History of English and American Literature* (see below, and Bibliography), and in the *Catholic Encyclopaedia* (website at http://www.newadvent.org/)
Chapter 4. p.73

The Later Genesis and Paradise Lost

The connecting link between *The Later Genesis* and *Paradise Lost* is the Gallo-Roman Avitus, Bishop of Vienne (Alcimus Ecdicius Avitus, AD 490-c:a 518, latterly St.Avitus), whose numerous writings included a poem of 2552 Latin hexameters, in 5 books, on the Origin of Sin (with the revolt of the angels), Expulsion from Paradise, the Deluge, the Crossing of the Red Sea. The Old Saxon poet evidently had access to it, and Milton is thought to have used the earlier books in drafting parts of *Paradise Lost.* Historians and theologians will find an introduction to the writings of Avitus in *Avitus of Vienne, Letters and Selected Prose,* ed. and transl. Danuta R.Shanzer and Ian Wood, Univ. Penn Press/ Liverpool Univ. Press, 2002. As far as I know, the poem is only accessible to those with ready access to the Abbé Migne´s *Patrologia Latinae Completus Cursus,* LIX, 191-398.
Chapter 4. p.75

Sir Thomas Browne

Sir Thomas Browne, *Pseudodoxia Epidemica, or Vulgar Errors,* London 1646, Book III; Browne makes no reference to theological interpretations of bestiary lore; his book is a massively learned assault on superstitions, old wive's tales, and pseudo-science. He makes reference, incidentally to the whale's "sweet breath", which he attributes to the presence of ambergris in the sperm whale's stomach.
Chapter 4. p.85

Aspidochelone - "shield turtle"

Aspidochelone, in Greek *aspido* + *khelon* The name means "shield turtle", from *aspis* (shield), whence *aspido-* (shield-shaped), and *chelone* (turtle). By a false etymology, deriving from another (Latin) sense of *aspis,* as "asp", this mythological monster is called by some the "Asp-turtle". Its ill repute, under diverse names – for example Zaratan - is ancient; some of Alexander the Great´s men are said to have

come upon a huge shield-turtle, big as an island, in the Indian Ocean, and to have landed on it, in expectation of finding the hoard of a dead king; whereupon the treacherous beast sank beneath them. Something of the sort is narrated of Sindbad the Sailor, who barely escaped with his life after an encounter with the beast. The Anglo-Saxon form, Fastitocalon, is as Tolkien has pointed out, essentially "astitocalon" (close enough to "aspidochelon") with an "F" to satisfy the demands of alliteration., in the line *fyrnstreama geflotan, Fastitocalon.* Tolkien employs Fastitocalon as a cautionary name in one of the songs of his character Tom Bombadil; whence the monster has taken on a new life in the conventicle seminars of modern Middle Earthers. There are several websites, eg. that of The Tolkien Wiki Community. See www.thetolkienwiki.org/wiki.cgi?Fastitocalon.
Chapter 4. p.85

marram grass

"marram grass" freely translates the text's *sáerýric*, apparently a *hapax legomenon*, or unique reading. In structure it divides into the elements *sáe*, "sea", and ? *rýric?*, meaning, at a guess, "reed". This corresponds to the formation in Old Norse of *marr*, "sea", and *halmr*, "straw", in the compound *marrhalmr*, "sea-straw", modern *marram*, a tough grass often found in sand-dunes.
Chapter 4. p.86

The land of the Finns

"the land of the Finns" : commentators doubt that this could be the same as modern Finland, or even, as in some translations, Lappland. A location somewhere further south on the Baltic coast of Sweden is preferred (see the note on line 580 in the Wyatt/Chambers 1914, repr.1948 edn. of *Beowulf*). But this line should be read in the full context of the swimming match episode. The contest begins off Geatland, in the south and south-west of Sweden. At first the two champions swim together and cannot be separated. Then wind and turbulent current divide them and they are borne their separate ways - Breca along the Swedish west coast to "the Heathoræmas land", in the south of Norway, Beowulf along the east (Baltic) coast to "the land of the Finns". But there is perhaps little point in ransacking the text for topographical precision.
Chapter 4. p.92

"a widow woman, her hair tied back"

"a widow woman, her hair tied back". The mark of her widowhood is that she us *bundenheord*, with her hair worn short and close. This part of the MSS (some eight lines) has been so badly damaged as to be in places almost indecipherable. The 19th century critic, Sophus Bugge, made a conjectural restoration, in which the relevant words defining the "widow" are *séo géo-méowle / æfter Beowulfe*, "the former maiden (spouse) after Beowulf". More recently J.C.Pope, in his *The Rhythms of Beowulf* (Yale, 1942) deciphered the phrase as *sé géatisc méowle*, "the Geatish woman". The inference left to be drawn is that this is a woman twice-widowed, Hygd, who was widow of the Geatish king Hygelac, and who later married Beowulf. But the documentation misses the poetic point, the "objective correlative". An image of desolation: here is a widow-woman, here is a funeral pyre. The rest is commentary.
Chapter 4. p.94

Judith

Catholic theology, numbering *Judith* among the canonical books, is obliged to consider it as a history with a divine purpose. Thus, "The purpose of the book is to give an example of heroic virtue and to show God's loving providence and care for His people." - John E. Steinmueller, *A Companion to Scripture Studies, Vol.II, p. 133;* New York, Joseph F. Wagner Inc., 1942. There are good grounds, however, for regarding the history as unhistorical. It amounts to what modern irreverence might call "a rattling good yarn", like many good yarns, morally ambiguous as it rattles.
Chapter 5. p.96

Hair styles

Hair styles: "braided locks" here translates *wundenlocc* compare this with the translation of *wunden gold* as "braided gold", see Postscripts p.144. But is it altogether certain that "braided" properly describes Judith's seductive *coiffure*? The Vulgate account describes her transformation, before her exploit, from the severe habit of the widow to the opulence of the total charmer. She bathes, anoints herself with "the finest myrrh", dresses lavishly, picks out a pair of sandals, puts on her jewels and her ear-rings, and - the Latin says - *discriminavit caput eius*, meaning, possibly, "braided" (or "plaited") her hair (*discriminare* = "to separate"), or perhaps "combed out" her hair, or even "let down" her hair. As a widow she would have worn her hair tied back close, (See Postscripts, p. 149) Her aim is to deceive Holofernus by presenting herself as a maiden footloose and fancy-free; perhaps her tresses, like those of a lass in an old song, "hung down in ringlets". Was it a curly-haired seductress, not a braided belle, who chopped off Holofernus' head?
Chapter 5. p.97

Tempering a sword

The blade is described as *scurum heard*, here literally translated as "shower-tempered". A first impulse, guided by the reminiscence of Othello's "sword of Spain, the ice-brook's temper", is to read this as meaning "tempered by plunging the forged blade into cold water". That would certainly indicate the swordsmith's practice of hardening the edge of a blade in the process of "annealing". Note, however, that the epithet *scurheard* (according to Clark Hall) means "made hard by blows" - the "shower" being the repeated hammer-strokes on the anvil.
Chapter 5. p.97

Maldon - Beginning the battle

The *Maldon* poet, describing the battle's first onset, says: *the time had come when doomed men must fall. A shout went up; ravens circled, and the eagle keen for carrion; there was uproar on earth. Then they let fly from their hands the file-hardened spears, the well-honed javelins; bows were busy; point struck shield; bitter was the storm of battle.* Behind its poetic rhetoric, this is a convincingly ordered account of what would happen in the opening moments of the battle.
Chapter 5. p.101

Is The Dream of the Rood a "heroic" poem?

Michael Swanton (op.cit.) writes, " Heroic elements in the poem are largely allusive and a matter of mere vocabulary. The poet is concerned to illuminate aspects of the Redemption rather than to linger on the theme of the victor prince." That the *Dream of the Rood* is a "Redemption" poem is undeniable, but Swanton dismisses perhaps too readily the sustaining importance, through much of the poem, of battle language and the warrior ethic . The "heroic elements" are matters of *invocation*, rather than mere *allusion*.
Chapter 5. p.107

Understating

The reading of the text's *máete werode* as "all alone" is confirmed by a line in the concluding section of the poem, where the poet describes himself, after his vision, as lying *þær ic wæs ana, mæte werode"*, "where I was alone, with little company" (ie "by myself"). For a comparable instance of "Anglo-Saxon understatement", see the poet's confession at the end, *Nah íc ricra feala freonda on foldan,* "I have not many rich and powerful friends on earth. By "not many" he means none at all - they have all passed away and are living in heaven.
Chapter 5. p.109

Robert Graves, The Crowning Privilege

(The Clark Lectures, 1954-1955). London: Cassell & Company. Graves elaborates his notion of the maritime origins of Germanic metre: "The function of the Nordic *scop* seems to have been twofold. Not only was he originally a "shaper" of charms, to protect the person of the king and so maintain prosperity in the realm; but he had a subsidiary task, of persuading the ship's crew to pull rhythmically and uncomplainingly on their oars against the rough winds of the North Sea, by singing them ballads in time to the beat. When they returned from a successful foray, and dumped their spoil of gold collars, shields, casques and monastic chalices on the rush-strewn floor of the beer-hall, then the *scop* resumed his song. The drunken earls and churls straddled the benches and rocked to the tune: "Over the whale's way, fared we unfearful...." To this, Graves adds the assurance that "Anglo-Saxon poetry is unrhymed because the noise of rowlocks does not suggest rhyme." (!)
Chapter 6. p.113

George Puttenham on "stirre"

George Puttenham on "stirre"; this is his name for the variable tempo which he perceive in quantity-based classical metres. The poetry of his own time ("our vulgar running verse", he calls it) he regards as strictly syllabic; it keeps a count ("time"), but it lacks any fluctuation of movement, or "stirre". Puttenham ascribes this to the monosyllabic base of common spoken English, which he regards as "Saxon". He knew nothing of Anglo-Saxon poetry, however, or the fact that "stirre", a fluctuating tempo, is implied in its metrical techniques – as Eduard Sievers first demonstrated in the late 19th century.
Chapter 6. p.115

Sweet on Sievers

Henry Sweet, *An Anglo-Saxon Reader,* 7th edn: Oxford, 1894. "I have tried to give a clear abstract of Sievers' views" - views which, with demure irony, he professes himself "obliged to accept in spite of the adverse criticism of some English critics. ... These critics seem to forget that Sievers' classification of the Old English metrical forms into types is not a theory but a statement of facts, and that the complexity and irregularity to which they object is a fact, not a theory." Sweet then adds an observation that deserves red letter status: "The truth is that we know very little of the details of the versification of most languages; and it is possible that if our modern English metres...were analysed in the same thorough way in which Sievers has analysed the Old English metres, we should have difficulty in realising that a modern poet should carry such a complicated scheme in his head." (Pref., pp. xi-xii)
Chapter 6. p.117

Siever's "five type" model of Old English poetic rhythms

Apart from Sievers. What is offered in this chapter is a very general account of Siever's "five type" model of Old English poetic rhythms. Andreas Heusler's *Deutsche Versgeschichte,* 1925 and J.C.Pope's *The Rhythm of Beowulf,* 1940, criticise Sievers' phrase-based, speech-based, method, and offer something more closely resembling the traditional concept of metre, ie a kind of musical "barring", foot by foot, the "bars" being isochronic (equal in time, just as in music), irrespective of the number of syllables each contains, and with one strong "beat" on the first syllable in the foot = note in the bar. The problems of metre in Old English continue to engage the attentions of scholars and break the wits of students. For some fairly recent discussions, see the Bibliography. Then adopt the counsel of Kemp Malone, to follow "the natural rhythm of the lines, with due heed given to the lift-patterns and in particular to those syllables which the poets by alliteration and rhyme mark for heightening." (In "The Old English Period", Book I Part I of A.C.Baugh (ed) *A Literary History of England.* London: Routledge & Kegan Paul Ltd, 1950, p.25.)
Chapter 6. p.118

Matters of metre

(1) First advice to the uncertain has to be, get the "beat" of the line first, and the rhythmic pattern will follow by and by. The "beat" of the line is carried by the alliterating syllables. The key alliteration is on the first accented syllable of the second half-line. There will be at least one, allowably two alliterating syllables in the first half-line. On the alliterating syllables the implied stress is greatest, the implied pitch highest. These are "full lifts". On these the song depends.

(2) A full lift thus combines accent and pitch. Accent falls on syllables which are long (a) by inherent quantity – they have long vowels which are long because they are long, or (b) by position – as when a normally short vowel combines with certain "lengthening groups" of consonants, eg n+cons., l+cons, r+cons. Long by quantity are *ár, gebídeþ, mód, lád, hréran, hrím, sǽ, -lást, (a)rǽd.* Long by position are *milts, long, sceold-, hond-, ceald- wyrd.*

(3) "Half lifts" are perceived in relation to full lifts. A full lift influences the pitch of an adjacent syllable, frequently in compounds, eg *hrímceald, módcearig* (compare modern English "ice-cold", "heartsore")

(4) Two short syllables may be "resolved", ie regarded as a single, lift-bearing syllable; thus, in the *Wanderer* passage, *metud, laguläd, wadan*. Resolutions of this kind may be regarded as a licence allowed to the versifier, but they may also reflect the current phonology of the spoken language. The latter is certainly the case with *lagu* in *laguläd* > "laoo", "law". (The same development of intervocalic guttural spirant *g* is observable in other words, eg *haguþorn* > "hawthorn") "Resolutions" are *roughly* comparable to the effects, in present-day spoken English, of *syncope*, when an accented and an unaccented syllable are elided, or assimilated, as in "wooden", pronounced "woodn"; or "general", pronounced "genrul"; or "jewellery", pronounced "jewelry", even when the conservative spelling persists. Syncope is an effect of sentence-rhythm, the metre of colloquy.

(5) A lift may be assigned, for "affective" or "performative" emphasis, to a word which would not otherwise bear the accent. This applies, in *The Wanderer*, to *Oft*, the first word of the poem. The first half-line, *Oft him anhaga* has an apparent metrical resemblance in metre to the first half-line of *Beowulf, Hwaet we gardena*. In the latter instance, however, *Hwaet* is regarded as extra-metrical, a mere exclamation or "listen up" call, whereas the *Oft* of *The Wanderer* is intrinsic to the narrative. As a short syllable it acquires its metrical "long" status in resolution with *him*.

(6) Do not suppose that all of the above is required to read five lines of Anglo-Saxon verse. Requirements are: a dictionary, or a good glossary; some basic grammar; patience, judgement, a sense of rhythm. (That´s all).
Chapter 6. p.120

Stops and spirants and things

This is of necessity a crude and cursory account of the spirant/stop, palatal/guttural variants of the consonants c and g, in word-initial positions, ie as relating to the practice of alliteration. A much fuller consideration of these sounds, in word-medial and word-final contexts, as well as in consonant groups, in Primitive Germanic and after, would lure the student away from mere verse and into the dense Teutonic boscage of the *Lautlehre* - an expedition well worth making for its own disciplinary interest, though perhaps not as an adjunct to literary criticism.
Chapter 6. p.123

On the question of intention

The sceptic might possibly wish to rebut the idea of the intentional or instinctive opposition of sounds in a phonetic/stylistic texture, as suggested here, with the argument that the opposition of spirant and stop is in any case "structural" - embedded in the forms of the grammar and the lexicon. Example, from verb conjugation: the verb *céosan* (choose) has palatal ç in the infinitive and guttural stop c in the past participle, *gecoren*. From lexical relationship (word formation): the verb *gadrian*, (to gather), guttural stop g, and the adverbial phrase *on geador*, (together), palatal spirant g > semivowel /j/, "on yador". Many such instances could be adduced, without suppressing altogether the intuition that in some poetic contexts, the opposition becomes a feature of style.
Chapter 6. p.123

Poetic diction

For a general treatment of the literary vocabulary of Anglo-Saxon, see Stephen A.Barney's *Word-Hoard, an Introduction to Old English Vocabulary*, 2nd edn, New Haven 1985. An excellent short introduction to the heroic vocabulary is J.R.R. Tolkien's essay "On translation and words", pp. ix - xxvii of his Prefatory Remarks to J.R.Clark Hall's *Beowulf and the Finnesburg Fragment, A translation into modern English prose*, revised edn. by C.L.Wrenn, London: George Allen & Unwin, 1950. "Kennings" in Old Norse and Anglo Saxon are concisely and informatively discussed in G.Turville-Petre's *Origins of Icelandic Literature*, OUP 1953, pp.27-31
Chapter 6. p.131

Brunanburh

Egil Skallagrimsson's Brunanburh poem (Chapter 2, p.44) typifies the complexity of skaldic verse-composition. The impromptu poem made by Egil in honour of Æthelstan is a strophe of 8 lines, divided into two half-strophes, each syntactically complete; each line containing six syllables; each line ending with a trochee; in each line two alliterating staves, in each line two fully rhyming or half-rhyming syllables; the whole package called the *Dróttkvætt*. There is nothing so intricate in Old English. The plain sense of Egill's strophe is "Æthelstan causes a gold bracelet to hang on my wrist; the warrior (thereby) wins greater glory." A series of kennings, some interlinked, conveys this simple sentiment: "hawk's tree" (wrist), "tinkling halter" (bracelet), "red flour" (gold), "hawk of battle" (raven), "feeder of ravens" (warrior, ie Æthelstan), "spear storm" (battle), "fish of battle" (sword), "gallows of the sword" (wrist).
Chapter 6. p.132

wunden - "curves are beautiful"

The aesthetic import of *wunden* - that "curves are beautiful" - appears not only in references to ships' prows and the damascening of swords, but even in architectural decoration and jewellery design. The *Wanderer's weall wyrmlícum fáh* - "wall adorned with serpentine shapes" suggests something like the intertwinings of the Byzantine vine-motif (seen in the panels of the Ruthwell Cross). An example from jewellery is the Sutton Hoo gold buckle, with its sinuous, endless ribbon-pattern.
Chapter 6. p.133

"broad and brown-edged"

The construction of the sword involved what is now called "pattern welding", with separate stages in the forging of the blade and the edge. The blade was created by taking iron rods, twisting them together, then hammering them flat. The edge, of metal made hard by a technically critical process known as annealing, was then added. The edge was then burnished with a file, which would give it the dull sheen the poets may have meant by "brown". This phrase, cited here from *Maldon*, has a previous history, in *Beowulf* .line 1548.
Chapter 6. p.134

Samples

These "samples" are representative extracts or gobbets, twenty-two in all, from poems cited in translation and commentary elsewhere in this book They are presented here in four thematic groups, as *Poetics, Wisdoms, Elegies,* and *Heroics. Poetics* includes varieties of verse-form and passages on the office and function of the poet, as discussed in chapter 1. *Wisdoms* relates to the recurrent observations on life, conduct, morals, faith and fate, which are a staple of Anglo-Saxon verse.*Elegies* are expressions of personal or general lamentation, as illustrated in chapter 3. *Heroics* includes varieties of the heroic stance, from the warrior-heroism of chapter 2, to the anti-heroics of chapter 4, to the religious heroism of chapter 5. Each group includes, as its final sample, a passage from *Beowulf*, in testimony to that great poem's power to involve and transcend all themes.

The purpose of this is to provide some access to texts in the original language, since poems seen only in translation are poems received but not possessed. The samples invite "close" reading, drawing attention to questions of grammar and syntax, to poetic idiom, to editorial emendations, and arguments to the prosody and punctuation of the text. Punctuation is a problem, since (as noted in chapter 6) editors may punctuate as they see fit, using the modern apparatus of stops and intonation marks, according to personal perceptions of the argument of the poem. This is true even of the great ASPR (*The Anglo-Saxon Poetic Records*, eds. G.P.Krapp and E.van K. Dobbie, New York, 1931-53) which, in its electronic form in the University of Georgetown's *Labyrinth Library* website, is the principal source of reference for the texts presented below. For the textual facts, I rely on ASPR/*Labyrinth*, but editorial punctuation is not a matter of fact; it is a tool of interpretation - and that must be my excuse for occasionally departing from the ASPR prescription. The departures, where they are of importance, are noted in due place.

The notes after each extract are for information and guidance, perhaps of the notemaker as much as his readers. If in some places they say rather more than is necessary, and in some rather less than might be helpful, and in others again make assertions that are open to question - not to say wrongheaded - I have to apologise. Confusions arise out of a wish to explain clearly. My personal experience of the Anglo-Saxon literary language, however, has been that after the first fifty hours of study it is wholly lucid; and after the first fifty years, all but impenetrable. *Wyrd bið ful aræd*

[**Note**: Here as elsewhere in the book, I have followed a common practice in the marking of long vowels: that is, I have not marked them in the Anglo-Saxon text, and in the apparatus have as a general rule reserved the accent mark [´] for the citation of words in their "dictionary", or "glossary" form. Very occasionally I use these marks in citing short phrases, of a half-line or less, to indicate an emphasis or a metrical pattern.]

I. Poetics

1. *Caedmon's Hymn*:   A poet's awakening

There are no less than 17 manuscript transcriptions of *Caedmon's Hymn*, including one in the Northumbrian dialect. Northumbrian and West Saxon versions are commonly available for comparison in anthologies, eg. the hardy perennial *Anglo-Saxon Reader* of Henry Sweet and his successors There is an excellent critical edition in *Eight Old English Poems, edited with a Glossary and Commentary*, by John C.Pope. The following is the West Saxon text used for translation in chapter 1, p.20 (in fact, the ASPR /*Labyrinth* text; however, see the notes below, at *eorþan*)

```
Nu sculon herigean    heofonrices weard              1
meotodes meahte    and his modgeþanc
weorc wuldorfæder    swa he wundra gehwaes
ece drihten    or onstealde.
He ærest scop    eorþan bearnum                      5
heofon to hrofe    halig scyppend
þa middangeard    moncynnes weard
ece drihten    æfter teode
firum foldan    frea ælmihtig.                       9
```

This is a bare text largely devoid of "editorial" punctuation, apart from the full stop at the end of line 4 (after *onstealde*) which demonstrates a division of the Hymn into two strophic sentences, rather like the verses of a Psalm. Compare, for example, Psalm 8, verses 1,3,4,6:

> O Lord our Governor, how excellent is thy Name in all the world: thou that hast set thy glory above the heavens!
> For I will consider thy heavens, even the works of thy fingers: the moon and the stars, which thou hast ordained.
> What is man, that thou art mindful of him: and the son of man, that thou visitest him?
> Thou makest him to have dominion of the works of thy hands: and thou puttest all things in subjection under his feet.

This is the very substance of *Caedmon's Hymn*, so much so as to invite the conjecture that the cowherd's theme was inspired by voices a little lower than the whisperings of the midnight angels; that he might have heard it propounded in church. Celebrating the Creation, however, is something of a *gradus* theme in OE verse. There is, for example, a Creation Hymn in *Beowulf*, 89-98, when a "sweet-voiced" scop, in the idyllic days of Heorot before the coming of the evil Grendel, lauds the work of the Creator in terms similar to those of Caedmon´s Hymn or Psalm 8.

Notes.

Line 1., *herigean* = *herian*, "to worship, praise, extol"; Line 2, *meotod* = *metod*, the first of the poem's six names for the Creator, the others being *wuldorfæder, éce drihten* (repeated), *hálig scyppend, moncynnes weard,* and *fréa ælmihtig.* The compound *módgeþanc*, literally "mind-thought", here signifies "intention", "purpose". Line 3, *wuldorfæder,* "glory-father", ie "glorious father", "father of glory." "The work of the father of glory". Read *faeder* as a genitive; the singular of this noun is usually undeclined in Old English. The sense of *swá* is that of the explanatory "for" - cf. the archaic "for that", the documentary "in that", "inasmuch as" Line 5, *eorþan bearnum,* "for the sons of earth"; some MS read *ælda bearnum,* "for the sons of men". The latter is thought by some to point a religious emphasis not necessarily present in the former; see Pope, ed.cit..

2. *Widsith*, lines 50-67, 135-143: A poet's travels

Widsith is a problem poem. The first problem is one of dating; we have it from the Exeter Book, a 10th century MS, but its recollections of the Teutonic migration period (4th-6th centuries AD) suggest a much earlier origin. One of its editors, Kemp Malone, regards it as having had "a long and eventful history". The second and larger problem concerns the discursive status of this poem. It reads like a "personation", a masquerade; its style, or near-strophic alternation of styles, suggests a poet (of later date) scripting a poem about a *scop* (of earlier times) In style there is a marked fluctuation between the primitive "end-stopping" of its lists of rulers and tribes and the "early run-on" style characterised by *Caedmon's Hymn*. For editorial commentary, see the editions of Kemp Malone and Joyce Hill, listed in the Bibliography.

These extracts describe the fictional scop's wanderings, his occupational philosophy - and his appreciation of a generous reward.

```
Swa ic geondferde fela    fremdra londa                    50
geond ginne grund.    Godes ond yfles
þær ic cunnade    cnosle bidæled
freomægum feor    folgade wide.
Forþon ic mæg singan    ond secgan spell,
mænan fore mengo    in meodohealle                         55
hu me cynegode cystum dohten.
Ic was mid Hunum    ond mid Hreðgotum,
mid Sweom ond Geatum    ond mid Suþdenum.
Mid Wenlum ic wæs ond mid Wærnum    ond mid wicingum.
Mid Gefþum ic wæs ond mid Winedum    ond mid Gefflegum.   60
Mid Englum ic wæs ond mid Swæfum    ond mid ænenum.
Mid Seaxum ic wæs ond Sycgum    ond mid Sweordwerum.
Mid Hronum ic wæs on mid Denum    ond mid Heaþoramum.
Mid þyringum ic wæs    ond mid þrowendum,
ond mid Burgendum    þær ic beag geþah                     65
me þær Guðhere forgeaf    glædlicne maþþum
songes to leane.    Næs þæt sæne cyning.


Swa scriþende    gesceapum hweorfað                        135
gleomen gumena    geond grunda fela
þearf secgaþ    þoncword sprecaþ
simle suþþe oþþe norþ    sumne gemetað
gydda gleawne    geofum unhneawne
se þe fore duguþe wile    dom aræran                       140
eorlscipe æfnan    oþþæt eal scæced
leoht ond lif somod    lof se gewyrceð
hafað under heofonum    heahfæstne dom.
```

Notes.

Line 51, *geond ginne grund,* "through the whole wide world". This phrase has the ring of a conventional formula, like other "far and wide" expressions occurring in OE., eg *betwux twæm seonum* , "from shore to shore" or "as far as land reaches", and *under swegles begong,* "beneath the expanse of heaven". For examples, see *Beowulf, 856-61.* In that passage, "the wide world" is called *eormengrund,* "the vast plain". A similar notion of vastness is implied in *gin(ne),* literally "yawning". In the *Snorra Edda* - the "Prose Edda" of Snorri Sturluson, the primal void of the universe is called *ginnungagap,* "yawning chasm".

Line 52, *cunnade.* Note, not from *cunnan,* but from the related weak verb, *cunnian,* in the sense "have experience of", "make trial of". It governs the genitive of *gódes* and *yfles.*

- *Cnósl* in this line signifies "kith and kin", or "native land" Thus *cnósle bidáeled* means both "separated from my kinsfolk" and "far from my country". - the compacted pathos of exile.

Line 53, *folgade wide,* "sought service everywhere"; *folgian,* "follow", as in "follow a master", "follow a cause", has a related noun, *folgað,* "service, employment, allegiance". See *The Wife's Lament,* line 9 - *ða ic me feran gewat folgað secan;* she sets out in the hope of joining her husband's "following".

Line 57, *cystum* - translate adverbially, "how men of noble rank treated me generously". Lordly generosity is a central motif in *Widsith.* *Dohten* is pret.3rd pers pl of the preterite-present verb *dugan,* commonly with the senses "to avail", "to be worthy", "to be strong" (see the noun *duguð*); here, however, in a transitive nuance, "to be kind [to]"

Line 67, *næs þæt sæne cyning*; said in praise of Guðhere's munificence, and thus might be rendered "no miser, that king" (which comes perilously close to "no tightwad, he!"). The usual meaning of *sáene,* however, lies within the semantic circle of "slack, lazy, negligent", even "cowardly". Guðhere was a great warrior, and Widsith's judgement is essentially in praise of the king's energy in prosecuting the wars that win the spoils that bring the largesse that followers enjoy and visiting poets share. Tacitus says of the Germans (*Germania, cap.14*) that they have no taste for peace, that they consider it spiritless and slack to work for a living instead of fighting for it, and that a large body of companions (the *comitatus,* in OE the *gesíðas*) can only be maintained by successful wars. Guðhere is by no means *sáene* - "spiritless", or "slack"; he fights for the good of his fighting men. A similar judgement on another fighting king occurs in line 10b of *Beowulf.* The king there is Scyld, dynastic ancestor of the Danes, renowned for his warlike prowess in exacting tribute from the surrounding nations. *Þæt wæs god cyning,* says the poet, This, like *ne wæs þæt sæne cyning,* is a sober, summary judgement, an expression of *dóm.* There is no call in either case for the admiring exclamation mark.

Lines 135-6. Read: "Wandering thus" (*swá scríþende*) "the world's gleemen" (*gléomen gumena*) "follow their destinies" (*gesceapum hweorfað*) "through many lands" (*geond grunda fela*). .

Line 214, *léoht ond líf somod,* "light and life together". A formulaic expression meaning "until the end of their days"

Line 142,3 on *lof* and *dóm,* see chapter 2, pp.49-50.

3. *Deor*: A poet's troubles.

"A poem's troubles" might well be the title of this section, for *Deor* is almost a song too far, straying beyond the grasp of conjecture. Like *Widsith*, it is evidently a "personation", the work of a poet imagining himself in another poet's place - a scribe playing a scop. It makes considerable play with mythical/historical allusions; one of which turns on a crucial reading in the MS (the Exeter Book), prompting a century and a half of zealous conjecture and counter-conjecture since 1842.

The text printed below is the text adapted for translation in our chapter 1, pp. 14-15. It is basically the *Labyrinth* text, though independent in punctuation and layout. At one important point (line 14, the beginning of the 3rd strophe) it adopts an MS reading apparently rejected by most modern editors and translators.

```
Welund him be wurman    wræces cunnade              1
anhydig eorl   eorfoþa dreag
hæfde him to gesiþþe   sorge ond longaþ
wintercealde wræce   wean oft onfond
siþþan hine Niðhad on   nede legde                  5
swoncre seonobende   on syllan monn.
þæs ofereode   þisses swa mæg.

Beadohilde ne wæs   hyra broþra deaþ
on sefan swa sar   swa hyre sylfre þing
þæt heo gearolice   ongieten hæfde                 10
þæt heo eacen wæs;   æfre ne mihte
þriste geþencan   hu ymbe þæt sceolde.
þæs ofereode   þisses swa mæg.

We þæt mæð Hilde   monge gefrugnon ·
wurdon grundlease   Geates frige                   15
þæt hi(m) seo sorglufu   slæp ealle binom.
þæs ofereode   þisses swa mæg.

Þeodric ahte   þritig wintra
Mæringa burg;   þæt was monegum cuþ
þæs ofereode   þisses swa mæg.                     20

We geascodan   Eormanrices
wylfenne geþoht;   ahte wide folc
Gotena rices.   Þæt wæs grim cyning.
Sæt secg monig   sorgum gebunden,
wean on wenan,   wyscte geneahhe                   25
þæt þæs cynerices   ofercumen wære.
Þæs ofereode   þisses swa mæg.
```

Siteþ sorgcearig,   sælum bidæled,
on sefan sweorceþ,   sylfum þinceð
ðæt sy endeleas   earfoða dæl.   30
Mæg þonne geþencan   þæt geond þæs woruld
witig dryhten   wendeþ geneahhe,
eorle monegum   are gesceaweþ,
wislicne blæd,   sumum weana dæl.

Þæt ic be me sylfum   secgan wile   35
þæt ic hwile wæs   Heodeninga scop,
dryhtne dyre, me was Deor noma.
Ahte ic fela wintra   folgað tilne,
holdne hlaford,   oþþæt Heorrenda nu
leodcræftig monn   londryht geþah   40
þæt me eorla hleo   ær gesealde.
Þæs ofereode   þisses swa mæg.

1. *A Commentary on Commentaries.*

For those seeking to emend the text of *Deor* there have been two principal points of speculation. The first involves the meaning of *wurman* in the line *Welund him be wurman wræces cunnade*, where *him* can be read as an "ethic dative", as in "Weland had him a bad time in/by/around/because of w------. But what/where/who is/ are/ w------? Down the years, the poem's editors have had them a hard time around *wurman*, attributing to it whatever meaning looked attractive in the context. C.W.M Grein, for example, suggested the reading *be wimman*, or *wifman*, implying that "Welund suffered on account of a woman", or in modern ellipsis, "had woman trouble". F.Klaeber, sensing a paradox, thought that the phrase should read *be wynnum*, "in pleasures", "through delights", ie., roughly speaking, "Welund had a bad time having him a good time". (Certainly a not uncommon human predicament).These and other speculations at length gave way to the one that now holds the conjectural field – which is that *wurman* is an inflected form of *wurm*, meaning "a serpent", "a snake" The usual word for "serpent" in Old English is *wyrm*, a strong masculine noun, the dative plural of which is *wyrmum*. *Wurm* may well be an alternative form of *wyrm*, but if so it apparently declines, here, like a weak noun. However, scholars and translators have increasingly favoured the meaning "by means of/ because of snakes" . Some translations have been: "Welund tasted misery among snakes"; "Welund knew wretchedness among the wyrm-like folk"; "Welund, from serpents, experienced misery". But wherefore all this wormy circumstance? Kemp Malone has suggested that the worms/snakes/serpents are the undulating patterns on the sword used by Nithhad to hamstring Welund; the serpents, then, are symbolic. (In *Beowulf*, line 1698 the hero's sword is described as *wyrmfah*). Others likewise catch a metaphorical drift. Bella Millett offers "Weland for his skill (as a sword-maker?) suffered exile". Louis J Rodrigues translates "Welund, entrammeled, understood wrack; "entrammeled" not inelegantly suggests that the *wurman* are the *swoncre seonobende*, the "supple bonds of sinew" at the close of the strophe. Among these readings, only one points to the semantic association of *wræc* ("misery", to be sure, "wretchedness", by all means, "persecution" if you will, and "wrack" if you must) with *exile* - as in The Wanderer's *wræclástas* - though it is a conjoint sense of suffering *and* isolation or alienation that suffuses the whole poem.

A conjecture that seems to have fallen by the way is a not unreasonable guess that *wurman* is the corrupted form of a place-name: "Welund suffered the pains of exile in, or near W" - "W" being, at a venture, the Swedish province of Värmland. This is the conjecture accepted, with some annotation, by Bruce Dickins in his *Runic and Heroic Poems* (Cambridge 1915). In support of that conjecture, the following information may be added, courtesy of Värmlands Släktforskarförening (The Genealogical Research Society of Värmland). The Society notes that there are several theories about the province's name, but opts, as the most likely reference, for "Värmernas land", the land of the Värmers, who took their name from the "Wärman" river, so called because it never froze in winter. (Though turbulence, rather than temperature, keeps this river, now called Borgviksälven, ice-free) By this "warm" river, Welund's *winterceald wræce*, his "wintry exile" may plausibly have been spent. Of geopolitical divisions in ancient Sweden we can know little or nothing, but a modern map shows Närke - Nithhad's attributed kingdom – as lying between Värmland, to the west and north, and Västergötland, to the east and south. As the latter name (- **göt**land) suggests, this is Gothic, or Geatish territory, making it a fair assumption that Nithhad was by kith a Geat. All this may be taken in support of the reading and translation "Welund in Värmland knew exile's pain"., or it may be taken for the merest leap in the dark; but no more of a leap than those conjectures that have our hero wrestling with women, snakes, or guilty delights.

The second major *crux* is of much greater consequence, since it marks a shift from a dubiously conjectured reading to a whole new story, at least in the third strophe. There, in line 14, the MS has *mæð hilde*, which some editors in the 19th and 20th century have construed as *mæð Hilde* - Hild being one with the *Beadohild* of the preceding strophe, and *mæð* signifying "violation, rape" - this on the original testimony of C.W.M.Grein's *Sprachschatz der angelsächsische Dichter*, the "reference glossary" to his (and Wülker's) *Bibliotek der angelsächsischen Poesie* (first, 1857). Grein supports his attribution with reference to an Old Norse *meiði*; but his attestation of *mæð* = "violation" as an Old English word has been questioned. For most editors, including Benjamin Thorpe in his 1842 text, the solution to *mæð hilde* has been to make two words into one, a personal name, *Mæðhild* ("Matilda"). This is not reckoned to be the same person as the *Beadohild* of strophe 2, but a new character in the catalogue of wrack, the heroine of a lost romance. Given that reading, the necessary restructuring, sometimes desperate, of the third strophe, may be illustrated from some recent translations, posted on academic websites:

We have heard of the laments of Mathild,
of Geat's lady, that they became countless
so that the painful passion took away all sleep.

    Stephen Pollington   http://glenavalon.com/deor.html

That for Maethhild, of us, many have heard
that boundless became Geat's desire
that him this sad love entirely deprived of sleep.

    Benjamin Slade   http://www.heorot.dk/deor

Many of us have heard that God's great love
for Maethild grew too great for human frame:
his sad passion stopped him from sleeping.

    G.Crane (?)   http://employees.oneonta.edu/craneg/elit200/sources.html

We have heard of the misery that Maethilde felt
who was wife to Geat; how it grew yet deeper
when her sleep was stolen by sorrowful love

    Bella Millett   http://www.soton.ac.uk/~enm/deor

These extracts present the sad story of the lovers Mæthild and Geat. Conservative reading takes the poem's *Geat* as "the Geat" - the tribal, kith-and-kin index of Nithhad. (So in *Beowulf*, line 788, the hero is called *Geat*; it is not his personal name, it is his folk-label). For the larger speculators, however, it is the name of a man (which may indeed be possible), and even the name of a god, for Snorri tells how Odin in his outings among strangers called himself *Gautr*. (This, by a misapprehension, if not by simple mistranscription, may be how "God" breaks into the third of the above extracts). In these versions of sad love and boundless desire, Mæthild is said to lose sleep over Geat (see Pollington, Millett); but then again, Geat is worried sleepless over Mæthild (see Slade, Crane) In cases of mutual passion, the syntax can perhaps be made to work both ways. However, it is the original emendation that has led to the verbal entanglements. Editors/translators choosing to go with the MS read *þæt mæð Hilde*, taking *þæt* as the definite article governing a (conjectural) neuter noun, *mæð*; the more adventurous take *þæt* as a subordinating conjunction, beginning the reported tale of what happened to Mæthild, leading into a ramble of dependent constructions - "that...that..", "who...how...when" The syntax has to be wrested in a quite unscoplike way.

What the story is, that was once known to many, we can only guess. Kemp Malone cites, from 19th century Norwegian and Icelandic ballad-sources, the tale of Gaute and Magnild in Norwegian, in Icelandic the story of Gauti and Magnhildur. In these tales, Gaute/Gauti marries Magnild/Magnhildur who prophesies her own death by drowning. When she indeed falls into a river, her husband, playing his lute in Orphic fashion, draws her to land - alive, as Magnhild, tragically dead as Magnhildur. The relevance of this sub-saga to the matter of *Deor* is something for a folklorist to assess (but see, for example, Norman E.Eliason, "The Story of Geat and Maethhild in *Deor*, *Studies in Philology* 62, 1965) and the "conservationists" – call them that - prefer to take the third strophe of the poem as it stands, in the interpretation defended by, for example, F.Tupper, in "The Song of *Deor*". *Modern Philology*, Oct.1911, and "The Third Strophe of *Deor*", *Anglia*, vol.37. This treats the third strophe as a sequel of the second. *Hild* is *Beadohild*, and *Geat* is the Geatish king *Nithhad*. We all know about Hild's trouble; so bad that she hardly dared to think what would become of it; and we all know - or should know - that what became of it was the hero Widia/Wudga. As for *the Geat*, that pitiless man, we know that he could not sleep, frantic as he was with love for his dead sons. That is a possible reading, as the other is a plausible reading, but the misery of it is, that in ceaseless conjecture the poem is lost: the plausible is less and less possible, and the possible becomes highly implausible. Eventually, there are as many poems as there are readers: to every doctor, or dunce, his/her own *Deor*. All this illustrates the serpentine ways of textual criticism, or what happens to makers when the menders go to work on them. As St.Paul says, "let all be done unto edifying"

2. Additional Notes

Line 5 *néde*, from *níed*, in the sense "compulsion", "necessity", "restraint". Clark Hall readers "fetter" with specific reference to this context.

Line 6 *swoncre*, from *swoncor, swancor*, "supple". The MS reading is *swongre*, from *swongor*, "heavy".

Line 7, In the refrain, *þæs oferéode þisses swá máeg*; *þæs* and *þisses* are genitives, of *þæt* and *þes*. Treat these as genitives of respect, or "as to that". Thus: *[the sorrow] of that passed over - so may [the pain] of this*. This construction is discussed in a recent article in *The Review of English Studies* (Vol.52, nr.28, Nov.2001) entitled "Genitive in *Deor*: Morphosyntax and Beyond". The author, Gwang-Yoon Goh, regards the genitives in this line as reflecting "a low degree of affectedness", meaning a sober "distancing" from passions past and gone. If that correctly assesses the rhetoric of the poem, it makes all the more inappropriate the exclamation mark that some editors are all too ready to foist onto this refrain - *þæs ofereode, þisses swa mæg!*

Line 9, *hire sylfre þing*. The appropriate translation for Beadohild's "thing", would be "case", or "condition"; the expression is perhaps a little coy - as is proper to a matter the maiden scarcely liked to think about.

Line 12, *hú ymb þæt sceolde*. The construction is awkward and elliptical - more coyness, perhaps? Translate *hú* as "what", and read the ellipsis as *hú ymb þæt [weorþan] sceolde* - "what would become of that"; or take Hild as the subject of *sceolde*, implying *geþencan* - "what she must think about that".

Line 14, *monge*. Usually taken as *monige (manige)*. The translator's choice is between *we monige*, "many of us", and *monige* = "many things, much"; thus, either "many of us have heard about...", or "we have heard much about..." Malone (1961), however, suggests that *monge* is the dat.sing. of a noun *mong* with the special meaning of "cohabitation", "intercourse" - Beadohild's *þing*, in fact.?

Line 14, *we....gefrugnon*, literally "we heard by asking", that is, "we have heard the story". There is a recurrent construction of *frignan* with accusative of direct object and genitive of indirect object eg *Beowulf*, line 2, *þeodcyninga* (gen) *þrym* (acc) *gefrugnon*. This is the construction postulated by the "conservationist" reading of *þæt mæð* (acc) *Hilde* (gen) *gefrugnon*.

Line 15, *frige*: "love", though this word commonly carries sexual/erotic connotations and might be considered inappropriate to Nithhad's fatherly love for his slaughtered sons. Yet we may read *frige* as "consuming love", a passionate extreme of feeling, not only for his murdered lads, but also for his violated lass.

Line 16. The MS reading is *þæt hi seo sorglufu* where *hi* may be taken as a contraction of *him*, or possibly of *híe*. The choice depends on the translator's gender-preferences

Line 21, *we geáscodan...etc*; *áscian* here constructs, like *frignan*, with an accusative (*geþóht*) and genitive (*Eormanrices*).

Line 24, *sæt secg monig*, translate "many a man sat" (that is, under Eormanric's oppression).

Line 28, *siteþ sorgcearig,* "a man sits, full of care", or "man endures, careworn". Here is a narrative transition from the specific instance in the past (sæt, l.24)to the present (general) state of *siteþ*

4. Riddle 28: The Harp

The text is ASPR/*Labyrinth*. Also the numbering, which differs from that of Craig Williamson's collection (see below). The riddles are another kind of textual puzzlement. They are not, like *Deor*, obscure through the mischances of time and loss; they are deliberately puzzling, in a literary way - a designed bafflement - and they achieve this by exploiting the resources of *polysemy*, the potential existence of words in diverse meanings, begetting a metaphorical process that both illuminates and obscures. "Why is a raven like a writing desk?", Alice wonders, and never gets an answer from the Mad Hatter. Nor do the authors or scribes of the Exeter Book riddles supply answers to their puzzles. The answers have come from numerous commentators. "Many of the proposed solutions" says Karl Young "rest on over a century's painstaking efforts and wild guesses by professors, poets and cranks."

```
Biþ foldan dæl    fægre gegierwed                          1
mid þy heardestan    ond mid þy scearpestan
ond mid þy grimmestan    gumena gestreona,
corfen, sworfen,    cyrred, þyrred,
bunden, wunden,    blæced, wæced,                          5
frætwed, geatwed,    feorran læded
to durum dryhta.   Dream bið in innan
cwicra wihta,    clengeð, lengeð,
þara þe ær lifgende    longe hwile
wilna bruceð    ond no wið spriceð,                        10
ond þonne æfter deaþe    deman onginneþ,
meldan mislice.   Micel is to hycganne
wisfæstum menn,    hwæt seo wiht sy.
```

This is the text translated in chapter 6, p.138. The following notes outline the rationale of that translation.

Notes.

Line 1, *biþ foldan dáel* Is *bið* existential - "There is (a part of the earth)?" Or is it, rather, declarative - "It is / This thing is"? A common habit of the riddles is to begin with a striking assertion about the thing the riddler has in mind - "A bug ate words", "These little chaps are airborne", "My folks left me for dead". So here, "This object is a piece of the earth"

Lines 2-3, note, the sequence of superlatives (- *estan*) after the instrumental [mid] *þy*. The problem is how to translate *heard, scearp, grymm*; more of a problem, how to understand the word they modify, *gestreon(a)*. The word *streon* can signify, variously, "treasure", "acquisition", "possession"; here interpret "human acquisitions, or possessions", and so, even "tools", as used in the various techniques listed in lines 4 – 6

Lines 4-6., *corfen, sworfen...frætwed, geatwed*. Imitating the emphases of the internal rhyme is one thing; saying for certain what these technical operations are is another. They are listed in pairs, the members of which may in some instances be perceived as in "complementary" relationship (as in *frætwed/geatwed*, "adorned and equipped"), in others "supplementary" (as in *corfen, sworfen*, "carved and filed"), or "implementary" (as in *blæced, wæced*, "bleached and ?cleansed?"). Evidently the whole sequence tends toward the happy condition of being cut and dried, or done and dusted. But taken word by word it adds up to a lexical/semantic problem.

Line 7. Although *dryht*, in heroic language, often means an army, or a body of retainers - the *comitatus* - in *dryhta* (gen.pl) it need not be read as "of heroes", but simply "of men", ie of mankind at large. Compare the similarly reduced or generalised meanings of *hæleþ, eorlas, duguð.*, in many poetic contexts.

Lines 7-8 *Dream biþ on innan cwicra wihta*. "Within [it]" (*on innan*) "is all the joy (*drēam*) of living men (*cwicra wihta*)"

Line 8, *clengeþ, lengeþ*. More problems with rhyming words; *clengan* has the straightforward dictionary sense, "to adhere", but the meanings of *lengan* include "lengthen, prolong, protract, delay". It may be allowed to take it as an intransitive, "linger".

Lines 8-12. There is a complex sentence-structure branching out of the subject *Dream cwicra wihta*, where *cwicra wihta* is paralleled by *þara þe ær lifgende*: *Dream bið on innan cwicra wihta; þara þe ær lifgende, clengeð, lengeð, longe hwile, wilna bruceþ ond no wiþ spriceþ, ond þonne æfter deaþe deman onginneð....*"The joy of living men is in this thing; while they live, it clings, lingers, indulges their desires, gainsays nothing - and then, after death, begins to judge..."

Line 11, *dēman*, "to judge"; Line 12, in parallel with *dēman, meldan*, "to announce, declare, proclaim", but also in a forensic sense "accuse", "inform against", "charge". (One of the senses of Swedish *anmäla*)

A very different interpretation of the poem's language and structure, is presented by Craig Williamson in the following version:

> Part of the earth grows lovely and grim
> With the hardest and fairest of bitter-sharp
> Treasures - felled, cut, carved,
> Bleached, scrubbed, softened, shaped,
> Twisted, rubbed, dried, adorned,
> Bound, and borne off to the doorways of men -
> This creature brings in hall-joy, sweet
> Music clings to its curves, live song
> Lingers in a body where before bloom-wood
> Said nothing. After death it sings
> A clarion joy. Wise listeners
> Will know what this creature is called.

This has no more than a casual correspondence with the version presented on p.138, explained in the Notes above. But the riddles are not propositions in logic; call them, rather, poetic challenges to the poetically inclined. They change colour from reader to reader; they tend to mean what the reader wants to see in them. They have attracted a great deal of translation and commentary; see Bibliography, section 3, particularly under Kevin Crossley Holland, John Porter, Louis J. Rodrigues, and Craig Williamson, whose *The Old English Riddles of the Exeter Book* is the version quoted above.

5. A Charm, Wið færstice ("For a sudden stitch"): A poem against pain

The text used here is the *Labyrinth*, Metrical Charms, 4 with the editorial punctuation, including exclamation marks. (For the latter it might for once be said, in justification, that this "poem" is a dramatic script for performance). I have ventured, however, to omit the caesura-spaces that customarily divide patterned half-lines. There is a rhythm beating throughout this poem, but no orthodox metrical pattern.

Hlude wæran hy, la, hlude, ða hy ofer þone hlæw ridan,	1
wæran anmode, ða hy ofer land ridan.	
Scyld ðu ðe nu, þu ðysne nið genesan mote	
Ut, lytel spere, gif her inne sie!	
Stod under linde, under leohtum scylde,	5
þær ða mihtigan wif hyra mægen beræddon	
and hie gyllende garas sendan;	
ic him oþerne eft wille sændan,	
fleogende flane forane togeanes.	
Ut, lytel spere, gif hit her inne sy!	10
Sæt smið, sloh seax lytel,	
iserna, wundrum swiðe.	
Ut, lytel spere, gif her inne sy!	
Syx smiðas sætan, wælspera worhtan	
Ut, spere, næs in, spere!	15
Gif her inne sy isernes dæl,	
hægtessan geweorc, hyt sceal myltan.	
Gif ðu wære on fell scoten oððe wære on flæsc scoten	
oððe wære on blod scoten	
oððe wære on lið scoten, næfre sy ðin lif atæsed;	20
oððe hit wære esa gescot oððe hit wære ylfa gescot	
oððe hit wære hægtessan gescot, nu ic wille ðin helpan.	
Þis ðe to bote esa gescotes, þis þe to bote ylfa gescotes,	
ðis ðe to bote hægtessan gescotes; ic wille þin helpan	
Fleoh þær on fyrgenheafde,	25
Hal westu, helpe ðin drihten!	

The MS source for the *Lacnunga* ("Leechdoms") is BM Harley 585. They are included in T.O.Cockayne's *Leechdoms, Wortcunning and Starcraft of Early England*. (London, 3 vols, 1863-65) At the present day there is a good deal of interest in leechdoms and pagan magic; see, for example, Bibliography 3, at S.Glosecki, Bill Griffiths, and Karen Jolly. Stephen Glosecki, in particular, offers an interesting reading of *Wið færstice* as the text of a shamanistic ritual, in which the shaman stands as defender, "under a light shield", between his client and the attacking furies, and counters their assault by throwing a "spear" of his own.

Notes

Line 3, *Scyld þú þe nú...*, "Shield yourself now"; the *láece*, "leech", warns himself; *genesan*, "escape from, avert" (this evil). NB *móte*, 2nd pers.pres. subjunctive, "that thou mayst".

Line 4, etc., *síe, sý*. Subjunctive, from *wesan*; in the conditional clause, "if thou beest".

Line 5, *Stod*, etc, "I stood under a light shield"; the leech describes his own measures of defence, his ritual preparations and actions = "I took certain precautions".

Line 6, *sændan* is 3rd pret.pl.; but in line 7, *sændan* is the infinitive [*sendan*].

Line 7, *oðerne* = *oðerne gár*, "another spear"; "they have thrown spears at me, I will throw one back at them" [*him*].

Line 8, *forane togeanes:* the preposition *togeanes*, "against", "back", governs the dative pl. *him*, "them" in the preceding line (so, "against them", or "back at them"); *forane* may be read either as meaning "opposite" (the phrase then becoming pleonastic, "back against them", or it may be read adverbially in the sense "beforehand" - "I will reply promptly/ I will forestall more attacks".

Lines 10-11. The lines are obviously unmetrical. Translate *sloh seax lytel iserna*, "he forged (*slóh* or *slóg*, 3rd pret.sing of *sléan*) a little iron knife (or blade)"; *iserna* is gen.pl,of *isern*, (*isen*), "iron", used adjectivally, "of/from iron". In the heroic vocabulary, *isen* is one of the synonyms for "sword"

Line 14, *næs in*; that is, *ne ealles in*, "not at all, by no means, absolutely not in."

Lines 16-18, *on fell...on fláesc...on blód...on lið scoten*; "in your skin...in your flesh...in your blood (ie with a deep wound)...in a limb (or member, or organ)"; the potential injuries, or penetrations, are listed in order of gravity.

Lines 19-20, *esa gescot...ylfa gescot....hægtessan gescot*; a taxonomy of malign powers, the gods, the elves (both supernatural), and human witches; *ésa* and *ylfa* are genitive plurals of *ós* and *ælf*, but *hægtessan* is the genitive singular of *hægtes[se]*, "a witch". So, "if the shot came from the gods, the elves, or a witch". Note that *gescot* in these lines is a noun, not a past participle (which would be *scoten*, see lines 16-18)

Line 20, *ic wille þin helpan*; *helpan*, as in "help you", takes the genitive, *þín*, of the personal pronoun. See also lines 22, 24

Line 21, *þis þe to bote esa gescotes*; the construction reads "this [is] to thee for a cure of the gods' shot". The many senses of *bót* in Anglo-Saxon include "remedy", "relief", "recompense", "amends", "atonement". The idiom *to bóte* in the sense of later English *to boot* - "moreover" - is also found in Old English.

Line 24, *fleoh þær on fyrgenheafde*: read *fléoh* as imperative sing. Of *fléogan*, "fly, fly away" - or, with the imputation of a foe defeated, "flee"; *fyrgenheafde*, "to the mountain-top (dat. sing of *fyrgenhéafod*; emended from *firen-* "?source of strife?, "?origin of the evil?")

6. *Beowulf,* lines 855b - 874: Poetry in praise

Here is Old English verse in the classical style. For a translator, this passage presents few problems, apart from the *word oþer fand soþe gebunden* of lines 879-80, a crux discussed briefly in chapter 1, p.13 The text is that of ASPR/ *Labyrinth* but in this instance with a punctuation supplied, or "applied", as a pointer to phrasing and sentence-structure.

Ðær wæs Beowulfes	855
mærðo mæned. Monig oft gecwæð	
þætte suð ne norð, be sæm tweonum,	
ofer eormengrund, oþer nænig	
under swegles begong selra nære	
rondhæbbendra rices wyrðra;	860
ne hie huru winedrihten wiht ne logon	
glædne hroðgar, ac þæt wæs god cyning.	
Hwilum heaþorofe hleapan leton,	
on geflit faran, fealwe mearas	
ðær him foldwegas fægere þuhton	865
cystum cuðe. Hwilum cyninges þegn,	
guma gilphlæden, gidda gemyndig,	
se þe ealfela ealdgesegna	
worn gemunde, word oþer fand	
soþe gebunden. Secg eft ongan	870
sið Beowulfes snyttrum styrian,	
ond on sped wræcan spel gerade,	
wordum wrixlan; welhwylc gecwæð	
þæt he from Sigemunde secgan hyrde.	

Notes

Lines 857-859, *suþ ne norþ...under swegles begong*. Here all the set phrases, worn cliches of location, each good to fill a half-line now and then, are assembled to create a trope of universality: in every quarter, says the poet, from sea to sea, over all the land, under all the heavens...

Lines 858-60. Not that there weren't never nobody like Beowulf; a double negative, for emphasis, is respectable in Old English. Take *nænig* as *ne ænig*, "not any", "none"; *náere* as *ne wáere*, "was not", or rather, "were not", *wáere* being 3rd sing. preterite subjunctive of *wesan*. Then in outline, from 856: "Many declared that under heaven there was no other hero, no better man, none worthier of rule For the subjunctive, *wáere*, in a clause of reported speech, cp. *Beowulf 3180-81, cwædon þæt he wære wyruldcyninga / monna mildust ...etc.*

Note the genitive plurals in *sélra, rondhæbbendra, wyrþra*, usual with expressions of number or quantity; also with the substantive verb ("be") in identifying type, property, sort. Cf. The coastguard's challenge to the voyagers, *Beowulf*, line 237.........*Hwæt sindon ge searohæbbendra.....?* - "What are you, men-at-arms...?

Line 859, *rondhæbbend*, a recurrent figure for "warrior" - indeed, more of a conventional synonym than a true kenning. Cp *lindhæbbend, searohæbbend, helmberend, æscberend, gárberend*.

Line 861, *ne...húru*, "nor, however", "nor yet"; *logon*, from *léogan*, "lie", but here in the sense "belie": "Nor yet did they in any way disparage their liege lord, the gracious Hrothgar, for he was a good king." The tribute recalls the judgement on Scyld, *Beowulf, 10*.

Lines 866-70 are summarily translated, with a dash of commentary, in chapter 1, p.13. To which add the following:

Line 870, *secg eft ongan*, translate *eft* as "then", or "presently".

Line 871, read *síð* in *sið Beowulfes* as "exploit"; *snyttrum* is dat.pl.of a noun *snyttru*, "wisdom, cleverness" - read it adverbially, as "deftly, cleverly, with skill"; *styrian*, primarily "stir", "move", here has the secondary meaning "tell". "Presently the man began a skilful telling of Beowulf's deeds".

Line 872, *on spéd* ["fluently"] *wræcan* ["devise"] *spel geráde* ["a poem"]. The meaning of the adjective *rad*, with or without the *ge-* prefix, is "straight", "direct". Clark Hall cites the phrase *geráde spræc* as meaning "prose" (ie "ordered speech"); then by inference *spel geráde* may be understood as "poem" (or "organised tale")

Line 873, *wordum wrixlan*, "to exchange words, ie "to converse" (again, Clark Hall is the voucher for this idiom); but the "conversation" in this instance is arguably a dialogue or colloquy of narratives, the Beowulf story and the Sigemund story.

II Wisdoms

7. *The Wanderer*, 62b-72, 106-15:
Counsel to survivors

       Swa þes middangeard   62
ealra dogra gehwæm   dreoseð ond falleð,
forþon ne mæg weorþan wis   wer, ær he age
wintra dæl in woruldrice.   Wita sceal geþyldig,
ne sceal no to hatheort   ne to hrædwyrde   65
ne sceal to wac wiga   ne to wanhydig,
ne to forht ne to fægen,   ne to feohgifre
ne næfre gielpes to georn,   ær he geare cunne.
Beorn sceal gebidan,   þonne he beot spriceð,   70
oþ þæt collenferð   cunne gearwe
hwider hreþra gehygd   hweorfan wille.

106-15

Eall is earfoðlic   eorðan rice,   106
onwendeð wyrda gesceaft   weorold under heofenum.
Her bið feoh læne,   her bið freond læne,
her bið mon læne,   her bið mæg læne,
eal ðis eorðan gesteal   idel weorþeð.   110
Swa cwæð snottor on mode,   gesæt him sundor æt rune.
Til bið se þe his treowe gehealdeþ,   ne sceal næfre his torn to rycene
beorn of his breostum acyþan,   nemþe he ær þa bote cunne,
eorl mid elne gefremman.   Wel bið þam þe him are seceð,
frofre to fæder on heofenum,   þær us eal seo fæstnung stondeð.   115

The text here reads with the ASPR, but the punctuation is my own preference. The two passages are from the second part of *The Wanderer*, in which "a wise man" ponders questions of blind fate and Christian duty. They are an outstanding example of how episodes of moral formulation - the so-called "maxims" - contribute to the shaping and structure of Old English poetic narrative.

Notes

Line 62b, *middangeard* - "the middle court", "the middle estate". Anglo-Saxon cosmology envisaged a three-tier universe, with Heaven and Hell at the extremes, and Earth between them. In the poem of *Genesis*, Paradise is described as lying "to the south and east" of Eden, Hell being "to the north and west".

Line 63, *ealra dogra gehwæm,* "each and every day", "with every day that passes"; *gehwáem* is dat. sing of the pronoun *gehwá*, "each one"; *ealra* and *dogra* are gen.pl., the latter of the noun *dógor*, "day". The literal rendering is thus "on each one of all days".

Lines 64-5, *ær he age wintra dæl in woruldrice*; *áge*, from *ágan*, "to own", is subjunctive, "ere he shall own"; *wintra dáel*, "[his] share of winters" (ie, years). The sentiment is perhaps not so much that men become wise with age - a commonplace, and a false one at that - as that a man cannot become wise until he has known the harsh trials of experience.

Lines 65-8, *wita sceal geþyldig*, etc. Here follows a tally of the qualities desirable in a wise man, only one of which (the first, *geþyldig*, "patient") is positively expressed. The rest are negative injunctions - "not *too* quick-tempered", "not *too* quick to speak", "not *too* easily influenced", "not *too* headstrong", etc., implying that it is in human nature to have these faults and that all a would-be-wise man can do is learn to know himself, and guard against them. Note that in these lines, *wita* alternates with *wiga*, "warrior"; the wise man is involved in the battle of living.

Line 68, *áer he géare cunne,* "before he knows for sure", "before he is wholly certain". But knows what? Is certain of what? Some understood object seems to be lurking here. One is supplied presently in Lines 70-72, *oððæt collenferð gearwe cunne / hwider hreþra gehygd hweorfan wille* "until the proud spirited man may know for certain where the heart's impulses are leading him" But line 68 might be simply translated as "before he truly knows himself". (Or even "before he knows what´s what")

Line 70, *collenferð*. This word, of obscure etymology, occurs quite often in OE, as a conventional epithet, meaning little more that "upstanding", "keen-spirited"; modern sporting slang would say "psyched-up" To be *collenferð* is a preliminary to action.

Line 71, *gehygd*. Commonly glossed as "thought, intention, mind, heart", in this context the sense seems closer to what Wordsworth calls the "motions" of the spirit - in the Latin phrase *motus animi*. Keeping emotion under restraint is the main point of this short sermon.

Line 107, *onwendeð wyrda gesceaft*. *Wyrd* in OE usage has diverse meanings and shades of meaning. Its etymological relationship is with *weorðan*, "to become", and its root-connection is with Latin *vertere*, "to turn, to change". Thus, along with the commonly apparent sense of "destiny", "fate", "fortune", *wyrd* carries an implication "change of destiny / fortune". *Wyrd* is the ordained course of events, but in some cases the ordinance may be changed. So in this line, "destiny's ordinance changes". In some cases, however, the ordinance is absolute - see *Wanderer*, line 5, *wyrd bið ful aráed,* "[the man's] lot is fixed".

Lines 108-9, *her bið féoh láene,* etc. The similarity of these lines to strophes 76, 77 of the Norse *Havamál* is pointed out in chapter 3, p. 66. The word *féoh* in OE can mean "cattle", "goods and chattels", "property", or "riches in general". In this *Wanderer* context "riches" or "wealth" is probably the most relevant sense. The phrase *bið láene* emphasizes transitoriness, a process of change, "friends pass away", as opposed to the Norse *deyr,* the defining fact of "die". In line 109, *mon* and *máeg* are in complement, "man and kinsman", where *mon* possibly means "serving man", or perhaps taking *mon* as *mon[drihten],* "lord and kinsman".

Line 109, *ídel.* Not meaning "idle", or "unused", but rather "useless", "empty", "vain", with reference to the *gesteal,* the worldly edifice.

Line 110. *Sæt him sundor æt rúne* - "sat apart, taking counsel with himself". In OE, *sittan æt rúne* is peculiar to this context. The usual idiom, *sittan to rúne,* means to sit in counsel (or council) with others.

Lines 113. *Til bið se þe his tréowe gehealdeþ,* "Good is the man who keeps his faith"; note the parallel, two lines later (115), *Wel bið þam þe him áre séceð,* "It is well for him who looks for grace." "Faith" (or "trust") and "grace" are key words; the latter, *ar,* occurs in the first line of the poem, *áre gebídeð,* "looks for grace", and is repeated here again in the last line but one., *áre séceð,* "seeks for grace". It is to be found, however, not in "the paths of exile", but with the Father in heaven, *þær us eal seo fæstnung standeð* - "where for us all our stronghold stands" - security is in heaven, not in any "foundation" (*gesteal,* see line 110) on earth.

8. *The Fortunes of Men*

1-14; 21-26; 58-63; 80-84, 93-98:

Man proposes, God disposes

"The Fortunes of Men" (*Be monna wyrdum*) and "The Gifts of Men" (*Be monna cræftum*) are well-structured poems designed, certainly, as homilies. They deal essentially with the operations of *wyrd,* as a force inherent in human life and nature and as a power controlled and directed by God. Some parts of this poetic homily are examples of "bad *wyrd*"; others are of "good *wyrd*"; the piece ends with the assurance of divine dispensation

1-14
Ful oft þæt gegongeð mid godes meahtum,	1
þætte wer ond wif in woruld cennað	
bearn mid gebyrdum ond mid bleom gyrwað,	
tennaþ ond tætaþ, oþþæt seo tid cymeð,	
gegæð gearrimum, þæt þa geongan leomu,	5
liffæstan leoþu, geloden weorþað.	
Fergað swa ond feþað fæder ond modor,	
giefað ond gierwaþ. God ana wat	
hwæt him weaxendum winter bringeð	
Sumum þæt gegongeþ on geoguðfore	10
þæt se endestæf earfeðmecgum	
wealic weorþeð. Sceal hine wulf etan,	
har hæðstapa; hinsið þonne	
modor bimurneð Ne bið swylc monnes geweald.	14

21-26
Sum sceal on holte of hean beame	21
fiþerleas feallan; bið on flihte seþeah,	
laceð on lyfte, oþþæt lengre ne bið	
westem wudubeames þonne he on wyrtruman,	
sigeð sworcenferð, sawle bereafod,	25
fealleþ on foldan, feorð biþ on siþe.	

58-63
Sum sceal on geoguþe mid godes meahtum	58
his earfoðsiþ ealne forspildan,	
ond on yldo oft eadig weorþan,	60
wunian wyndagum ond welan þicgan,	
maþmas ond meodoful mægburge on,	
þæs þe ænig fira mæge forð gehealdan.	

178

80-84

Sum sceal mid hearpan   æt his hlafordes   80
fotum sittan,   feoh þicgan,
ond a snellice   snære wræstan,
lætan scralletan   sceacol, se þe hleapeð,
nægl neomægende; bið him neod micel.

93-98

Swa wrætlice   weoroda nergend   93
geond middangeard   monna cræftas
sceop ond scyrede   ond gesceapo ferede   95
æghwylcum on eorþan   eormencynnes.
Forþon him nu ealles þonc   æghwa secge,
þæs þe he for his miltsum   monnum scrifeð.   98

Notes

Line 3. The phrases *mid gebyrdum* and *mid bléowum* are not co-ordinates. This is a child *mid gebyrdum* (= "of high birth", "with the advantages of rank") His parents bring him up in luxury (*gyrwað mid bléoum*, literally "dress him in colours")

Lines 5-6. Observe the half-lines in parallel, *séo tíd cymeþ / gegæð géarrímum*, both dependent on *oððæt*, then *geongan limu / liffæstan leoðu*, joint subjects of *geloden weorþað*. *Limu* and *leoþu* are near-synonymous, *leoþu* being the nom.pl of *liþ*, "limb, member, joint"; *geloden* is the past participle of *léodan*, meaning, in this poetic context, "to grow strong", "to wax".

Line 9, *him weaxendum winter*. Read *winter* as nom.pl, take *him weaxendum* together, "him growing", a somewhat Latinate construction.

Line 10, *sumum*...etc. This line is the first of the long "*sum*-series" ("this one...this one...these...those....in the fashion of Latin *hic* and *ille*). This indefinite pronoun is declinable; here in line 10 it is in the dative sing, "for one".

Line 12, *sceal hine wulf etan*, "the/a wolf shall eat him". Understand *hine* as the personal correlate of the impersonal *sum* in line 10; or take it as a separate theme - either "for one, the end of life is miserable;him the wolf shall eat", or "for this one life ends in wretched suffering; this one the wolf shall eat."

Line 14, *Ne bið swylc monnes geweald*: "such things are not in man's power" - ie his power to anticipate or prevent. In these cases, *wyrd* is fixed.

Lines 21-27. For a translation of these, see chapter 1, p.24. In line 22, *fiþerléas* may be rendered "without feathers", as in the translation, but a more accurate reading would be "wingless". A feather is *feþer*, a wing *fiþer*.

Line 24, *westem* = *wæstm*, "growth", "increase", "produce"

Line 25, *sworcenferð*, "dark-spirited"; *sworcen*, past participle of *sweorcan*, "to grow dark, to become obscured"; but also, "to be troubled", "to be sad". This is the last darkness, the ultimate trouble - this is blackout.

Line 27, *on síðe*, "on his journey". In this, as in many other contexts, *síð* and its compounds refer to the soul's final journey; eg *hinsíþ*, "departure hence" (this poem, line 14).

Lines 58-63 preach the point that with God's help a man may recover from misfortunes of his own making and recover his destiny.

Line 59, *earfoðsíþ*, another kind of *síþ*, man's travels in travails; *forspildan*, "waste", "lose", "let go for nothing" - "he lets the toils and pains of growing up all go to waste".

Line 61, *þicgan*, "to receive"; also "partake of", "taste", "consume", "eat"; see the note on *áþecgan* in *Wulf and Eadwacer*. He "dwells in joyous days and tastes prosperity". But for *þicgan* as plain "receive", see line 81, on the harper, *féoh þicgan*, "take his pay".

Line 62, *máegburge on*: literally, "in the kinsman cities", ie among his own people. There is a comparable formulation in *The Husband's Message*, where the lovers are described as delighting in each other's company *on meduburgum*, "in the mead-boroughs", ie civil society.

Line 63, *þæs [þe]*, "the more [than]", *forð*, "thenceforward": "the more [wealth] than any man thereafter might possess".

Lines 80-84, translated in chapter 1, p.9, with a note at Postscripts, *Happy Harpist* p.139. Add here, that the unusual form *néomegende* is the present participle of a verb *néomian*, glossed in Clark Hall as "to sound sweetly"

Lines 93-98 summarise the message of the homily (there is a comparable summary at lines 64-67, not cited here), which is that God alone dispenses the fortunes of men the world over

Line 93, *wráetlice*, "curiously". God works in a mysterious way; an intricate design or pattern may be described as *wráetlic*; *weoroda nergend*, the Saviour of mankind. It is God's saving function that is emphasised in these closing lines of a poem on fates, fortunes, and destinies.

Line 94, *cræftas*; means primarily "gifts", "talents", "skills", as in the title of the companion-poem, *Be monna cræftum*; but here may nevertheless be rendered "fortunes".

Lines 97-98. The poem closes on a liturgical formula, of the kind "now to God may thanks be given". *Ealles* = "wholly"; *ealles þonc* = "thanks in full", "all thanks"; *áeghwá* = "all men", "people everywhere"; *secge*, subjunctive, "let say"; *þæs þe* = "since", "because", "for that"; *fore his miltsum* = "for his mercies' sake"; *monnum scrífeð*, = "cares for men" "is troubled on their account", or, at a venture, "hears their confessions" ("shrives" them). So, "Now let each one of us give due thanks to God, since for his mercies' sake he has regard to men, and pardons their sins". The sentiment is that of Psalm 106: "O give thanks unto the Lord, for he is good: for his mercy endureth for ever".

9. The Exeter Maxims, 93-106
Good wives and gadabouts

Chapter 1, p.23, cites what are probably the best-known lines from the Exeter Maxims, the charming sketch of the Frisian wife and her seafaring man. Those lines, however, are part of a longer passage, a minor homily on wifeliness; the good woman keeps house and attends to her duties, the hussy makes the most of her husband's absence. The first line-and-a-half of the following extract may at first seem to have no connection with the rest. The connection lies, after the usual manner of the *Maxims*, in declaring the properties of "how it ought to be". A properly built ship ought to be riveted; a properly-made shield, even of the lightest kind, ought to be bound at the rim, to prevent splitting. So, then, a wife....

```
Scip sceal genægled,   scyld gebunden,              93
leoht linden bord,   leof wilcuma
Frysan wife  þonne flota stondeð;                   95
biþ his ceol cumen   ond hyre ceorl to ham,
agen ætgeofa,   ond heo hine in laðaþ,
wæscaþ his warig hrægl,   ond him syleþ wæde niwe,
liþ him on londe   þæs his lufu bædeð.
Wif sceal wiþ wer wære gehealdan, oft hi mon wommum belihð;  100
fela bið fæsthydigra,   fela bið fyrwetgeornra,
freoð hy fremde monnan,   þonne se oþer feor gewiteþ.
Lida biþ longe on siþe;   a mon sceal seþeah leofes wenan,
gebidan þæs he gebædan ne mæg.   Hwonne him eft gebyre weorðe,
ham cymeð, gif he hal leofað,   nemne him holm gestyreð,   105
mere hafað mundum   mægðegsan wyn.
```

Notes

Line 98, *hrægl*: in the heroic vocabulary, *hrægl* is commonly a synonym for body-armour, eg ring-mail. Here, however, the sense is less exalted. The good wife washes her man's work-shirt.

Line 100, *wáere gehealdan*, "keep faith with", "be true to"; *hi mon wommum beliho*, "she wickedly deceives her man"; *hi = héo, wommum* (from *wóhmum*) dat.pl, used adverbially, of the adj *wóh*, "wicked, wrongful, deceitful"; *beliho*, from *[be]léogan*, "belie, betray". In an earlier passage (at line 63) the poet declares, *widgongol wif word gespringeð, oft hy mon wommum beliho*, "a gadding wife gives rise to talk....etc".

Line 101, *fæsthýdig...fyrwetgeorn*; the opposed characteristics are "constant" and "fickle", from "single-minded" and "inquisitive".

Line 102, *fréoð*, "cherishes", from *freoðan (friðian)*. She "takes up with", or "sets up house with", another.

Line 103, "The sailor is a long time at sea, yet a man will always have hopes of his love, desiring [*gebidan*] what he cannot command [*gebædan*]

Line 104, *eft gebyre weorþe*, "becomes a husband again", from *gebúr*, "farmer", "freeholder"; that is, in opposition to *lída*, he stops being a seaman and becomes a landlubber.

Lines 105-6, Take as parallel, depending on *nemne*, "unless", the clauses *him holm gestyreð* and *mere hafað mundum* - "unless the sea claims him, the ocean takes a hand" In line 106, *máegðegesan wyn* is in parallel with *holm* and *mere*, but the meaning of *máegðegesa* is dubious. Clark Hall suggests "viking"; thus, "unless the sea claims him, the ocean, the viking's joy, takes a hand."

10. *The Whale,* 49b-70:
The mortal desires of the flesh

Much of this homily is translated, with incidental commentary, in chapter 4; for the passage below, see p.88. The tale is of the whale's sweet breath and the gullibility of mortal fish (or fishy mortals).

                He hafað oþre gecynd,
wæterþisa wlonc,   wrætlicran gien   50
þonne him on holme   hungor bysgað,
ond þonne aglæcan   ætes lysteþ,
ðonne se mereweard   muð ontyneð,
wide weleras,   cymeð wynsum stenc
of his innoþe,   þætte oþre þurh þone,   55
sæfisca cynn,   beswicen weorðaþ,
swimmaþ sundhwate   þær se swete stenc
ut gewiteð. Hi þær in farað
unware weorude, oððæt se wida ceafl
gefylled bið,   þonne færinga   60
ymbe þa herehuþe   hlemmeð togædre
grimme goman. Swa bið gumena gehwam,
se þe oftost his   unwærlice
on þæs lænan tid   lif bisceawað,
læteþ hine beswican   þurh swetne stenc,   65
leasne willan,   þæt he bið leahtrum fah
wið wuldorcyning. Him se awyrgda ongean
æfter hinsiþe helle   ontyneþ,
þam þe leaslice   lices wynne
ofer ferhtgereaht   fremedon on unræd   70

Notes

Line 50, *wráetlicra[n]*, "more wondrous". But see *The Fortunes of Men*, line 93 and note, where the rendering "curiously", or "intricately" is suggested for the adverb *wrætlice*. The same meaning may apply here: *He hafað oþre gecynd....wrætlicran gien* - "He has another way, yet more curious..." He gets, in Alice's phrase, curiouser and curiouser.

Lines 51, 53, *þonne...ðonne*; coordinating adverbs, "when...then"; "when he feels hunger, then the sea-beast opens his mouth."

Lines 55b-56a, *þæt oþre þurh þone, sæfisca cynn*, a Latinate construction.; the word-order is *þæt þurh þone, oþre sæfisca cynn*, "so that as a result, other kinds of fish, etc."

Line 59, *weorud[e]*. The *werod* is the shoal of fish, designated in a term usually reserved for a martial/heroic company. This is a further example of the poem's repeated "re-grading" of the vocabulary, in words like *duguð, hæleþ, eorlas*.

Lines 63-4, *his unwærlice on þæs lænan tid lif besceawað*. More quasi-Latin or semi-Anglo Saxon. Translate as though the order were *unwáerlice bescéawað his líf on þæs láenan tíd*.

Line 65-6, *læteð hine beswican þurh swetne stenc, leasne willan*. A similar patchwork. Unpick in this order *láeteð léasne willan beswícan hine, þurh swétne stenc*.

Line 66, *leahtrum fáh*, "spotted/stained/blemished/blotched with sins". The adjective *fáh* (or *fág*) is one that takes its fair-or-foul colouring from its context. A damascened sword-blade is *fáh*, "adorned", or "gleaming"; a lost soul is *fáh*, "besmirched".

Lines 69-70 *lices wynne ofer ferhtgereaht fremedon on unræd*. *Líces wynne*, "the pleasures of the flesh"; *ferhtgereaht* (*ferhðgeriht*) "the law of the spirit"; *on unráed*, "in folly". "In their folly they preferred the pleasures of the flesh above the law of the spirit." The adjective from *unráed, unráedig*, is well known as Æþelred's epithet - though in his case it signifies not so much "foolish" - and certainly not "unready" - as "ill-advised, ill-counselled", or possibly "unadvised". On *ráed*, see below, note on *Beowulf*, 1760.

11. *Beowulf,* 1758-68: The mortal pride of war

This little sermon, preached by the good King Hrothgar in friendly admonition to a winsomely warlike Beowulf, is clearly a Christian scribe's intrusion upon the text. Old Germanic heroes enjoy fighting, and can make a whole moral meal of it; but here the newly-triumphant champion is urged to consider the ways of peace. In the line numbering, 1758 > 58, etc.

<pre>
Bebeorh þe þone bealonið,   Beowulf leofa,   58
secg betsta,   ond þe þæt selre geceos,
ece rædas;   oferhyda ne gym,   60
mære cempa. Nu is þines mægnes blæd
ane hwile. Eft sona bið
þæt þec adl oððe ecg   eafoþes getwæfeð,
oððe fyres feng,   oððe flodes wylm,
oððe atol yldo,   oððe eagena bearhtm   65
forsiteð ond forsworceð;   semninga bið
þæt ðec, dryhtguma,   deað oferswyðeð
</pre>

Notes

Line 58: *Bebeorh þe....* "shield yourself" [from]" "be on your guard [against]". The prefix *be-* here has intensive force ("*do* be on your guard"); the verb *beorgan* constructs with a dative of person (*þe*, "thee") and an accusative of object, *þone bealonið*, "the urge to savagery". It is as though Hrothgar were gently reproving Beowulf for taking too much pleasure in his recent work.

Line 60 *éce ráedas,* "eternal counsels", ie divine guidance - a better resort, Hrothgar says, than the exultant zeal of *bealoníð*.

Line 60, *oferhýd = oferhygd,* "pride, arrogance."; *ne gym* (from *gíeman*), "have no regard for".

Line 63 (also 68), *þec*, older accusative of *þú*, direct object of *forsiteð, forsworceð* (and *oferswýðeð*)

Lines 63...65, *adl oððe ecg...oððe atol yldo*. There is a formulaic echo of this in *The Seafarer, adl oððe yldo oððe ecghete*. Line 63, *eafoð*, "power", "might", synonymous with *mægen* in Line 61.

Lines 67-68, *forsiteþ, forsworceþ, oferswyðeð,* "will beset [thee], darken [the brightness of the eye]; death will overpower" [thee]; the prefixes *for* and *ofer* have intensifying force - the shutdown will be total.

Line 68, *dryhtguma,* "warrior"; with such emphasis as to imply "great soldier though you are".

III. Elegies

12. *Wulf and Eadwacer*: A fenland tragedy

This poem is translated and discussed at some length in chapter 3, pp.54-56. It was at one time assumed to be a riddle - the first of the Exeter riddles - but its secretiveness, its desperate privacy, could never be the riddling talk of someone deliberately aiming at deception. It is the language of one who talks to herself and for herself, passionately, yet hardly caring who might overhear her. The style lacks the formal procedure of "establishment" poetry; it suggests, rather, the spoken tongue, allusively creating the poetry that might be, the latent figure, the lost idiom. This is a piece that has attracted increasing interest during recent decades - and with that, some variety of interpretation and translation.

Leodum is minum swylce him mon lac gife,	1
willað hy hine aþecgan, gif he on þreat cymeð.	
Ungelic is us.	
Wulf is on iege, ic on oþerre.	
Fæst is þæt eglond, fenne biworpen.	5
Sindon wælhreowe weras on iege,	
willað hy hine aþecgan, gif he on þreat cymeð.	
Ungelic is us.	
Wulfes ic mines widlastum wenum dogode;	
þonne hit wæs renig weder ond ic reotugu sæt,	10
þonne mec se beaducafa bogum bilegde,	
wæs me wyn to þon, wæs me hwæþre eac lað.	
Wulf, min Wulf, wena me þine	
seoce gedydon, þine seldcymas,	
murnende mod, nalæs meteliste.	15
Gehyrest þu, Eadwacer? Uncerne earne hwelp	
bireð wulf to wuda.	
Þæt mon eaþe tosliteð þætte næfre gesomnad wæs,	
uncer giedd geador.	

Notes

Line 2, *on þréat*. There are two ways of taking this: i), as *cymeð / on þreat* an adverbial phrase, with the meaning "with a troop", "in force", or in the modern slang phrase, "team-handed", or ii),.*cymeð on / þreat* "comes upon", "comes across a troop" - he being single-handed. The first seems more convincing as Anglo-Saxon idiom; the second more consistent with the implied narrative of the poem, as suggested on p.55.

Line 6, *fæst is þæt eglond..* The translation on page 54 takes *fæst* as an adjective, "firm", in opposition to *fenn* at the end of the line. Another possibility, however, adopted by some translators, is that *fæst* is a noun, = *fæsten*, "fortification". Then: "the island is a stronghold, begirt by fen".

Line 9, *Wulfes ic mines widlastum wenum dogode*. This line resists convincing translation, mainly because it turns on a little-attested verb, *dogian*, conjecturally meaning "endure, suffer, undergo", apparently governing the dative case, in *wénum* primarily, then "comitatively" in *widlástum*. The suggested order would be: "*ic dogode*, "I endured", "pined in" *wénum*, "hopes", *widlástum* "for the long journeys" *Wulfes mines* ("of my Wulf") = "I fretted in longing for my Wulf to make his long journey ". This is arguable from the data, but whether the data are arguable in the first place is another matter.

Lines 10-11 *þonne...þonne*. The editorial punctuation, with a full stop after *dogode* at the end of line 9, affects the interpretation of this part of the poem. If there were no full stop there, the sense would run on through line 10, with a stop at the end: "I endured in hope when (=while) it rained and I sat weeping". If the text is taken as printed above, then *þonne...þonne* is a coordinating construction, "when...then": "when it was raining and I sat weeping, then the bold captain came."; OR *þonne* and *þonne* are a sequence- "then it rained and I sat there howling, and then the bold captain...etc. The question is, reader, what is the authentic rhythm of her speech?

Line 10. *reotugu*, nom.sing.fem of *reotig*. "Mournful", "tearful", etc may be inadequate renderings - too genteel, too ladylike - for this forlorn condition. She sits boo-hooing, she wails. The related verb is *reotan* - cp. Swedish *ryta*, "to shout, cry out, bawl".

Line 11, *bógum*, "in his arms". It is suggested by some commentators (eg by Anne Klinck, in *The Old English Elegies,* Montreal, 1992) that *bóg* denotes in its primary sense the shoulder and forearm of an animal. This might imply that Eadwacer "mounts" rather than kindly "embraces" the poor woman. But there is some play with "animal" connotations elsewhere in the poem - eg the pun on "Wulf – wolf", the reference to the child as a "whelp" (line 16).

Line 12, *to þon*. However delicately we may translate it, or avoid translating it in this sensitive context, *to þon* signifies "to an extent"; and what she says of Eadwacer's embrace is "I loved it in a way, and yet I loathed it."

Lines 13-14. In these lines, two phrases, , *wéna me þíne* and *þíne seldcymas* are the parallel subjects of the predicate *séoce gedydon*. In these two instances, *þíne* has different grammatical functions. In one, it is the dative of the pronoun *þú*, eg "my longing for you"; in the other it is the nom.pl of the pronominal adjective, *þín,* as in "your rare visits".

Line 16, *earne.* So the ASPR. Most editors amend to *eargne* (*earg*, "wretched = vile") or *earmne* (*earm,* "wretched = poor, pitiful").How does she feel about her child? Is she sorry for the poor little thing? Or does she recoil from it, the reminder of a repulsive "love"?

Line 18, *giedd* - "song", yes, or "tale", but with irony - "so much for us, Eadwacer; end of story". Note, by the way, that *uncer* is the dual form of the possessive *úre*. She is talking about the two of them, she and Eadwacer.

13. The Wife's Lament, 21-41

Possibly because of its curriculum status in most college English Departments, *The Wife's Lament* is a much-discussed poem, one that has prompted many articles and numerous web-pages, with such a diversity of conjectures and preferred scenarios - feminist, fantasist, homoerotic (the gay's lament) - as to suggest, in some instances, the triumph of creative accounting over philological fact. The pathos of the following passage, at least, is not controversial.

```
Bliþe gebæro    ful oft wit beotedan                    21
þæt unc ne gedælde    nemne deað ana
owiht elles;    eft is þæt onhworfen,
is nu    swa hit no wære
freondscipe uncer. Sceal ic feor ge neah                25
mines felaleofan    fæhðu dreogan.
Heht mec mon wunian    on wuda bearwe,
under actreo    in þæm eorðscræfe.
Eald is þes eorðsele,    eal ic eom oflongad,
sindon dena dimme,    duna uphea,                       30
bitre burgtunas,    brerum beweaxne,
wic wynna leas. Ful oft mec her wraþe begeat
fromsiþ frean.    Frynd sind on eorþan,
leofe lifgende,    leger weardiað,
þonne ic on uhtan    ana gonge                          35
under actreo    geond þas eorðscrafu.
Þær ic sittan mot    sumorlangne dæg,
þær ic wepan mæg    mine wræcsiþas,
earfoþa fela;    forþon ic æfre ne mæg
þære modceare    minre gerestan,                        40
ne ealles þæs longaþes    þe mec on þissum life begeat.
```

Notes

Line 21, *Bliþe gebæro*, etc; *gebáer* suggests a certain restraint, a "bearing" towards each other consistent with the usual warmth of *fréondscipe*. It may be implied that they are lovers behaving discreetly; on the other hand, *fréondscipe* occurs elewhere in the sense "conjugal love".

Lines 21, 22. Note the dual forms of personal pronouns, *wit*, "we two", *unc* "us two". So also in line 25, *fréondscipe uncer*, "the love we two had".

Lines 22-3, *þæt unc ne gedælde nemne deaþ ana owiht elles*. Take *ne* with *owiht* and make "nowt", or "naught" of it. Then, [we vowed] "that naught else but death alone should separate us"; *gedáelde* is pret.subjunctive.

Line 24. The *Labyrinth* reading, as shown above makes a metrically defective line; it is metrical only as a half-line, *is nu swa hit no wære*. On *swá hit nó wáere*, see the comment, below, at lines 95b-96 of *The Wanderer*.

Lines 25-6, *sceal ic feor ge néah*. Far or near, near or far - render "wherever I am". "Wherever I am I must suffer the feuds of my dearly beloved" - meaning that she must bear the brunt of his quarrels: whether this signifies being blamed *along with* him, or being held responsible for his plight (by the vindictive kinsfolk), or even held to blame by the man himself.

Line 31, *bittre burhtúnas*, in our translation (chapter 3, pp.56-57) "sullen townships". A *burhtún* (as in names like "Burton", "Bourton") should be a settlement, within an enclosure. Some translators read it as meaning the enclosing hedges or palisades, which are *bitre* - "sharp, cutting", from the overgrowing briars.

Lines 32b-33, *ful oft...fromsiþ frean*. The translation on p.56 reads "So often I rage against the absence of my lord", but the Anglo-Saxon text puts the process in reverse, the subject of the sentence being *fromsíþ fréan*, "my lord's absence", which *mec begéat*, "has seized me", *wráþe*, "wrathfully" - or "grievously". Thus a closer translation might be "So often has my lord´s absence deeply grieved me".

Lines 39-41. Tense: render *begéat* as a perfect, with the nuance "seize", "possess": "I may never have rest from my care, nor from all the yearning that has filled my life"; *módceare* is gen.sing.feminine, whence *þære*, *mínre*, and *longaþes* gen. sing masculine, hence *þæs* The verb *[ge]restan*, in the sense "rest from" takes a genitive.

14. *The Wanderer,* 73-96:
A vision of world's end

See Chapter 3, pp.63-65), for a translation of part of this passage from *The Wanderer*, with some commentary on the poem's general significance. This is indeed a "deep" poem; as with icebergs, its apparent surface is a mere fraction of what lies beneath. Any effort of description and annotation must therefore be regarded as exploratory.

```
Ongietan sceal gleaw hæle   hu gæstlic bið                    73
þonne ealre þisse worulde wela   weste stondeð,
swa nu missenlice   geond þisne middangeard                   75
winde biwaune   weallas stondaþ,
hrime behrorene,   hryðge þa ederas.
Woriað þa winsalo,   waldend licgað
dreame bidrorene,   duguþ eal gecrong
wlonc be wealle.   Sume wig fornom,                           80
ferede in forðwege,   sumne fugel oþbær
ofer heanne holm,   sumne se hara wulf
deaðe gedælde,   sumne dreorighleor
in eorðscræfe   eorl gehydde.
Yþde swa þisne eardgeard   ælda scyppend                      85
oþþæt burgwara   breahtma lease
eald enta geweorc   idlu stodon.
Se þonne þisne wealsteal   wise geþohte
ond þis deorce lif   deope geondþenceþ,
frod in ferðe,   feor oft gemon                               90
wælsleahta worn,   ond þas word acwið:
"Hwær cwom mearg? Hwær cwom mago? Hwær cwom maþþumgyfa?
Hwær cwom symbla gesetu?   Hwær sindon seledreamas?
Eala beorht bune! Eala byrnwiga!
Eala þeodnes þrym! Hu seo þrag gewat,                         95
genap under nihthelm,   swa heo no wære.
```

Notes

Line 73, *gæstlic* may be "ghostly" or even "ghastly", but more to the point would be "terrifying" The topic is the end of the world - not ghastly like London in the rush hour, but appalling, like the devastation of great cities.

Line 74, *ealre*. This is an emendation from *ealle*. The text so amended reads "the wealth of all this world"; with *ealle,* it might suggest "all the wealth of this world" - except that *wela* is nom.sing.masc. and *ealle* is acc.sing.fem. As Americans say, "go figure".

Line 76, *winde biwaune*, "buffeted by the wind"; *biwáune*, pres.particip.pl. of *biwáwan,* "to blow on".

Line 77, *hrime bihrorene*; *bihrorene,* past.particip.pl. of *+hréosan,* "fall". The *be-* prefix has a transitive effect - "befallen with frost", ie "covered with frost", "hoarfrosted". Compare this poem's line 48, where *hréosan* is not prefixed: *hréosan hrím and snáw, hagle gemenged,* [the wanderer sees] "frost and snow falling, mingled with hail".

Line 78, *woriaþ*, the usual reading, with the attributed meaning "crumble to pieces".Clark Hall lists this meaning under *worigan*, but at least two editors (T.M.Dunning and A.J.Bliss, 1969) assert that the central meaning of *wori[g]an* is "to wander",and reject as unattested the secondary meaning "crumble". The verb appropriately meaning "crumble" is, they suggest, *wonian* (listed in Clark Hall under *wanian,* "wane, diminish, dwindle, decay, etc").

Lines 80-84. The *sum* series. See the note on *The Fortunes of Men*, line 10. *Be monna wyrdum* and *Be monna cræftum* are poems, or addresses, constructed round the *sum-* device. The *Wanderer* passage is brief, but powerfully evocative; see p.64 and Postscripts, p.147 – "Those who hope for name and fame"

Lines 86-7 *oþþæt burgwara breahtma lease, eald enta geweorc, idlu stodon.* This is a tricky passage, all too easy to translate "until the cities, the ancient work of giants, stood empty, their revelry gone.". The problem is, however, that *burgwara* does not mean "cities", but is the gen.pl of *burgware,* "citizens" . One solution is to take *burgwara breahtma léase,* "devoid of the revelry of citizens" as a parenthetical phrase, between the subject of the clause, *eald enta geweorc,* and the predicate, *ídlu stódon*: "till those ancient works of the mighty, bereft of the revelry of their citizens, stood empty" (or "idle", or "useless").

Lines 92-3, *Hwaer cwom...?* That is, "what became of...?" The usual construction (for *ubi sunt*) reads *hwáer sindon...?,* but *hwáer c[w]om* is not unique.

Lines 94-5, *Eala...!* This is commonly rendered as "alas!", which, as to style, is almost as infelicitous as "woe is me!" or "lackaday!". The exclamation mark appears in most editions, but not all rueful expressions are exclamatory. This one is certainly rather more serious than "dear me" - but would a simple "invocative" O or Ah not serve? See the translation on p.65.

Line 97, *nihthelm* means "the shades of night", or "the cover of night", but it is tempting to translate literally, "the helm of night", perhaps because of a lurking association with the *tarnhelm* of Norse mythology, a helmet which, when worn, made the wearer invisible.

Line 97, *genáp...swá héo nó wáere*; compare, from *The Wife's Lament,* lines 23-24, *eft is þæt onhworfen, is nu swa hit no wære.* The *Wanderer* 's *héo = þrag, f.,* "time"; the Wife's *hit = þæt =* the promise (*béot,* n) *þæt unc ne gedælde...*"that nothing should part us".

15. *The Ruin,* 1-11; 25-37

These passages are translated in chapter 3, pp.68-69. The MS, in the Exeter Book, is badly marred, obscuring what was evidently a very fine elegiac poem. Some lines not cited here tell of hot springs and baths, obviously suggesting the Roman city of Bath; but to insist on a topography would be to deny the play of the poet's imagination. The style is "late" - at least from the second half of the tenth century. Note, for instance, the dynamic play of the internal rhymes.

```
Wrætlic is þes wealstan;    wyrde gebræcon,         1
burgstede burston,    brosnað enta geweorc.
Hrofas sind gehrorene,    hreorge torras,
hrungeat berofen    hrim on lime,
scearde scurbeorge    scorene, gedrorene,           5
ældo undereotone.    Eorðgrap hafað
waldend wyrhtan    forweorone, geleorene,
heardgripe hrusan    oþ hund cnea
werþeoda gewitan.    Oft þæs wag gebad
ræghar ond readfah    rice æfter oþrum              10
ofstonden under stormum; steap geap gedreas.


Crungon walo wide,    cwomon woldagas,              25
swylt eall fornom    secgrofra wera,
wurdon hyra wigsteal    westen staþolas,
brosnade burgsteall.    Betend crungon
hergas to hrusan.    Forþon þas hofu dreorgiað,
ond þæs teaforgeapa    tigelum sceadeð              30
hrostbeagas hrof.    Hryre wong gecrong
gebrocen to beorgum,    þær iu beorn monig
glædmod on goldbeorht    gleoma gefrætwed,
wlonc ond wingal    wighyrstum scan;
seah on sinc, on sylfor, on searogimmas,            35
on ead, on æht,    on eorcanstan,
on þas beorhtan burg    bradan rices.
```

Notes

Lines 1,2. *Labyrinth* punctuates with a semi-colon after *gebræcon*. It makes better sense to place one after the first half-line: *Wrætlic is þes wealstan; wyrde gebræcon, burgstede burston, brosnað enta geweorc.* "Wonderful is this stone-built wall; dire events have broken it, have destroyed the castle, the work of giants falls into ruin". Compare the first lines of the Cotton Tiberius *Gnomics* (*Maxims II*): *Ceastra beoð feorran gesyne / orðanc enta geweorc, þa þe on þysse eorðan sindon,/ wrætlic weallstana geweorc* The plural *wyrde* suggests that this is not the great *Wyrd*, "destiny", but the smaller *wyrd* of things that just so happen - the *wyrd* of Ecclesiastes' sentence, "time and chance happeneth to all".

Line 3, *hreorge* = *hréorige*, nom.pl.f., "ruined", "in ruins".

Line 4, *hrungeat*, most probably *hrung-geat*, a gate with "rungs", or bars; the great gate of the fortress, or city. *Lamentations, 2.9*: "Her gates are sunk into the ground; he hath destroyed and broken her bars."

Line 4, *hrím on líme* - see the same "painterly" detail in *Wanderer*, 76-7, *weallas stondað hríme behrorene*. "Frost" may be thought more likely to show in patches on the brickwork/stonework than on the *lím*, the mortar - but this is here for the sake of the rhyme, one of those chiming half-lines that occur throughout the poem.

Line 5, *sceard[e]*, adjective related to *scieran*, "to cleave, cut"; the past participle *scoren* occurs in the second half-line. *Scearde* agrees with *scúrbeorge*, nom.pl.f; the latter word is commonly translated "roofs", or in part-for-whole relationship, as "houses". The etymology identifies *scúrbeorg* as "a shelter from the weather".

Line 10, *ræghar ond readfah*: *ráeg* from *ragu*, lichen, + *hár*, "hoary"; *réadfáh* = "red-coloured,", "red-stained", perhaps from the nature of the building material, whether sandstone or brick; or, let us not overlook it, from the quality of the poet's visual imagination.

Line 11, *stéap géap gedréas* - another "chiming half-line", the chime here extending to the vowel of the verb (pret. of *dreéosan*, "fall"). So, "the tall wall is fallen". The meaning of *géap* here and in other contexts where buildings are described appears to be "wall", or rather "a stretch/expanse of wall"; in *Beowulf*, for example, Hrothgar's palace of Heorot is called *héah ond horngéap*, and *horngéap* is glossed as "broad between the gables". There, however, *géap* is an adjective; in this line from the *Ruin* it is a noun, or an adjective with nominal function. But see further *téoforgéap* at line 30, note below.

Line 25, *walo*, nom.pl of *wæl*, "the dead", or "dead in battle". Cp. *The Wanderer*, line 7, *wráþra wælsléahta*, "of fierce battles/cruel slaughters". This is the Norse *val-*, as in *valkyrjor*, "Valkyries", "choosers of the slain", and *valhöllr*, "Valhalla", "the hall of the slain". More prosaic is the recurrent *Chronicle* formula, *þa wearð micel wæl geslægen*, "a lot of people were killed".

Line 26, *swylt eall fornom secgrofra wera*: it might be possible to take *eall* as an adverb = "wholly", "entirely", but that would not explain how *forniman* comes to govern the genitive plural of the adjective *secgróf* and the noun *wer*. As an expression of number or quantity (like *sum, fela, monig*, etc), *eall* may take a genitive: so - "all of the brave men"

Line 27, *wígsteal(l)* = "ramparts". *Staþolas* = "foundations". The foundations of a rampart wall may be its "footings", or possibly its "buttresses" - in either event, its supporting structures. The words used to designate the architecture and plan of this ruined town suggest the elements of a "burhtun" as described in the Chronicle for 757 - the "Merton" episode, see chapter 2, p.29: centrally, the *burgsteall*, or *burgstede* - "steading", as in "homestead", "farmstead", but here the command centre, the "hall"; round about, the smaller dwellings, the *scúrbeorge*, called in the Merton episode (as also in *Beowulf*) the *buras*; enclosing the whole, the *wígsteall* (literally "war-site"), or in Merton simply the *burg*, the rampart, in which is found the *hrungeat*, the "barred gate", a somewhat more modest affair in the Merton episode, where it is simply *þa duru*, "the door(s)". Though the poet may allowably claim to be describing the *eald enta geweorc*, its details look a good deal like those of the kind of "borough" he must have known.

Line29, *dreorigiað*, from *dréorigian*, a denominative verb, from *dréorig*, "sad, melancholy, dismal, etc" Not "to sadden", but "to grow sad", "to become dismal". An example of an "inchoative" sense; cp. the similar instance of *woriað* at *Wanderer*, line 78 (or *woniað*, see note).

Line 30, *teaforgeapa*: *téafor* = red, or vermilion, or purple; for *géap*, see note 11 above. Here *téaforgéapa*, "red" + "broad", is apparently an adjective, declined weak, after *þæs* = *þes*, modifying the noun *hrof*. Translate in the order *þes teaforgeapa hrof sceadeþ tigelum hrostbeages*, "the broad red roof (or "the broad red span of the roof") sheds its tiles from the supporting timbers". For the dative (*tigelum*) as object of a verb denoting consequence, effect, etc, compare the *fætum befeallan* of Beowulf 2255-56, *Sceal se hearda helm hyrsted gold fætum befeallan.* See note below, on passage 16

Line 31, *hrostbeages*, genitive of *hróstbéag*, "roof-timbers", "beams".

Line 31, *hryre wong gecrong* : *cringan*, "to die", commonly has the nuance "to fall in battle"; see *Wanderer*, lines 79-80, *duguþ eal gecrong, wlonc bi wealle*. In the *Ruin*, it is the noble city itself, or its site (*wong*, "field, place", cp. Norse *vangr*) that is laid low: "the ground sank down in death"

Line 32, *gebrocen to beorgum* is from *beorg*, in the sense (assumed for this context) of "mound", "burial place". Then *gebrócen to beorgum* may mean "broken down, reduced, to a graveyard" For *beorg* in the sense of "barrow", see *Beowulf*, line 3156 (in extract 22 below, p.228)

16. *Beowulf,* 2247-2266:   The fall of pride

This passage is translated in chapter 3, p.71. The text follows the ASPR/ *Labyrinth,* except for the punctuation, which I have modified. In the line numbering, 2247 > 47, etc.

>Heald þu nu, hruse,   nu hæleþ ne moston,   47
>eorla æhte. Hwæt, hyt ær on ðe
>gode begeaton.   Guðdeað fornam,
>feorhbealo frecne,   fyra gehwylcne   50
>leoda minra,   þara þe þis lif ofgeaf;
>gesawon seledream. Ic nah hwa sweord wege,
>oððe feormie   fæted wæge,
>dryncfæt deore; duguð ellor sceoc.
>Sceal se hearda helm   hyrsted golde   55
>fætum befeallan;   feormynd swefað,
>þa þe beadogriman   bywan sceoldon,
>ge swylce herepad,   sio æt hilde gebad
>ofer borde gebræc   bite irena   60
>brosnað æfter beorne.   Ne mæg byrnan hring
>æfter wigfruman   wide feran
>hæleþum be healfe.   Næs hearpan wyn,
>gomen gleobeames,   ne god hafoc
>geond sæl swingeð,   ne swifta mearh   65
>burhstede beateð.   Bealocwealm hafað
>fela feorhcynna   forð onsended.

Notes

Line 47, *ne moston*, that is "may not", with the implication "may no longer".

Line 49, *góde*, pl, "good men"

Line 50, *feorhbealo frecne*, "baleful, deadly evil" But it is always a little difficult to tease out the particular meaning, literal or affective, of the *bealo-* compounds, recurrent in heroic poetry, eg *bealoníþ, bealocwealm*. The same is true of other heroic nouns, eg those compounded on *heoro-* or *beado-*.

Lines 50-52. [*Guðdeað fornam*] *fyra gehwylcne leoda minra þara ðe þis lif ofgeaf, gesawon seledream*. The sense is clear as far as *ofgeaf*: "[Death in battle took] each one of my people who quit this life." On the genitives *fyra , léoda mínra, þára*, after *gehwylc*, see the note on the *Ruin*, line 26. After *ofgeaf*, we might punctuate with a full stop or a semicolon, making *gesáwon seledréam* a free-standing clause (as in the translation on p.70); or it can be taken in tandem with *þis líf ofgeaf*, "those who departed this life, who had seen ("known") all the joys of the hall". The rendering on p.70, "They had their feasts and have seen the end of them", is somewhat free, but (I hope) true to the sense of the text.

Line 52, *ic ná*, from *ne-ágan > nágan*, "not to own, not to have". Here *ic náh hwá sweord wege*, literally "I have not who might wield a sword", is a type of existential construction, "There is no one to wield a sword". (So in modern English, "I have no friends who might help me" = "There are no friends to help me")

Line 53, *feormie*, subj, from *feormian*, to polish. This is the generally accepted reading, but some scholars have objected to it on palaeographical grounds, and have suggested the emendation *fægrie*, from *fægrian*, in the sense "to adorn". (It otherwise has an "inchoative" meaning - see the *Ruin*, line 29 - "to become beautiful")

Line 53, *fáeted wáege*. A *fáet* is an embossed dish, or bowl; the word also means an ornament, of the kind seen in the form of embossed rectangular plates on the replica of the Sutton Hoo helmet. The *fáeted wáeg* is then an ornamental (or ornamented) chalice. See further below, line 56.

Line 54, *ellor sceoc*, "departed elsewhere".The sense is derived through *sceacan*, meaning basically "shake", then "move rapidly", then "move away".

Line 55-6, *sceal se hearda helm, hyrsted golde, fætum befeallan*: *hyrsted golde*, "encrusted with gold"- the *hyrste* are decorative "trappings" of the armour. *fáetum befeallan*, "lose (be deprived of) its ornaments".

Line 58, *ge swylce*, "in like manner", "in the same way that"

Line 59, *[gebád] bite írena*; "of irons" = "of swords". See the note on lines 10-11 of extract 5, above.

Line 60, 61, *æfter beorne, æfter wígfruman*, "after [the death of] the warrior"

Line 62., *hæleþum be healfe* "side by side with", or "shoulder to shoulder with". Here is a typical example of Anglo-Saxon ironic understatement, "nor may the mailcoat, after the warrior's death, go marching in the ranks".

Line 65, *burhstede béateþ*: translated "stamps in the yard", on p.70 on the assumption that the *stede* includes a "hall" and the space around it, the "yard". But "gallops through [or round] the town" may be the intended, and indeed sufficient, meaning.

IV Heroics

17. *The Battle of Brunanburh*, 57-73: After a victory

See chapter 2, pp.31-33 The text is from the *Anglo-Saxon Chronicle,* where it is the sole entry for the year 937. It exists, however, in four manuscript versions, one of which, via ASPR/*Labyrinth,* is represented below. This passage describes, in high heroic style, how the royal brothers, Æþelstan and Edmund, return victorious from their day's fighting.

Swylce þa gebroþer begen ætsamne,	57
cyning ond æþeling, cyþþe sohton,	
Westseaxna land, wiges hremige.	
Letan him behindan hræw bryttian	60
salowigpadan, þone sweartan hræfn,	
hyrnednebban, and þane hasewanpadan	
earn æftan hwit, æses brucan,	
grædigne guðhafoc and þæt græge deor,	
wulf on wealde. Ne wearð wæl mare	65
on þis eiglande æfre gieta	
folces gefylled beforan þissum	
sweordes ecgum, þæs þe us secgað bec,	
ealde uðwitan, siþþan eastan hider	
Engle ond Seaxe up becoman,	70
ofer brad brimu Brytene sohtan,	
wlance wigsmiþas, Wealas ofercoman,	
eorlas arhwate eard begeatan.	

Notes

The language of *Brunanburh* throughout the text of the poem as shown here is a casual scribal mixture of West Saxon and non-West Saxon (perhaps Anglian, or other dialectal) forms. There are one or two of these scribal deviants in the present passage.

Line 57, *Swilce*. A narrative sentence connector. Read as "likewise", or simply "too": "The brothers, too, king and prince together, returned to their people." The point of this "too", and this togetherness, is ironic; the preceding lines of the poem describe how the Vikings have fled in disorder to their base in Ireland. In narrative parallel to this, see an earlier passage, line 37, *Swilce þær eac se froda mid fleame com/ on his cyþþe norð, Constantinus*, "There, too, the old one, Constantine, took flight to his people in the north" Constantine has left his son dead on the battlefield - no kinsmanlike "togetherness" for him, then.

Line 57 *begen ætsamne*, "both together", or "united". The triumphal emphasis of this is noted above.

Line 59, *wiges hrémige*, lit. "boastful of their warfare", ie "rejoicing in their victory". There is, hower, a feeling of triumphalism ("exulting", "vaunting") in *hrémig* that goes some way beyond civilised rejoicing; also *wíg* may have the sense of "valour", or "prowess". It is a fair example of how a conventional phrase may be coloured by various meanings, or aspects of meaning.

Line 60, *bryttian*, "divide", as in "divide the spoils", the spoils in this case being the corpses divided among the attendant birds and beasts. There is something of a parody here, of the courtly treasure-giving after a won battle, when the *duguð* receive their dues from the *sinces brytta*. But Æthelstan and Edmund do not stay behind to do the division; they leave the beasts to manage that for themselves.

Line 62, *þane* [WS þone] *hasewanpadan*, an adjectival phrase, modifies *earn* in line 63. Metrically, *hasewanpádan* makes the half-line pattern (cp. *saluwigpadan* in line 61), of an A-type, / x / x, with a resolution of two short syllables in *hase(w)* [*hasu*] to make the first "lift". (NB *hasewa* is grammatically the "weak" form of *hasu*). The unaccented syllables *and þane* in 62 are an anacrusis.

Line 63, *earn æftan hwít* - "eagle-from-behind-white" = "the white-tailed eagle"

Line 65, ff, *ne wearþ wæl máre*....etc. On *wæl*, see the note on The Ruin, line 25. The common idiom of battlefield reportage is *wæl... sléan*, literally "to slay the slain", that is, "to do/make/inflict slaughter or carnage". In such phrases, *wæl* is usually quantified, as *micel wæl, þæt máest wael, ungemetlic wæl* - "great slaughter", "the greatest slaughter, "immense slaughter. A typical example is this, from the Chronicle entry for the year 851, recording a battle at *Ac-lea* (?Oakley?): *and þær þæt mæst wæl geslogon on hæþnum herige þe we secgan hierdon oþ þisne andwearne dæg*, "and there they inflicted the greatest slaughter on the heathen host that we have ever heard tell, until this present time".

The elegantly versified communiqué of Brunanburh is quite similar in style and content to the report from *Ac-lea*. Instead of *sléan*, however, it uses *fyllan*, "strike down, cut down, destroy, kill": *ne wearþ wæl máre [folces] gefylled*; in full, "from what books tell us, the writings of learned men of old, never yet on this island have more people perished by the sword, until this battle".

Line 70, *up becóman* (pret., 3rd plur), "arrived", more particularly "landed"; the particle *up*, in accounts of troop movements, etc., usually conveys the sense "up country", "inland".

Line 71, *ofer brád brimu*. Though the *Labyrinth* text has a comma after this half-line, an acceptable, perhaps rhetorically preferable, punctuation might be to make a full stop, before the triumphant emphasis of the final sentence.

Lines 70-73, *becóman, sóhtan, ofercóman, begeatan,* all 3rd plur pret (but note *sohton* in line 58).

18. *The Battle of Maldon,* 42-61; 309-319 : Two vows

Byrhnoth's speech of defiance is translated on p.35; Byrhtwold's affirmation of loyalty to the last, is reported on p.43. Both speeches are examples of the soldierly significance of *beot*.

Byrhtnoth's boast

Byrhtnoð maþelode, bord hafenode,   42
wand wæcne æsc,   wordum mælde
yrrum, and anræd   ageaf him andsware.
"Gehyrst þu, sælida,   hwæt þis folc segeþ?   45
Hi willaþ eow to gafole   garas syllan,
ættryne ord   and ealde swurd,
þa heregeatu   þe eow æt hilde ne deah.
Brimmanna boda,   abead eft ongean,
sege þinum leodum   miccle laþre spell,   50
þæt her stynt unforcuð   eorl mid his werode,
þe wile gealgean   eþel þysne
Æþelredes eard,   ealdres mines,
folc and foldan.   Feallan sceolon
hæþene æt hilde. To heanlic me þinceð   55
þæt ge mid urum sceattum   to scype gangan
unbefohtene,   nu ge þus feor hider
on urne eard   in becomon.
Ne sceole ge swa softe   sinc gegangan.
Us sceal ord ond ecg   ær geseman,   60
grim guðplega   ær we gafol syllon."

Byrhtwold's vow

Byrhtwold maþelode   bord hafenode
(se wæs eald geneat),   æsc acwehte,   310
he ful baldlice   beornas lærde
"Hige sceal þe heardra   heorte þe cenre
mod sceal þe mare   þe ure mægen litlað.
Her lið ure ealdor   eall forheawen,
god on greote. A mæg gnornian   315
se þe nu fram þis wigplegan   wendan þenceþ.
Ic eom frod feores   fram ic ne wille,
ac ic me be healfe   minum hlaforde,
be swa leofan men   licgan þence."

Notes

Line 42, *maþelode*: *maþelian* indicates formal speech, or declamation - "he proclaimed". The posture of the line is theatrical; note the gesture, repeated elsewhere, of the uplifted shield (and in the next line, the brandished spear); also the near-rhyme, *maþelode-hafenode*. In line 43, *máelde*, though still formal, is closer to a simple "he spoke".

Line 43, *æsc* - "ash", that is, "spear". In heroic diction, weapons are often designated by the material from which they are made - other examples being *lind*, "limewood" (shield), and *iren*, "iron" (sword) In other cases, the naming device is synechdoche (part for whole), as in *ord* (point, of sword or arrow) and *ecg* ("edge", ie of the sword-blade), cf line 63, *us sceal ord ond ecg ær geséman*; or some component property is cited, as in *bord*, for the flat of the shield, or *rond*, for its round shape.

Lines 43-44. The punctuation here is mine, enclosing the construction *wordum máelde yrrum (= ierrum)*, "spoke in angry words"; then, *ond ánráed, ageaf him andsware*, " and resolute, gave him his answer"; or more freely, make *ánráed* a transferred epithet - "speaking in angry words, gave him a resolute answer".

Line 46, *syllan (= sellan)*: not "sell", but "give, present, bestow", or simply "pay".

Line 47, *attryne ord*, "poisoned points" (from *attren*); but Byrhtnoth does not necessarily mean that the arrow-tips are actually poisoned, rather that they are painfully sharp In the poem of *Judith*, a kenning for "arrows" is *hildenæddran*", literally "battle-vipers" - the points are sharp as snake-bite. Byrhtnoth´s defiance is tipped with venomous feeling.

Line 47, *ealde swurd*: this is the sword as heirloom, so not "old swords", or even "well-used swords", but something closer to "ancestral swords". (Byrhtnoth himself is carrying one). Throughout this passage, B. speaks with aristocratic contempt for the opposing rabble. "Who d'you think you are dealing with?", his words imply. It is this same contempt that leads to his fatal error of allowing the invaders a bridgehead at the ford.

Line 48, *þa heregeatu þe eow æt hilde ne deah*, "war-gear that will be of no use to you in battle" The pronoun of address has shifted from *þú* (sing) to *gé* (pl, acc. éow); through the messenger B. speaks to the messenger's masters. The verb *dugan*, "to be worth, to be good for, to avail", is one of the preterite-present group, hence *déah*. A related noun is *duguð*, the seasoned warriors, the body of noble retainers round the chief. From their chief the *duguð* receive gifts of arms and weapons - war gear - that will avail them in battle. No such gifts will be made to the contemptible Vikings; sharp arrows and the wrong end of ancestral swords will be all their reward.

Line 52, *éþel*, "native land", "ancestral home", the abode of kith and kin.

Lines 53-54, *eard, folc, folde*: these are conjoint elements of *éþel*, corresponding to "region", "nation" (or "kith"), and "soil".

Line 61, *in becómon*: "now that you have come this far inland" - cp *up becóman* in *Brunanburh*, line 72. Byrhtnoth's irony is apparent here - "this far", "so far", but the invaders are sitting on an island in midstream and have yet to make a crossing of the ford; or perhaps - still ironically - *nu ge þus feor hider on urne eard in becomon* means "now you have come *all this way* to visit our country".

Line 309, repeats line 42; line 310, *æsc ácwehte*, "shook his spear", cp *wand wácne æsc*, line 43. Byrhtwold has his own moment of theatre, imitating his master's.

Line 311. Byrhtwold's verb of formal address, however, is not *maþelian*, but *láeran*, "to teach", here in the sense of "urge", "exhort".

Lines 312-13, *Hige sceal þe heardra....etc*. In these poignant lines, enshrining the spirit of the poem, the key words are *hige, heorte, mód* and *mægen*. *Mægen* is "main strength", referring to the collective power of the dwindling band. The others all refer to the individual will, but what they mean separately is not easily determined. A dip into the dictionary in search of relevant senses yields the following:

Hyge: thought, mind, heart, intention, courage, pride.
Heorte: spirit, will, desire, courage, mind.
Mód: heart, mind, spirit, temper, courage.

It appears from this that the words mean, centrally, the same thing, or the same sort of thing, with peripheral possibilities of difference. It also appears, rather disturbingly, that one of the most celebrated passages in Old English heroic verse is clear as to purpose but elusive as to particulars. We may perhaps suggest that *hyge* corresponds to "mind", *heorte* to "spirit" and *mód* to "courage".

Lines 315-16 *Á mæg gnornian...etc*: "Ever may [he] rue [it] who (*se þe*) now thinks to turn away from this fight."

Line 316, *fród féores*, "old of life"= old in years, aged. Byrhtwold says "I am old, but..", meaning, perhaps, "I have lived long enough, and now..."

Line 318, *be swá léofan men*, etc: *men* is dative singular; "but I intend to lie side by side with my chief, with so beloved a man". The verb *þencan* here has the specific sense of "intend", "purpose". Byrhtwold's mind is made up, his intention firm. *Hige sceal þe heardra...*

19. *The Later Genesis*, 277-296 :
Renegade sentiments

Here Satan renounces his vows of thaneship to his supreme Lord, and speaks of his intention to lead his own *genéatas*, his band of companions. Some of this passage is translated in chapter 4, p.74-7. Text, ASPR/*Labyrinth*, with modified punctuation.

    "Hwæt sceal ic winnan?" cwæð he.   Nis me wihta þearf   277
hearran to habbanne.   Ic mæg mid handum swa fela
wundra gewyrcean.   Ic hæbbe geweald micel
to gyrwanne   godlecran stol,   280
hearran on heofne   Hwy sceal ic æfter his hyldo þeowian,
bugan him swilces geongordomes?   Ic mæg wesan god swa he.
Bigstandað me strange geneatas, þa ne willað me æt þæm stride geswican,
hæleþas heardmode. Hie habbað me to hearran gecorene,
rofe rincas;   mid swilcum mæg man ræd geþencan,   285
fon mid swilcum folcgesteallan.   Frynd sind hie mine georne,
holde on hyra gesceaftum.   Ic mæg hyra hearra wesan,
rædan on his rice.   Swa me þæt riht ne þinceð,
þæt ic oleccan   awiht þurfe
god æfter gode ænegum.   Ne wille ic leng his geongra wurþan."   290
Þa hit se allwalda   eall gehyrde,
þæt his engel ongan   ofermede micel
ahebban wið his hearran   and spræc healic word
dollice wið drihten sinne,   sceolde he þa dæd ongyldan,
word þæs gewinnes gedælan,   and sceolde his wite habban,   295
ealra mordra mæst.

Notes

Line 277, *winnan*: as between two possible senses, "strive" and "serve", the meaning here is almost certainly the latter. *Nis me wihta þearf*, "For me there is no need", "I have no need, not a whit". [*wihta þearf* = "need of anything"].

Line 278, *héarran*, from *héah*, comparative (weak form) *héahra* > *héarra*, "one higher", "an overlord". *To habbane* is the "inflected infinitive", commonly used to complement the sense of verbs like "have", "do", (as in modern colloquial or dialect speech, "to be having", "for to be doing") or in other instances to express purpose (see below, line 280, *to gyrwanne*).

Line 281, *æfter his hyldo*:"under his favour" - "in allegiance to him"- "in his service".

Line 280-81 The inflected infinitive, *to gyrwanne*, here expresses purpose: "I have great power to establish a goodlier throne, higher in heaven". Both *gódlecra*, "goodlier" (from *gódlic*) and *héarra* (see note at 278) modify *stól*.

Line 282, *geongordomes*: *geongordóm* = "discipleship" - ie the service expected from the *geoguð*. (*geongra* = a dependent, a servant, a vassal). Satan speaks contemptuously of his high position, *primus inter pares*, in the ranks of heaven. For this angel, a feast is never as good as enough.

Line 285, *ráed geþencan*, "take counsel". In line 286, *fón* is in apposition with *geþencan*, but suggests "make" rather than "consider". Read, perhaps, "take counsel, make plans".

Line 287, *holde on hyra gesceaftum*, "loyal in their natures", ie because they were created that way (*gesceaft* also means "destiny"); odd, for Satan to be praising the loyal natures of his disloyalists.

Lines 288-90: *me...þinceþ*, "it seems to me" (*þincan*, not *þencan*); *oleccan*, read "flatter", "be obsequious": "So it hardly seems right to me that I should need (*þurfe*) to be at all (*áwiht*) beholden to God for any good gift".

Line 292-3 the construction is *ongan oferméde micel áhebban*, literally "began to raise up great pride", ie "began to pit his great pride against...."

Line 293-4, *wið*: there are two major senses of the preposition or particle *wið* in Old English. One is oppositional, as in modern "withstand" = "stand against"; the other is "directional" as in modern "withdraw" = "draw from", "draw back"-. The sense here is oppositional, in both occurrences: he pitted his pride against God, he fought with his lord = against his lord. For an instance of the directional sense, see below, *Judith*, line 98.

Lines 294-95. The words to take in tandem here are *dáed*, "deed", and *word*, "word": "deed" being the act of rebellion for which he must be punished (*ongyldan = ongieldan*, "to be punished for, atone for"), and "word", the judgement of which he must partake (*gedáelan*). This interprets *word* in the sense of Latin *sententia* = pronouncement. The punishment and the sentence are *þæs gewinnes*, "on account of the strife".

Line 296, *ealra mordra máest*, not "worst of all murders", but "worst of all punishments", or "torments".

20. *Judith,* 96b–120:   Maidenly vengeance

This passage is described and translated in part in chapter 5, p.99. It represents the poem's disturbing, quasi-erotic pleasure in sanctified violence

                        Þa wearð hyre rume on mode,   96
haligre hyht geniwod;   genam þa þonne hæðenan mannan
fæste be feaxe sinum,   teah hine folmum wið hyre weard
bysmerlice,   ond þone bealofullan
listum alede,   laðne mannan,   100
swa heo þæs unlædan   eaðost mihte
wel gewealdan.   Sloh ða wundenlocc
þone feondsceaðan   fagum mece,
heteþoncolne,   þæt heo healfne forcearf
þone sweoran him,   þæt he on swiman læg,   105
druncen ond dolhwund.   Næs dead þa gyt,
ealles orsawle;   sloh ða eornoste
ides ellenrof   oðre siðe
þone hæðenan hund,   þæt him þæt heafod wand
forð on ða flore.   Læg se fula leap   110
gesne beæftan,   gæst ellor hwearf
under neowelne næs   ond ðær genyðerad wæs,
susle gesæled   syððan æfre,
wyrmum bewunden,   witum gebunden,
hearde gehæfted   in hellebryne   115
æfter hinsiðe.   Ne ðearf he hopian no,
þystrum forðylmed,   þæt he ðonan mote
of ðam wyrmsele,   ac ðær wunian sceal
awa to aldre   butan ende forð
in ðam heolstran ham,   hyhtwynna leas.   120

Notes

Line 97b - 98: *wearþ hyre*, "[it] happened to her" = "she became"; *rúme*, fem.acc.sing of *rúm*, "ample", "large". "She became great in spirit, her sacred trust renewed". (On p.98 we translate, "her spirit was eased") On such words as *mód* and *hyht* ("hope", "trust", "expectation", a relative of *hyge*), see above, on *The Battle of Maldon*, lines 312-13. A half-line similar to 97a occurs in *The Dream of the Rood*, 148b: *hiht was geniwad*. There, the renewed hope is that of those rescued from Hell by the victorious Christ.

Line 98, *wið hyre weard*, "to her ward" = "towards her". On *wið* see above, in comment on *The Later Genesis*, line 294 where the "oppositional" sense of *wið* is remarked. Here the sense is "directional".

Lines 102-3, *swa heo þæs unlædan eaðost mihte wel gewealdan*; the verb *wealdan*, here in the sense "control", "direct", governs a genitive, hence *þæs unláedan*. The whole construction reads a little awkwardly in modern English: [with her fists she pulled him towards her, and cunningly positioned the wretch]"so that she could most easily carry out the terrible act". This assumes that *unláed* refers adjectivally to the action from which she shrinks, not the victim of the act, Holofernus (the *láðne mannan* of line 101).

Line 104, *fágum méce*, "with the ornamented blade"; on *fáh*, see, for example, the note on line 66 of *The Whale*.

Line 105, *heteþoncolne*, acc.sing.masc of *heteþoncol*, "hostile"; used as noun, in apposition to the preceding line's *feondscaðan*, acc.sing of weak masc *féondsceaða*, "enemy". "She struck the enemy, the hostile one..."

Line 105., *healfne*, accusative, in agreement with *þone swéoran* in line 106.

Line 106, *þone swéoran him*, literally "the neck to him"; his neck, or as modern folk- English might say, "*the neck of him*". This use of a "possessive dative" is quite common in Old English.

Lines 110b-111, *þæt him þæt heafod wand forð on ða flore*, "so that his head [or "the head of him", see above] spun away to the floor." Important here to stress the force of *windan*; this is no mean blow.

Lines 111-112. The counterpoised words are *léap*, "[foul] trunk [of his body] and *gáest*, "spirit". The dead body (*gesne* = adj. *gáesne*) remained behind (*beæftan*), while the spirit (*gáest*) departed elsewhere (*ellor*).

Lines 113-116 depict a conventional landscape and mindscape of damnation: the *neowol næs*, "precipitous cliff" at the foot of which the outcast lies condemned and helpless, *súsle gesáeled*, "sealed up in torture", *hearde gehæfted in hellebryne*, "painfully fettered in hellfire", *wyrmum bewunden*, "by serpents encircled", *wítum gebunden*, "in torments bound". The principal feature of this lodging of the damned is the condemned's utter helplessness: compare the situation of the fallen Lucifer in Genesis B, described in chapter 4, p77-8.

Line 117, *þearf* is the present tense ("nor need he"), as is *móte* (may) in line 118, and *sceal* ("must") below in line 119. The poet has shifted from the historic narrative tense to the eternally valid present, the language of overseeing judgement. The double negative, *ne þearf he...nó* in line 117 is emphatic - "nor need he in the least expect..."

Line 119. The two halves of the line conjoin liturgical formulae, *áwa to aldre*, "for ever and ever", and *bútan ende forð*, "world without end".

Line 120, *in þam heolstran hám*, "in the house of darkness" (from *heolstor*, noun, weak masc); *hyhtwynna léas*, "bereft of joyful hopes".

21. *The Dream of the Rood:* 39-56.
The Saviour's Fight

The poem is treated at length, in almost continuous translation, in chapter 5, pp.106-111. The following passage is the most obviously "heroic" part of the text.

Ongyrede hine þa geong hæleð   þæt wæs god ælmihtig,
strang ond stiðmod.   Gestah he on gealgan heanne,   40
modig on manigra gesyhðe,   þa he wolde mancyn lysan.
Bifode ic þa me se beorn ymbclypte,   Ne dorste ic hwæðre bugan to eorðan,
feallan to foldan sceatum,   ac ic sceolde fæste standan.
Rod ic wæs aræred.   Ahof ic ricne cyning,
heofena hlaford,   hyldan me ne dorste.   45
Þurhdrifan hi me mid deorcan næglum.   On me syndon þa dolg gesiene,
opene inwidhlemmas. Ne dorste ic hira nænigum sceððan.
Bysmeredon unc butu ætgædere.   Eall wæs ic mid blode bestemed,
begoten of þæs guman sidan,   syððan he hæfde his gast onsended.
Feala ic on þam beorge   gebiden hæbbe   50
wraðra wyrda.   Geseah ic weruda god
þearle þenian.   Þystro hæfdon
bewrigen mid wolcnum   wealdendes hræw,
scirne sciman,   sceadu forðeode
wann under wolcnum.   Weop eall gesceaft,   55
cwiððon cyninges fyll.   Crist wæs on rode.

Notes

Line 39, *Ongyrede hine*. On *gyrwan* in its martial context, see chapter 4, p.80, discussing the "girding for battle" of, respectively, Beowulf and the Tempter. Of Beowulf, arming for a liberating mission, it is said *nalæs for ealdre mearn*, "he cared nothing for his own life"; so here, the "young hero" is *strang ond stiðmód*, "brave and unflinching" as he prepares for the fight to redeem mankind.

Line 42, *ymbclypte*, "embraced". This is touched with ambiguity. Is it the embrace of an opponent - he *grappled* with me?; or that of a comrade in arms - he *clasped* me?

Line 43, *to foldan scéatum* - if read literally "to the corners of the earth", but idiomatically, "to the ground"; the phrase occurs much earlier in the poem, at line 8, where *æt foldan scéatum* appears to refer simply to the ground at the base of the cross. Yet there is the shadow of an iconographic sense, if the image of the Cross is conceived as all-embracing, its cross-beam extending over all, its shaft rising to heaven above and descending to earth below.

Line 44, *Ród ic was áráered*. Here for the first time in the poem, the Cross receives its sacred name. A few lines earlier (line 40), it has been called *gealga*, "gallows". Now it stands in the dignity of its sanctified thaneship - "As the Cross I was raised up; I bore the great King, the Lord of Heaven; I dared not bow down".

Line 44, *deorc*: interpretations vary around a theme - black, bloodstained, cruel: see comment and note at chapter 6, p.135.

Line 47, *inwidhlemmas*: from *inwid*, or *inwit* = "evil", and *hlemman* "to wound". The wounds evilly inflicted are still *opene*, "open". Compact translation is not easy; perhaps, "terrible, open scars" or "gashes".

Line 48, *bestémed*, "drenched" [with steaming fluid, ie blood]; *begoten* is the pp, not of *begietan*, "beget", but of *begéotan*, to pour [on or from].

Line 49, *gást onsended*, "gave up the ghost" (the phrase used in the AV text of the Gospels, eg Mark 15, 37, Luke 23, 46, John, 19, 30. Matthew 27, 50 has "yielded up" which, indeed, is the sense of Anglo-Saxon *onsendan*).

Line 50, *fela...wraðra wyrda* : gen.pl with *fela*; *ic gebíden hæbbe*, expresses the simple past, "I endured", in a "periphrastic" form, with *habban* - cp the use of "do" in later English, eg "I did endure", "did I endure".

Lines 51-2, *weruda god....þearle þénian*. The point here is surely to emphasize, in soldierly terms, the paradoxical contrast between Christ as supreme commander and Christ as humble servant. The Lord of Hosts, *weruda god*, does painful service as a thane (*þegn*; whence the verb *þegnian > þénian*).

Line 52, *þystro*, plural form with singular meaning, "darkness"; *bewrigen*, pp of *bewréon*, "envelop, cover, wrap"; *wolcnum* (dat pl of wolcen) at this point signifies "clouds" - "darkness had swathed in cloud the Master's body, that shining ray".

Line 54, *sceadu forðeode*: possibly from *forðéon*, "oppress", more plausibly from *forðgan*, "go forth"; the choice is between "the/a shadow loomed [that is, oppressively], dark under the heavens", and the/a shadow went forth....etc. The Gospel accounts of the darkness from the sixth to the ninth hour say "over all the land", "over the whole land", "over all the earth"; the indication of extent and movement in "over" would seem to support the suggested reading with *forðgan* in the Old English poem.

Line 55, *wann under wolcnum.* Here (contrast line 52 above) *wolcen* means "the heavens" - the whole sky - the antique sense of "the welkin"

22. *Beowulf,* 3156 – 3182: A hero's burial

This is the poem's final scene. A memorial barrow, "tall and broad", "clearly visible to seafarers" has been made for Beowulf. The preceding narrative tells how the loyal thane Wiglaf calls for the building of a great funeral pyre, while he and seven brave men go into the dragon's hoard and bring out all its treasures, having pushed the dragon's body over a cliff into the sea. This passage now tells how a pyre was made on the burial mound, and how from its remnant timbers, a walled enclosure was constructed, into which all the treasure from the hoard was brought, with the chief's body. The style is classical run-on - indeed, late run-on: note the length of the sentence from *Geworhton* to *findan mihton*, a continuous structure, but lucidly measured throughout. For the line-numbering, 3156 > 56, etc.

```
Geworhton ða    Wedera leode                    3156
hleo on hoe,    se wæs heah ond brad,
wægliðendum    wide gesyne,
ond betimbredon    on tyn dagum
beadurofes becn,    bronda lafe                  60
wealle beworhton,    swa hyt weorðlicost
foresnotre men    findan mihton.
Hi on beorg dydon    beg ond siglu,
eall swylce hyrsta,    swylce on horde ær
niðhedige men    genumen hæfdon,                 65
forleton eorla gestreon    eorðan healdan,
gold on greote,    þær hit nu gen lifað
eldum swa unnyt    swa hyt æror wæs.
Þa ymbe hlæw riodan    hildediore,
æþelinga bearn    ealra twelfe,                  70
woldon ceare cwiðan    ond kyning mænan,
wordgyd wrecan    ond ymb wer sprecan;
eahtodon eorlscipe    ond his ellenweorc
duguðum demdon,    swa hit gedefe bið
þæt mon his winedryhten    wordum herge,         75
ferhðum freoge,    þonne he forð scile
of lichaman    læded weorðan.
Swa begnornodon    Geata leode
hlafordes hryre,    heorðgeneatas,
cwædon þæt he wære    wyruldcyninga              80
manna mildust    ond monðwærust,
leodum liðost    ond lofgeornost.
```

Notes

Line 60, *becn*, "beacon", whether the sense of "landmark" (visible from far out at sea), or "signal fire, on a hill or promontory". In *The Dream of the Rood*, the shape of the Cross in the poet's dream, *léohte bewunden*, "wreathed in light", is called *þæt béacen*. It seems that "bright light" is a usual component of the meaning of this word. However, *beadurófes bécn* in this context must mean "the warrior's memorial" - built in ten days by his faithful subjects.

Lines 60 - 62 *bronda láfe*, (from *brand*, "fire, flame") the timbers left over from the pyre. These are *wealle beworhton*, "made into a wall", *swa hyt weorðlicost foresnotre men findan mihton*, = "of which experts might wholly approve", or, in the actual terms of the text, "such that very wise men might find it most worthily done".

Line 63, *beg ond siglu...hyrsta*: in the nom.sing, *béah* ("ring"), *sigle* ("collar"), *hyrst* ("armour") - the spoils of war.

Line 65, *niðhédig*, (*niðhýdig*), "valorous"; the *niðhédige men* are the seven who went into the hoard-chamber with Wiglaf, to bring out the treasure.

Line 66, *eorla gestréon*, "the precious possessions of rich men". All these riches are "left for the earth to hold".

Line 67, *gold on gréote*, "gold in the ground", has something of a formulaic ring: see Byrhtwold's mourning for the fallen Byrhtnoth (*Maldon*, line 315), *gód on gréote*, "good man on the ground"; in both instances, however, *gréot* is something less like "ground" and more like "grit" - ie the common dirt underfoot.

Line 69, *riodan* = *ridon*; *ealra twelfe*, "twelve in all".

Line 72, *wordgyd*, "dirge", "lament"

Lines 73-4. Read thus: (i) *eahtodon eorlscipe*, "praised his manhood", (ii) *ond his ellenweorc duguðum démdon*, and "nobly judged his heroic deeds" Take *duguðum* adverbially, "in a manner proper to the *duguð*". From *déman*, to deem, adjudge, comes the noun *dóm* - the "judgement on each of the dead" of which the *Havamál* poet speaks. The twelve riders speak their hero's praise (*lof*) and accord him his judgement (*dóm*).

Line 76, *ferhðum fréoge*, "should honour in their minds" - that is, they should praise with their words, *wordum herge*, and cherish in their hearts, *ferhðum fréoge*.

Lines 76-7, *þonne he forð scile of lichaman læded weorðan*, literally, "when he shall be led forth from his body", ie "when he shall pass away"; *scile=scyle*, *scule*, subjunctive of *sceal*.

Select Bibliography

Of the items in this list, most are printed books, some "electronic texts", and some internet pages on Anglo-Saxon poetry. Such is the bibliographical value of the internet to students of Old English that a search engine will turn up a great many useful websites. A few of them are listed here or have been mentioned in the Notes. They may be serviceable to readers living at a distance from major libraries and bookshops. Note, however, that URLs (internet addresses) not infrequently change. I have done my best to confirm those listed here and elsewhere. When in doubt, consult the indispensable Google.

1. Basics

Godden, M., and M. Lapridge, *The Cambridge Companion to Old English Literature*. Cambridge U.P, 1991. (A recent publication, with articles by specialists in every aspect of the subject, a valuable companion to study).

The Cambridge History of English and American Literature, Vol.I: From the beginning to the cycles of Romance. Cambridge U.P., 1927

Quirk, R., et.al., *Old English Literature: A Practical Introduction.* London, 1976. ("Practical" in its emphasis on reading texts)

Online: The University of Georgetown's *Labyrinth Library*, Old English Section. URL: http://www.georgetown.edu/labyrinth This is a corpus of Old English texts, including the contents of Krapp, G.P. and E.V.K Dobbie, eds., *The Anglo-Saxon Poetic Records: A Collective Edition, 6 vols,*

New York, 1931-53. It is an invaluable resort; the poems come as a plain text, however, with no apparatus or glossary.

Online: Biggam, C.P., ed., *A General Bibliography of Anglo-Saxon Studies.* URL: http://bubl.ac.uk/docs/bibliog/biggam. This originated as the *Bocgetæl engliscra Gesiða,* "Book-list of the English Companions" - on which, see below. It is now a huge bibliography, regularly updated, and can fairly be called indispensable.

Online: Journals, etc., of study-groups interested in Old English life and literature. They include *Maþeliende,* The Newsletter of Anglo-Saxon Studies at the University of Georgia, a quarterly issue with a long back-list and many scholarly papers. URL: http://www.parallel.park.uga.edu/~abruce

Ða engliscan Gesiþas (see above) is a "society for people interested in all aspects of Anglo-Saxon language and culture". It publishes a journal, *Wiðowinde.* Its URL is http://www.kami.demon.co.uk/gesithas.

Other sites of this kind are *English Heathenism,* URL http://:www.englishheathenism.homestead.com and *Winlandes Scir,* "the United States chapter of *Ða engliscan Gesiðas.* URL: http://www.dnaco.net/~sirbill/information/html

Dictionaries. Though some printed editions of texts supply glossaries, a good dictionary - but "portable"- is necessary. Used throughout the preparation of this book was Clark Hall, John R., *A Concise Anglo-Saxon Dictionary*, 4th edn. with a supplement by Herbert D. Merritt, Cambridge 1960. A more recent, and therefore more readily accessible issue, is published by the University of Toronto Press.

2. Beowulf: text, editions, translations, commentaries

Because *Beowulf* remains the central study of Old English poetics, it calls for a separate section in the Bibliography. The following is a summary of resources.

A. Hasenfratz, Robert J., *Beowulf Scholarship: an Annotated Bibliography 1979-1990* New York, 1993. Updated as a website, *Beowulf Bibliography, 1979-1994*: http://spirit.lib.uconn.edu/medieval/beowulf.html. This valuable undertaking documents the state of the critical art in recent decades.

   Bjork, Robert E., and John Niles, eds. *A Beowulf Handbook,* Exeter, 1997

B. Editions: A standard text is Klaeber, F., ed. *Beowulf and the Fight at Finnsburg*. 3rd ed. With supplement, Boston, 1950. More recently, Wrenn, C.L and W.F.Bolton, *Beowulf with the Finnsburg Fragment*, revised edn., Exeter, 1988, and Jack.,G., *Beowulf: A Student Edition,* Oxford 1994.

C. Translations: Numerous, some noble, many competent, a few verging on the gorblimey. The best general guide is online, Syd Allan's Beowulf website at http://www.jagular.com   Allan lists 89 translations and provides extracts from each. The list includes Seamus Heaney's Whitbread Prize-winning *Beowulf: A New Verse Translation,* London, 2000

E. Critical Studies: for recent studies, consult Hasenfratz, above. However, note, as a classic text, Chambers, R.W., *Beowulf, an Introduction to the Study of the Poem*, Cambridge, 1921, rev.edn.1932. Also, in connection with Chapter 6 of this book, Tolkien, J.R.R. *Beowulf and the Monsters*, British Academy Lecture, 1936

3. Poetic texts in translation: heroic poems, elegies, wisdoms, riddles, allegory

These are single works, or short anthologies of Old English poems or extracts from poems. In some cases text is included with translation. They embrace, collectively, most of the works discussed in this book. The translations vary a good deal in style and poetic quality.

Bolton, W.F., *An Old English Anthology*, London, 1963

Bradley, S.A.J, *Anglo-Saxon Poetry: an Anthology of Old English Poems in Prose Translation*. London, 1982

Crossley-Holland, K., and B.Mitchell, *The Battle of Maldon and other Old English Poems*. London, 1965

Crossley-Holland, K., *The Seafarer*. Llandogo, 1988

Crossley-Holland, K., transl. *The Exeter Book Riddles*, revised edn., London 1993

Fowler, R., *Old English Prose and Verse,* London, 1966

Griffiths, Bill, *Guthlac B*, a Translation of the Old English Poem on the Death of St.Guthlac. Peterborough, 1985

Griffiths, Bill, *The Battle of Maldon*, text and translation. Hockwold-cum-Wilton (Anglo-Saxon Books) 1996. This qualifies as an "edited" edition (see section 4 below). It performs a very useful service in reviewing the numerous critical writings on this poem.

Hamer, R.A., *A Choice of Anglo-Saxon Verse,* London, 1970

Pope, J.C., *Eight Old English Poems,* ed. with Commentary and Glossary, 3rd edn, revised by R.D.Fulk, New York, 2001. Contains *Caedmon's Hymn, Brunanburh, The Dream of the Rood, Maldon, Wanderer, Seafarer, Deor, The Wife's Lament*. A very useful resource.

Porter, J. *Anglo-Saxon Riddles*. Hockwold-cum-Wilton (Anglo-Saxon Books) 2002. Texts and translations of the 95 riddles of the Exeter Book.

Raffel, B. *Poems from the Old English*. Nebraska, 1961. Raffel translates with flair; he makes poems out of poems.

Rodrigues, Louis J., transl. *Anglo-Saxon Religious Verse Allegories*. Felinfach, 1966. (includes a translation of *The Whale*).

Rodrigues, Louis J., transl, *Anglo-Saxon Verse Charms, Maxims and Heroic Legends,* Lampeter, 1995.

Rodrigues, Louis J, transl. *An Anglo-Saxon Verse Miscellany* Felinfach, 1997

Rodriguez, Louis J., *Sixty-five Anglo-Saxon Riddles* Felinfach, 1998

Shippey, T.A., ed. and transl. *Poems of Wisdom and Learning in Old English.* Cambridge, 1976

Waddington-Feather, J., *Visions in the Winter Dark: Three Old English Poems.* With an Introduction by Walter Nash. Shrewsbury, 2000.

4. Critical editions, commentary, and "background"

Cockayne, T.O., ed. *Leechdoms. Wortcunning and Starcraft in Early England:* 3 vols., London, 1864-6. Repr. Thoemmes Press, 2001. A source-book for charms, spells, and medical magics.

Cooper, Janet, ed., *The Battle of Maldon, Fiction and Fact.* London, 1993

Doane, A.N., ed., *The Saxon Genesis*: an Edition of the West Saxon Genesis B and the Old Saxon Vatican Genesis. Madison, Wisconsin 1991

Dickins, Bruce, ed.and transl., *Runic and Heroic Poems,* Cambridge U.P., 1915

Bibliography

Dickins, B., and A.S.C. Ross, *The Dream of the Rood*, 4th edn, repr. London 1963

Dunning, T.P. And A.J.Bliss, *The Wanderer*, Methuen 1969, repr 1973 This enormously instructive edition of the poem has a critical rival (or "gesith") in that of R.F.Leslie – see below

Griffith, M., ed., *Judith*. Exeter, 1998

Griffiths, Bill, *Aspects of Anglo-Saxon Magic*. (in connection with charms and spells, runes, etc.) Hockwold-cum-Wilton, Anglo-Saxon Books, 1996

Hill, Joyce, ed. *Old English Minor Heroic Poems*. Durham Medieval Texts 4, revised. University of Durham, 1994

Jolly, Karen L., *Popular Religion in Late Saxon England: Elf Charms in Context*. Chapel Hill, North Carolina, 1996. Text online at: http://www2.hawaii.edu/~kjolly/unc.

Klinck, Anne L., *The Old English Elegies: A Critical Edition and Genre Study*. London, 1992

Larrington, Carolyne, *A Store of Common Sense: Gnomic Theme and Style in Old Icelandic and Old English Nature Poetry*. Oxford, 1998

Leslie, R.F., *The Wanderer*, revised edn., University of Exeter, 1985

Leslie, R.F., *Three Old English Elegies*, revised edn., University of Exeter, 1988

Linsell, Tony, *Anglo-Saxon Mythology, Migration and Magic,* Pinner, 1996

Malone, Kemp, ed. *Widsith*, revised edn., Copenhagen, 1962

Malone, Kemp, ed. *Deor*, revised edn., University of Exeter, 1977

Muir, Bernard J., ed., *Leoð*: Six Old English Poems, a Handbook. New York, 1989

Muir, Bernard J., ed. *The Exeter Anthology of Old English Poetry: an Edition of Exeter Dean and Chapter MS 3501*, Exeter, 1962

O´Keefe, Katherine O´Brien, *Old English Shorter Poems: Basic Readings,* London, 1994

Scragg, D.G. ed., *The Battle of Maldon, AD 991*, Oxford, 1991. This extensive survey of the poem includes Wendy E.J.Collier´s "A Bibliography of the Battle of Maldon", pp.294-301

Squires, Anne, ed. *The Old English Physiologus*. Durham Medieval Texts, V. University of Durham, 1988

Swanton, Michael, ed., *The Dream of the Rood*. University of Exeter 1996, repr.2000. The latest edition of this great poem, and by far the best, almost overloaded with information and critical perceptions.

5. Poetics, literary theory, textual criticism

Barney, Stephen A., *Word-Hoard, An Introduction to the Old English Vocabulary.* 2nd edn. New Haven, 1985

Bliss., A.J., *An Introduction to Old English Metre.* Oxford, 1962

Bragg, Lois, *The Lyre Speakers of Old English Verse,* London 1991

Clemoes, Peter, *Interactions of Thought and Language in Old English Poetry,* Cambridge, 1995

Doane, A.N., and Carol Braun Pasternak, eds. *Vox Intexta: Orality and Textuality in the Middle Ages.* Univ. of Wisconsin Press, 1992

Frank, Roberta, *The Search for the Anglo-Saxon Oral Poet,* Manchester, 1993

Fulk, R., *A History of Old English Metre,* Philadelphia, 1992

Greenfield, Stanley B., *Hero and Exile: the Art of Old English Poetry,* ed. George H. Brown, London, 1989.

Hutcheson, B.R., *Old English Poetic Metre,* Cambridge 1995

Lapidge, M., *Textual Criticism and the Literature of Anglo-Saxon England,* Manchester, 1991

Lerer, S., *Literacy and Power in Anglo-Saxon Literature,* London, 1991

Momma, H., *The Composition of Old English Poetry,* Cambridge, 1997

O'Keefe, Katherine O'Brien, *Visible Song: Transitional Literacy in Old English Verse.* Cambridge 1990

O'Keefe, Katherines O'Brien, ed., *Reading Old English Texts,* Cambridge, 1997

Pope, J.C., *The Rhythm of Beowulf.* Yale University Press, 1942.

Raw, Barbara C., *The Art and Backgrounds of Old English Poetry,* London, 1978

Russom, Geoffrey, *Beowulf and Old Germanic Metre,* Cambridge 1998

Shippey, T.A., *Old English Verse.* London, 1972

Sisam, Kenneth, "Dialect Origins of the Earlier Old English Verse", in his *Studies in the History of Old English Literature,* London 1953. Argues powerfully his view of the evolution of an independent literary dialect, above regional origins, "Anglian forms", etc.

Bibliography

6. Allusions and quotations

Sources of casual references are generally cited in the notes. In a few instances, matter "alluded to" is extensively or repeatedly quoted. The following is a summary of this background material.

Anglo-Saxon Chronicle Translations: Currently in print is Michael Swanton, ed and transl, *The Anglo-Saxon Chronicle; the Monks of the Monasteries of Winchester, Canterbury, Peterborough, Abingdon and Worcester*. London (Phoenix Press) 2000. This is excellent, alike for students or general readers .Translations online include http://sunsite.berkeley.edu/OMACL/Anglo (in the Berkeley Digital Library of Classical and Medieval Texts); http://www.britannia.com/history/docs/asintro; and http://www.northvegr.org/lore/anglo. These are all based on old translations, eg the Everyman translation, 1912, or the Revd.James Ingram's translation d. 1823. Use with allowances. Texts: for an online text see Tony Jebson's edition at http://jebbo/home.texas.net/asc . This is an edition of a major manuscript, MS A, the Parker Chronicle. For a description and history of Chronicle manuscripts, see http://www.georgetown.edu/labyrinth/library/o

Bede. Colgrave, Bertram, and R.A,B. Mynors, eds., *Historia Ecclesiastica Gentis Anglorum*, Oxford (Oxford Medieval Texts 1969 repr. 1988) has in parallel Latin text and English translation. Bertram Colgrave's English translation, *The Ecclesiastical History of the English People,* is published in the Oxford World Classics series, 2000. For an online translation, see http://www.fordham.edu/halsall/basis/bede-book. See also http://englishheathenism.homestead.com/bede
(For the Caedmon story, see Bk IV, xxiv)

Tacitus. His *Germania* is frequently cited in Chapter 2 and elsewhere. A good translation is that of Mattingly, H., and S.A.Handford, *Tacitus: the Agricola and the Germania* London (Penguin Classics) 1970. On-line translations of this text, an indispensable source for students of things Germanic, are to be found at http://www.englishheathenism.homestead.com/tacitus.html and at http://www.northvegr.org/lore/tacitus , which also supplies the Latin. For the Latin text, see further http://www.fordham.edu/halsall/source/tacitus and http://www.patriot.net/~lillard/cp.tac.html.

Old Norse *Havamál* is cited here. For the Norse text of this poem, see the Runeberg Project at http://www.lysalor.liu.se./runeberg/eddais. (but there are many versions on line, of text and translations) For an English translation of the Eddaic poems, see Carolyne Larrington's *The Poetic Edda,* Oxford (World's Classics) 1999. A guide to the Eddaic world is Andy Orchard´s *Cassell Dictionary of Norse Myth and Legend*, London, 1997. Snorri Sturluson's *Heimskringla* is in online translation at http://sunsite.berkeley.edu/OMACL/Heimskringla. The best translation in print is Lee M.Hollander's *Heimskringla: History of the Kings of Norway*, University of Texas, 1964, repr. 1991 *Egil's Saga* has been translated, with an Introduction, by Herman Pálsson and Paul Edwards (Penguin, 1976) and more recently by Christine Fell & John Lucas (Everyman, 1998).

Vulgate For the Latin text of the Apocryphal Book of Judith, see http://www.sacred-texts.com/bib/vul

Some of our other titles

The English Warrior from earliest times to 1066
Stephen Pollington

This is not intended to be a bald listing of the battles and campaigns from the Anglo-Saxon Chronicle and other sources, but rather it is an attempt to get below the surface of Anglo-Saxon warriorhood and to investigate the rites, social attitudes, mentality and mythology of the warfare of those times.

> "An under-the-skin study of the role, rights, duties, psyche and rituals of the Anglo-Saxon warrior. The author combines original translations from Norse and Old English primary sources with archaeological and linguistic evidence for an in-depth look at the warrior, his weapons, tactics and logistics.
>
> A very refreshing, innovative and well-written piece of scholarship that illuminates a neglected period of English history"
>
> *Time Team Booklists* - Channel 4 Television

Revised Edition

An already highly acclaimed book has been made even better by the inclusion of additional information and illustrations.

£16.95   ISBN 1-898281-42-4   245 x 170mm   over 50 illustrations   304 pages   hardback

The Mead Hall   The feasting tradition in Anglo-Saxon England
Stephen Pollington

This new study takes a broad look at the subject of halls and feasting in Anglo-Saxon England. The idea of the communal meal was very important among nobles and yeomen, warriors, farmers churchmen and laity. One of the aims of the book is to show that there was not just one 'feast' but two main types: the informal social occasion *gebeorscipe* and the formal, ritual gathering *symbel*.

Using the evidence of Old English texts - mainly the epic *Beowulf* and the *Anglo-Saxon Chronicles*, Stephen Pollington shows that the idea of feasting remained central to early English social traditions long after the physical reality had declined in importance.

The words of the poets and saga-writers are supported by a wealth of archaeological data dealing with halls, settlement layouts and magnificent feasting gear found in many early Anglo-Saxon graves.

Three appendices cover:

- Hall-themes in Old English verse;
- Old English and translated texts;
- The structure and origins of the warband.

£14.95   ISBN 1-898281-30-0   9 ¾ x 6 ¾ inches   248 x 170mm   288 pages   hardback

First Steps in Old English
An easy to follow language course for the beginner
Stephen Pollington
A complete, well presented and easy to use Old English language course that contains all the exercises and texts needed to learn Old English. This course has been designed to be of help to a wide range of students, from those who are teaching themselves at home, to undergraduates who are learning Old English as part of their English degree course. The author is aware that some individuals have difficulty with grammar. To help overcome this and other difficulties, he has adopted a step-by-step approach that enables students of differing abilities to advance at their own pace. The course includes practice and translation exercises.

There is a glossary of the words used in the course, and 16 Old English texts, including the Battle of Brunanburh and Battle of Maldon.

£16.95   ISBN 1-898281-38-6 10" x 6½" (245 x 170mm) 256 pages

Ærgeweorc   Old English Verse and Prose
read by Stephen Pollington
This audiotape cassette can be used with *First Steps in Old English* or just listened to for the sheer pleasure of hearing Old English spoken well.

Tracks: 1. Deor. 2. Beowulf – The Funeral of Scyld Scefing. 3. Engla Tocyme (The Arrival of the English). 4. Ines Domas. Two Extracts from the Laws of King Ine. 5. Deniga Hergung (The Danes' Harrying) Anglo-Saxon Chronicle Entry AD997. 6. Durham 7. The Ordeal (Be ðon ðe ordales weddigaþ) 8. Wið Dweorh (Against a Dwarf) 9. Wið Wennum (Against Wens) 10. Wið Wæterælfadle (Against Waterelf Sickness) 11. The Nine Herbs Charm 12. Læcedomas (Leechdoms) 13. Beowulf's Greeting 14. The Battle of Brunanburh 15. Blacmon – by Adrian Pilgrim.

£7.50   ISBN 1–898281–20–3   C40 audiotape

Wordcraft: Concise English/Old English Dictionary and Thesaurus
Stephen Pollington
This book provides Old English equivalents to the commoner modern words in both dictionary and thesaurus formats. The Thesaurus presents vocabulary relevant to a wide range of individual topics in alphabetical lists, thus making it easily accessible to those with specific areas of interest. Each thematic listing is encoded for cross-reference from the Dictionary. The two sections will be of invaluable assistance to students of the language, as well as to those with either a general or a specific interest in the Anglo-Saxon period.

£9.95   A5   ISBN 1–898281–02–5   256pp

An Introduction to the Old English Language and its Literature
Stephen Pollington
The purpose of this general introduction to Old English is not to deal with the teaching of Old English but to dispel some misconceptions about the language and to give an outline of its structure and its literature. Some basic knowledge of these is essential to an understanding of the early period of English history and the present form of the language.

£4.95   A5   ISBN 1–898281–06–8   48pp

Anglo-Saxon Runes
John. M. Kemble

Kemble's essay *On Anglo-Saxon Runes* first appeared in the journal *Archaeologia* for 1840; it draws on the work of Wilhelm Grimm, but breaks new ground for Anglo-Saxon studies in his survey of the Ruthwell Cross and the Cynewulf poems. It is an expression both of his own indomitable spirit and of the fascination and mystery of the Runes themselves, making one of the most attractive introductions to the topic. For this edition new notes have been supplied, which include translations of Latin and Old English material quoted in the text, to make this key work in the study of runes more accessible to the general reader.

£4.95   A5   ISBN 0–9516209–1–6   80pp

Looking for the Lost Gods of England
Kathleen Herbert

Kathleen Herbert sifts through the royal genealogies, charms, verse and other sources to find clues to the names and attributes of the Gods and Goddesses of the early English. The earliest account of English heathen practices reveals that they worshipped the Earth Mother and called her Nerthus. The tales, beliefs and traditions of that time are still with us in, for example, Sand able to stir our minds and imaginations.

£4.95   A5   ISBN 1–898281–04–1   64pp

Rudiments of Runelore
Stephen Pollington

This book provides both a comprehensive introduction for those coming to the subject for the first time, and a handy and inexpensive reference work for those with some knowledge of the subject. The *Abecedarium Nordmannicum* and the English, Norwegian and Icelandic rune poems are included in their original and translated form. Also included is work on the three Brandon runic inscriptions and the Norfolk 'Tiw' runes.

£4.95   A5   ISBN 1–898281–16–5   Illustrations   88pp

Rune Cards
Brian Partridge & Tony Linsell

> "This boxed set of 30 cards contains some of the most beautiful and descriptive black and white line drawings that I have ever seen on this subject."
>
> *Pagan News*

30 pen and ink drawings by Brian Partridge

80 page booklet by Tony Linsell gives information about the origin of runes, their meaning, and how to read them.

£9.95   ISBN 1-898281-34-3   30 cards 85mm x 132mm - boxed with booklet

Dark Age Naval Power
A Reassessment of Frankish and Anglo-Saxon Seafaring Activity
John Haywood

In the first edition of this work, published in 1991, John Haywood argued that the capabilities of the pre-Viking Germanic seafarers had been greatly underestimated. Since that time, his reassessment of Frankish and Anglo-Saxon shipbuilding and seafaring has been widely praised and accepted.

In this second edition, some sections of the book have been revised and updated to include information gained from excavations and sea trials with sailing replicas of early ships. The new evidence supports the author's argument that early Germanic shipbuilding and seafaring skills were far more advanced than previously thought. It also supports the view that Viking ships and seaborne activities were not as revolutionary as is commonly believed.

> 'The book remains a historical study of the first order. It is required reading for our seminar on medieval seafaring at Texas A & M University and is essential reading for anyone interested in the subject.'
>
> F. H. Van Doorninck, *The American Neptune*

£16.95 ISBN 1-898281-22-X   approx. 10 x 6½ inches (245 x 170 mm) Hardback 224 pages

English Martial Arts
Terry Brown

Little is known about the very early history of English martial arts but it is likely that methods, techniques and principles were passed on from one generation to the next for centuries. By the sixteenth century English martial artists had their own governing body which controlled its members in much the same way as do modern-day martial arts organisations. It is apparent from contemporary evidence that the Company of Maisters taught and practised a fighting system that ranks as high in terms of effectiveness and pedigree as any in the world.

In the first part of the book the author investigates the weapons, history and development of the English fighting system and looks at some of the attitudes, beliefs and social pressures that helped mould it.

Part two deals with English fighting techniques drawn from books and manuscripts that recorded the system at various stages in its history. In other words, all of the methods and techniques shown in this book are authentic and have not been created by the author. The theories that underlie the system are explained in a chapter on *The Principles of True Fighting*. All of the techniques covered are illustrated with photographs and accompanied by instructions. Techniques included are for bare-fist fighting, broadsword, quarterstaff, bill, sword and buckler, sword and dagger.

Experienced martial artists, irrespective of the style they practice, will recognise that the techniques and methods of this system are based on principles that are as valid as those underlying the system that they practice.

The author, who has been a martial artist for twenty-eight years, has recently re-formed the Company of Maisters of Defence, a medieval English martial arts organization.

£16.95   ISBN 1–898281–29-7   10 x 6½ inches - 245 x 170 mm   220 photographs   240 pages

Anglo-Saxon Riddles
Translated by John Porter
Here you will find ingenious characters who speak their names in riddles, and meet a one-eyed garlic seller, a bookworm, an iceberg, an oyster, the sun and moon and a host of others from the everyday life and imagination of the Anglo-Saxons. Their sense of the awesome power of creation goes hand in hand with a frank delight in obscenity, a fascination with disguise and with the mysterious processes by which the natural world is turned to human use. This edition contains **all 95 riddles of the Exeter Book in both Old English and Modern English.**

£4.95   A5   ISBN 1–898281–13–0   144 pages

Tolkien's *Mythology for England*
A Guide to Middle-Earth
Edmund Wainwright
Tolkien set out to create a mythology for England and the English but the popularity of his books and the recent films has spread across the English-speaking world and beyond.

You will find here an outline of Tolkien's life and work. The main part of the book consists of an alphabetical subject entry which will help you gain a greater understanding of Tolkien's Middle-Earth, the creatures that inhabit it, and the languages they spoke. It will also give an insight into a culture and way-of-life that extolled values which are as valid today as they were over 1,000 years ago.

This book focuses on *The Lord of the Rings* and shows how Tolkien's knowledge of Anglo-Saxon and Norse literature and history helped shape its plot and characters.

£9·95   ISBN 1-898281-36-X   approx. 10 x 6½ inches (245 x 170 mm)   Hardback   128 pages

Anglo-Saxon Books
Tel. 0845 430 4200   Fax. 0845 430 4201   email: enq@asbooks.co.uk

Please check availability and prices on our web site at www.asbooks.co.uk

See website for postal address.

Payment may be made by Visa / Mastercard or by a cheque drawn on a UK bank in sterling.

UK deliveries add 10% up to a maximum of £2·50

Europe – including **Republic of Ireland** – add 10% plus £1 – all orders are sent airmail

North America add 10% surface delivery, 30% airmail

Elsewhere add 10% surface delivery, 40% airmail

Overseas surface delivery 6 – 10 weeks; airmail 6 – 14 days

Most titles can be obtained through North American bookstores.

Latest Titles

Anglo-Saxon Attitudes – A short introduction to Anglo-Saxonism
J.A. Hilton

This is not a book about the Anglo-Saxons, but a book about books about Anglo-Saxons. It describes the academic discipline of Anglo-Saxonism; the methods of study used; the underlying assumptions; and the uses to which it has been put.

Methods and motives have changed over time but right from the start there have been constant themes: English patriotism and English freedom.

£6.95   A5   ISBN 1–898281–39-4   Hardback 64pp

The Origins of the Anglo-Saxons
Donald Henson

This book has come about through a growing frustration with scholarly analysis and debate about the beginnings of Anglo-Saxon England. Much of what has been written is excellent, yet unsatisfactory. One reason for this is that scholars often have only a vague acquaintance with fields outside their own specialism. The result is a partial examination of the evidence and an incomplete understanding or explanation of the period.

The growth and increasing dominance of archaeological evidence for the period has been accompanied by an unhealthy enthusiasm for models of social change imported from prehistory. Put simply, many archaeologists have developed a complete unwillingness to consider movements of population as a factor in social, economic or political change. All change becomes a result of indigenous development, and all historically recorded migrations become merely the movement of a few hundred aristocrats or soldiers. The author does not find this credible.

£19.95   A5   ISBN 1–898281–40-2   304pp

A Departed Music – Readings in Old English Poetry
Walter Nash

The *readings* of this book take the form of passages of translation from some Old English poems. The author paraphrases their content and discuses their place and significance in the history of poetic art in Old English society and culture.

The authors knowledge, enthusiasm and love of his subject help make this an excellent introduction to the subject for students and the general reader.

£16.95   A5   ISBN 1–898281–37-8   240pp

English Sea Power 871-1100 AD
John Pullen-Appleby

This work examines the largely untold story of English sea power during the period 871 to 1100. It was an age when English kings deployed warships first against Scandinavian invaders and later in support of Continental allies.

The author has gathered together information about the appearance of warships and how they were financed, crewed, and deployed.

Price £14.95   144 pages   hardcover   ISBN 1-898281-31-9

Organisations

Þa Engliscan Gesiðas

Þa Engliscan Gesiðas (The English Companions) is a historical and cultural society exclusively devoted to Anglo-Saxon history. Its aims are to bridge the gap between scholars and non-experts, and to bring together all those with an interest in the Anglo-Saxon period, its language, culture and traditions, so as to promote a wider interest in, and knowledge of all things Anglo-Saxon. The Fellowship publishes a journal, *Wiðowinde,* which helps members to keep in touch with current thinking on topics from art and archaeology to heathenism and Early English Christianity. The Fellowship enables like-minded people to keep in contact by publicising conferences, courses and meetings which might be of interest to its members.

For further details see www.tha-engliscan-gesithas.org.uk or write to: The Membership Secretary, Þa Engliscan Gesiðas, BM Box 4336, London, WC1N 3XX England.

Regia Anglorum

Regia Anglorum was founded to accurately re-create the life of the British people as it was around the time of the Norman Conquest. Our work has a strong educational slant. We consider authenticity to be of prime importance and prefer, where possible, to work from archaeological materials. Approximately twenty-five per cent of our members, of over 500 people, are archaeologists or historians.

The Society has a large working Living History Exhibit, teaching and exhibiting more than twenty crafts in an authentic environment. We own a forty-foot wooden ship replica of a type that would have been a common sight in Northern European waters around the turn of the first millennium AD. Battle re-enactment is another aspect of our activities, often involving 200 or more warriors.

For further information see www.regia.org or contact: K. J. Siddorn, 9 Durleigh Close, Headley Park, Bristol BS13 7NQ, England, e-mail: kim_siddorn@compuserve.com

The Sutton Hoo Society

Our aims and objectives focus on promoting research and education relating to the Anglo Saxon Royal cemetery at Sutton Hoo, Suffolk in the UK. The Society publishes a newsletter SAXON twice a year, which keeps members up to date with society activities, carries resumes of lectures and visits, and reports progress on research and publication associated with the site. If you would like to join the Society please see website: www.suttonhoo.org

Wuffing Education

Wuffing Education provides those interested in the history, archaeology, literature and culture of the Anglo-Saxons with the chance to meet experts and fellow enthusiasts for a whole day of in-depth seminars and discussions. Day Schools take place at the historic Tranmer House overlooking the burial mounds of Sutton Hoo in Suffolk.

For details of programme of events contact:-
Wuffing Education, 4 Hilly Fields, Woodbridge, Suffolk IP12 4DX
email education@wuffings.co.uk   website www.wuffings.co.uk
Tel. 01394 383908 or 01728 688749

Places to visit

Bede's World at Jarrow

Bede's world tells the remarkable story of the life and times of the Venerable Bede, 673–735 AD. Visitors can explore the origins of early medieval Northumbria and Bede's life and achievements through his own writings and the excavations of the monasteries at Jarrow and other sites.

Location – 10 miles from Newcastle upon Tyne, off the A19 near the southern entrance to the River Tyne tunnel. Bus services 526 & 527

Bede's World, Church Bank, Jarrow, Tyne and Wear, NE32 3DY

Tel. 0191 489 2106; Fax: 0191 428 2361; website: www.bedesworld.co.uk

Sutton Hoo near Woodbridge, Suffolk

Sutton Hoo is a group of low burial mounds overlooking the River Deben in south-east Suffolk. Excavations in 1939 brought to light the richest burial ever discovered in Britain – an Anglo-Saxon ship containing a magnificent treasure which has become one of the principal attractions of the British Museum. The mound from which the treasure was dug is thought to be the grave of Rædwald, an early English king who died in 624/5 AD.

This National Trust site has an excellent visitor centre, which includes a reconstruction of the burial chamber and its grave goods. Some original objects as well as replicas of the treasure are on display.

2 miles east of Woodbridge on B1083   Tel. 01394 389700

West Stow Anglo-Saxon Village

An early Anglo-Saxon Settlement reconstructed on the site where it was excavated consisting of timber and thatch hall, houses and workshop. There is also a museum containing objects found during the excavation of the site. Open all year 10am–4.15pm (except Yuletide). Special provision for school parties. A teachers' resource pack is available. Costumed events are held at weekends, especially Easter Sunday and August Bank Holiday Monday. Craft courses are organised.

For further details see www.stedmunds.co.uk/west_stow.html or contact:

The Visitor Centre, West Stow Country Park, Icklingham Road, West Stow,

Bury St Edmunds, Suffolk IP28 6HG   Tel. 01284 728718